JIANYANG
CODE
OF TIANFU
CULTURE

谭平——著 彭蕴希——译

天府文化之

简阳密码

中国出版集团有限公司
研究出版社

图书在版编目（CIP）数据

天府文化之简阳密码：汉英对照 / 谭平著；彭蕴
希译 . -- 北京：研究出版社，2023.6
ISBN 978-7-5199-1517-9

Ⅰ.①天… Ⅱ.①谭… ②彭… Ⅲ.①地方文化－简
阳－汉、英 Ⅳ.① G127.714

中国版本图书馆 CIP 数据核字 (2023) 第 107283 号

出 品 人：赵卜慧
出版统筹：丁　波
责任编辑：张　琨

天府文化之简阳密码

谭平　著　彭蕴希　译

研究出版社 出版发行
（100006 北京市东城区灯市口大街 100 号华腾商务楼）
北京隆昌伟业印刷有限公司　新华书店经销
2023 年 9 月第 1 版　2023 年 9 月第 1 次印刷
开本：710 毫米 ×1010 毫米　1/16　印张：19.5
字数：210 千字
ISBN 978-7-5199-1517-9　定价：79.00 元
电话 010-64217619　64217612（发行部）

→ 三岔水库主坝河床清基
Sancha Reservoir main dam
bed clearing

↑ 首届茅盾文学奖获得者周克芹
Zhou Keqin, winner of the 1st Mao Dun Literature Award

↑ 天府雄州——简阳
Tianfu Xiongzhou—Jianyang

↑ 一江两岸流光溢彩
On both sides of a river, lights shine brightly.

↑ 东来印象
Donglai Impressions

↑ 状元台（简州四状元）
Top Scholar Platform (Jianzhou's four top scholars)

↑ 2019 中华龙舟大赛（成都·简阳站）
2019 China Dragon Boat Competition (Jianyang, Chengdu)

↑ 简州八景之一——塔凌云

One of the eight scenic spots in Jianzhou: Tower Lingyun

深化四川文化研究的新探索

　　简阳，自古号称巨邑雄州，大多数时间属于成都的一部分。2016年，在行政上重新"回归"成都，迎来崭新的发展机遇。在国家赋予成都"成渝地区双城经济圈"建设、世界文化名城建设、公园城市示范区建设等重大使命的背景下，简阳也面临各方面加速与时俱进的任务，立足于四川、成都的文化版图和文化追求，对自身文化个性、文化魅力的梳理、传承与弘扬成为一项重要的工作。由成都大学天府文化研究院院长谭平教授精心撰写的《天府文化之简阳密码》一书，便是这方面卓有成效的一次探索。读罢书稿，感受颇受。

　　一是深化对四川、成都、简阳文化的研究，注重对具有代表性、典型性市县的区域文化进行个案研究。这样以中、微观视野为主的研究，对乡土中国活力的多视角揭示，满足了对中国特色、川蜀风韵的现代化追

求需要，具有传统、宏大的历史著述不可替代的价值。此外，它不仅可以使当地城乡的文化建设取得更好的成效，实现民众不断增长的文化生活、文旅产品的获得感、满足感和幸福感，而且可以举一反三，带给兄弟市区县有益的启示，并在与国内外同类城乡文化交流中，更好地介绍、展示自己，讲好简阳、成都、四川，甚至"中国故事"。正因为有这样的追求，本书的写作手法注重深入浅出，采用中、英文双语呈现的方式，搭配精美的图片，突出其独特性。

二是县域文化个性研究，具有极大的难度，但只有迎难而上，才能推动其向前发展，具备巴蜀文化、天府文化的共性，也能彰显自己独特、优良的个性，形成百花齐放的勃勃生机。分析其难度，首先是四川盆地的市区县生存发展环境变化、族群的构成与变动、历史际遇以及当今发展中面临的主要问题大同小异；其次是史料和其他相关联的文献十分有限，高水平学者对这类中、微观研究积累甚少，对简阳的历史文化个性进行精准梳理、总结、呈现也同样如此，尤其是把这样的梳理、呈现努力对接今日简阳和成都、四川的文化追求，站在历史的高点，提出一些学术可靠，具有前瞻性、启示性的观点和建议，更是难能可贵。这种介于理论和应用之间的学术范式，在服务地方文化传承的事业中，应该予以提倡。

这部书稿的谋篇、布局简明扼要，内容逻辑连贯、详略得当，其独创的研判城市文化水准的四个层次理论、城市文化生态的河流理论具有启发性。对儒、释、道内涵的生动解读，对运用它来审视简阳的天府文化资源的论述，对简阳文化与巴蜀文化、天府文化的逻辑关系的论述；以及对最具有简阳个性的八大文化的内涵和价值的解读，都显示了作者对成都、四川文化资源的探索以及如何实现其创造性价值的转化和创新性发展的深度思考和作为四川人扎根四川乡土，切实助益、推动天府文化在简阳开出绚丽花朵的拳拳之心。

学术，既是智慧，也是情感的结晶。简阳文化内涵丰富，个性独特，值得继续梳理、总结和表达。这本"小"书，无疑开了一个好头，并走在时代前沿，值得鼓励。作者于1978—1982年在川大历史系读本科，1985—1988年在川大历史系读研究生，都是我的学生。乐见其一直在努力用科研助力成都、四川文化事业的发展与进步，谨此为序。

四川大学历史文化学院博士生导师　冉光荣

2022年9月27日

冉光荣：1938年12月出生于四川重庆。1959年于四川大学历史系本科毕业，1962年四川大学历史系先秦史专业研究生毕业，获硕士学位，留系工作。1983年任副教授，1987年晋升为教授，1995年任博士生导师。1984～1993年任历史系副主任、历史研究所副所长，1994～1998年任历史研究所所长，1993年获国务院特殊津贴，1993年至今任四川省人民政府参事，1998年至今任省人大常委、教科文卫专门委员会委员，2000年任四川大学西部开发研究院学术委员。

简阳文化研究概述

谭　平

简阳文化是巴蜀文化、天府文化的一颗耀眼的明珠。历经千百年的积累与发展，这里逐渐形成了深厚且不乏特色的地方文化。龙垭遗址的发掘更是将简阳人类活动的历史追溯到 3 万年前，极大地增添了简阳历史的厚重感。研究简阳文化意义非凡、很有必要。

简阳融入成都后，迎来全新的发展机遇，简阳干部群众开始了新的历史征程。面向现实和未来，不管是从成渝地区双城经济圈建设、四川省"一干多支"和成德眉资同城化发展的战略，还是从全面建设践行新发展理念的公园城市示范区、成都都市圈、世界文化名城的需求来讲，简阳都具有不可忽略的重要地位、重大影响和理应肩负起的历史使命。习近平总书记指出：中华优秀传统文化是中华民族的突出优势；文化自信是更基础、更广泛、更深厚的自信。因此，深化以"东灌文化"为代

表的优秀传统文化的挖掘阐释，有助于推进简阳文化的总结提炼和传承创新，提升城市文化软实力，推动特色鲜明、充满活力的成都东部区域中心城市进一步"雄起"。

给国内外读者介绍简阳的文化个性，并非易事。首先要正确运用"文化"的概念。"文化"一词，在全世界的不同词典里，有两百余种文字解释，对其精准地理解与运用，是简阳文化阐释的理论基础。所谓文化，在汉语中是"人文教化"或"以文化人"的简称，前者强调其资源和事业属性，是一个名词性词组，后者强调文化价值必须在人的素质的优化上得以体现，是一个动词性词组。大部分学者认同，文化包括物质、制度、精神三个层面，尤其强调以价值观和生活方式为核心内涵的人类精神活动，唯有它可以穿越古今，引领或支撑未来的发展。优良的文化具有使人远离假恶丑、走向真善美的推动力量。必须传承、弘扬的文化基因，主要体现在名人生平、有强大正能量的重大事件和典籍名篇中。简阳的八大文化，既有长期在历史的发展和沉淀中形成的重要遗迹和精神共识，如龙垭文化、农耕文化、商道文化、状元文化、名人文化、非遗文化等，也有对现当代简阳群众的集体价值选择和生活方式的提炼与总结，如东灌文化、群众文化等。把简阳八大文化放在这样的坐标里来分析、阐述、研判，既有利于从文化范畴找准八大文化形成的坐标，也有利于从现实角度影显八大文化的城市特色。

其次要选择正确的视角。在城市化、现代化、全球化的背景下说文化，除了合作、融通，也要强调竞争的概念，一个城市的文化建设水准，可以通过纵向比较梳理自身进步与发展，也必须通过横向比较，才能看到自己的差距，从而找准自己的定位，努力彰显城市个性、塑造城市特质。城市的文化水准，当然表现在生活于此地的人民，在文化生活中普遍感受到的安全感、获得感、幸福感以及自信心、自豪感的高低上，但更突出地表现在与情况大致相当的竞争城市相比较，本城优质的人财物是流出多，还是流入多。而城市对于外部优质的人财物的吸引力大小，比照其城市综合形象，可以分为四个层次：被忽略、被记住、被向往、被仰望。因为没有或缺乏优良个性而被关联者忽略的城市，不仅不能吸引外部优质人财物，自身优质的人财物也会大量"逃离"，没有任何发展机会。因为具有某些优良个性而被记住的城市，情况会明显好得多，但吸引力有限，除非你的竞争对手比你给人印象更差。被向往的城市往往具有众多优良个性，并得以成功表达、传播，因此在吸引优质人财物方面会处于优势地位。被仰望，是城市优质人财物竞争力的最高境界，也是"世界文化名城"的核心内涵，当一座城市，因为具有价值观和生活方式的崇高、伟岸、庄严、高雅、包容等外在气质，并得到公认以后，全世界优质的人财物会自动向它汇聚，这样的城市，将立于不败之地。城市在这四个层次中的高低，与本地人民的文化获得感、幸福感、自信心、自豪感的高低，完全成正比。成都不仅志在被人向往，更要成为被仰望的世界文化名城，简阳作为"蜀都东来第一州"，必须要梳理好自身历史文化资源的丰富内涵和当代价值，分别放在天府文化、巴蜀文化、中华文化的版图上，找准自身坐标和定位，既脚踏实地，也志向高远地确立自己的文化发展战略，选择适合自身的发展路径，聚集并用好比较优势资源，实现文化软实力的稳步提升，文化竞争力的逐步增强。

谭平：1961年生，教授。籍贯四川武胜，四川大学本科和研究生毕业，一直供职于成都大学，先后担任学校党委宣传部长和文学与新闻传播学院院长等职，主要从事中国古代史、巴蜀文化和天府文化的研究、教学。单独或排名第一获得省市政府科研、教学成果奖八项，有专著十余部（多部翻译成英语和西班牙语），大型文学作品两部，论文近百篇。兼任成都市天府文化传承发展促进会会长，天府文化研究院院长，省社科院四川研究院学术委员，四川省李冰、杨慎研究会副会长，四川武则天研究会学术委员会主任等职。

目　录

导　论

在中国 960 万平方公里百花齐放的文化地图上，基于思考和研究，生动介绍一个县级城市的地域文化魅力，既要阐明其与中华文明、巴蜀文化的共性，也要指出其能够与时俱进的文化个性，绝非易事。如果还要助力实现城市钩沉历史、回应现实、引领未来的志向和追求，更是对论述者的巨大考验。这首先取决于作者研究、阐释的视野和方位，必须把简阳放在中华文明及其区域分支巴蜀文化、典型都市表达天府文化的主坐标上加以衡量，才能够形成科学严谨的总体研判。其次，研究者最好有独具个性的理论，才容易在人们耳熟能详、司空见惯的史料和资料上，产生新的具有启发性的论述和结论，而不是对已有事实和研判的重新组装，或新瓶子里依然装着"老白干"。再次，如何谋篇布局也至关重要。韩愈说过，写作要"惟陈言之务去"，没有人愿意读陈词滥调，更没有人愿意接受冗长、乏味的"鸡汤"，因此，必须以干练、简洁、生

动为原则，实现资料、论述的详略取舍的尽可能优化。

第一节　在文化版图上认识简阳文化

一、问题的提出

众所周知，中华文明是地球上唯一没有中断过的古老文明，它历经无数天灾人祸和悲欢离合，至今依然生机勃勃，在奉行丛林法则的西方文明的强烈刺激和冲击中，凤凰涅槃，浴火重生。习近平总书记一再强调，传承、弘扬中华优秀传统文化是我们的根与魂，文化自信是最重要的自信和力量之源。中华文化作为一个精神家园，由儒、释、道共同建构，儒家为主，释道为辅。我们在研究简阳文化的历史渊源和当代表达时发现，在简阳的文化中，儒、释、道既是活水之源，其践行也有精彩的呈现。因此，研究和阐释简阳文化，首先要深刻理解儒释道共同构建的中华文化，精准认识其丰富价值内涵，唯有如此，文化遗产（包括文物）和文化景观的保护、利用才能打动人心、形成共识、建立个性。在新时代传承弘扬简阳历史文化，是在中华文化坐标体系下构建简阳城市特质的文化选择，是形成城市发展广泛共识和展现群众生活方式的文化表达，意义重大，影响深远。

二、认识儒、释、道是理解简阳文化的基础

所有文化（或文明），如欲在与其他文化（或文明）的冲击、竞争中与时俱进，生生不息，必须最智慧地解答三大问题：人与自然的关系、人与人的关系、人与自己的关系。中华文化恰恰在这一点上显示了巨大的优势，分属于儒释道或在儒释道中实现着融会贯通的列祖列宗与时贤，为我们建构了一个具备海纳百川、开放自信、吐故纳新气度和功能的进退有据的文化体系和精神家园。可以说，这在人类历史上是独一无二的。

以孔子、孟子为符号的儒家文化，是世界上对如何处理人与人（含族群与族群、国家与国家）的关系，认识最温暖、最人性、最智慧的文化。《礼记》中描绘的"大同"世界，是人类命运共同体意识的最早发端；《论语》中记载的孔子弟子子夏所言"四海之内皆兄弟也"，是人类最早的反种族主义意识；"君子和而不同"是抛弃文化傲慢与偏见的最早宣示；"皇天无亲，唯德是辅""修文德以来之"是必须以德服人、以理服人（而不是丛林法则）的文明礼义之邦的高尚气度。正是因为秉持这样的价值观念和交往心理，中国在两千多年中，始终是地球上版图最为辽阔的国家之一，今天的56个民族能够相亲相爱，和谐共处，并在改革开放40年以后重新走近世界舞台的中央，"和平崛起"势不可当。包括简阳在内的天府成都，依靠"一带一路"、成渝地区双城经济圈、公园城市示范区建设等宏大战略，与国内以及世界各地建立了广泛良性交融，实现了历史巨变。儒家的核心价值观是仁义礼智

信和忠孝廉耻，都是处理人与人关系的金玉良言。儒家核心价值观，从各个方面、层面确立了人际交往应遵循的准则，成为今日社会主义核心价值观丰厚的历史滋养。在简阳的名人文化、状元文化、东灌文化、农耕文化中，都能感受到鲜明的儒家精神影响。

为更好地以儒家精神来解读简阳文化，我还建立了一个这样的系统表述——儒家的强大正能量有：以爱和忠诚为核心的情感世界；以仁义礼智信为核心的价值观；以立德立功立言为标准的人生观；以诗词歌赋琴棋书画为主的生活方式；天行健君子以自强不息，地势坤君子以厚德载物的人生态度。把简阳历史上具有代表性的人物和有重大影响的事件，放在这样一个坐标中去加以检验和审视，便不难形成较为客观公正的评判。事实上，在2100余年建置史中，很长一个时期，推动简阳时代进步和文化形成的，都是儒家的传人和信奉者。不深刻认识儒家文化的价值，很难全面深入地解读状元文化、名人文化和东灌文化的活水之源。

以老子（他最后的隐居地应该是在成都或成都附近）和庄子为主要标签的道家，以及后来在成都平原率先形成的道教，在论述并践行人与自然的关系方面，作出了独到的贡献。儒家、道家都有"天人合一"的观念，而《道德经》将其进一步描述为"人法地，地法天，天法道，道法自然"。道家思想是世界历史上最早主张人类必须顺应、尊重自然，与自然和谐相处的伟大哲学。道家和道教把人的肉体也看成自然的一部分，它认为最成功的人生是拥有健康的身体、自由的个性。道家和道教认为：如果人生的其他目标妨碍了健康的身体、自由的个性，都是可以放弃的；只有在兼容的情况下，才会去追求。如果说儒家是人类历史上最成功的集体主义的话，道家就是人类历史上最温和、最善良的个人主义，是对个性各异、人生风险莫测、命途难以自主的芸芸众生提供的独到关怀，没有道家和道教，就不可能有严君平、扬雄、陶渊明、李白、苏东坡等历史名人的独特精神体系，也不可能有《西游记》《聊斋志异》等名著的独特文化风貌。成都平原是地球上道教和道家的大本营，也是深受道家文化影响的城市，崇尚自然的道家哲学及其实践留下的诸多遗产，也是成都建设公园城市示范区、世界文化名城的重要资源。简阳人民历史上捐资兴建、重修道教寺庙史不绝书。由此可见，在漫长的历史中，简阳这片土地深受道家观念和主张的影响，后来形成的"大道至简，阳光致远"的简阳城市精神，或多或少还有一些道家思想的身影。

人应该怎样与自己相处？佛学、佛教作出了独到的贡献。佛学、佛教出自古代的印度、今天的尼泊尔，东汉前期，它经丝路来到中国，经历了与儒家、道家及道教的碰撞与融合，在隋唐时实现汉化（简阳的庙宇多数开始于这一时期，说明四川盆地，尤其是成都平原的佛教变革与中原完全同步），禅宗和净土宗成为绝对的主流（简阳也不例外）。如果说儒家修身，道家养性，佛教则是宁心之学。佛教、佛学博大精深，但浓缩其要旨，不外净心、宁心之学。佛教认为，人生最重要的价值，是能经常保持内心的洁净和宁静，能否做到，决定人是否幸福（无烦恼），以及来世的状态。这与人的身份、地位无关。汉化的佛教主张"众生平等""慈航普度"（大乘佛教），主张行善积德，主张与儒家伦理尽量兼容、适应，总体上使人向善。至于佛教在哲学、美学、语言学、神话建构、建筑及园林、服饰等诸多领域对中华文明的独

到贡献，在简阳，我们也能够有深刻的感受。如果说儒家是集体主义、道家是个人主义，那么佛教、佛学则是面对众生的慈悲与关怀。其净心、宁心的自我关怀、自我激励、自我升华留下了许多故事与传说。简阳历史上佛教寺庙众多，也不乏高僧大德的身影，涌现出许多捐资、出力兴建、重建寺庙的行为，也相继出现过一批诸如简州双孝子等体现佛教理念的践行者，把这些历史发展中的简阳特征放在天府文化乐观包容、友善公益的视角下，也能够在当代找到充分的呼应。

四川大学著名学者舒大刚先生，用如下的语言总结儒释道给炎黄子孙持续提供的正能量：儒家使人拿得起，道家使人放得下，佛家使人想得开。这无疑是最精辟的总结。我们审视今天简阳的儒释道三教遗产、景观以及影响，这样的评价也可以借鉴。

总之，准确认识和把握儒释道文化对中华文明的影响，是认识、理解甚至把握简阳历史上的状元、名人现象以及在历史上以集体行动产生了引人注目现象的普通民众行为的关键所在，也是理解近现代以来简阳城市、乡村文脉演变的重要依据。

三、简阳文化与巴蜀文化、天府文化的逻辑关系

（一）巴蜀文化与简阳

巴蜀文化是天府四川的地域文化。产生、活动于四川盆地及其周边部分区域，其中心和首府，绝大部分时间都在成都，是多元一体的中华文明中不可替代的一元，源远流长，底蕴非常深厚。据考古工作者论证：巴蜀文化距今已有5000余年的历史，与中原文化、齐鲁文化、

三晋文化一起构成了中国上古时代的几大文化体系，对整个中华文明的创造和发展产生了不可磨灭的作用。立体的山水、丰富的物产、多样的族群、频转的灾祥、反复的移民，是巴蜀文化产生和演进的五个主要基础，其综合性的作用，形成了巴蜀人从容自信、兼容并包、张弛有道、重商崇文、热情浪漫的基本价值观和生活方式，并能够代代传承。

毫无疑问，简阳的人文个性也几乎完全吻合上述成因（除了多样的族群这一特点稍弱以外）和特征，并在山水、物产、移民等方面展现出优良的个性魅力、历史传承与现代表达。今天我们研究、阐释、传播简阳文化，就是为了彰显简阳与其他县市既有共性，也不乏个性的城市人文魅力。如果以四川众多同级别市县为参照，一直号称巨邑和蜀都门户的简阳，其综合性成就和影响力，使其无疑是巴蜀文化区域的一个强势存在，是有多方面代表性、影响力的"天府雄州"。而简阳文化，正是巴蜀文化在简阳的区域性表达和生动的诠释，找准简阳文化在巴蜀文化传承中的坐标体系，有利于彰显简阳在巴蜀地区的城市地位和提升简阳人的文化自信。不过，包括原资阳市各县（区）在内的四川各县（市）区，以及全国各地与简阳有经济文化交流的同级别县（市）区，都知道简阳融入成都以后，将获得更加优越的物质和文化资源，各界对简阳的期望值也随之大幅提升，简阳能否保住其在巴蜀文化版图上的经济文化"雄州"地位，未可盲目乐观。

（二）天府文化与简阳

天府文化是天府成都的文化，这一概念及其行动，出自 2017 年 4

月召开的成都市第十三次党代会，2022年4月召开的成都市第十四次党代会，对传承弘扬这一文化又提出了新的深化要求。天府文化主要是指成都行政区域的地域文化，在一些语境下，其产生、活动区域，也包括在历史上曾经纳入成都府（市）管辖或对天府文化有决定性影响的一些区域，如今天的成德眉资大都市圈的部分区域，以及甘孜州、阿坝州的紧密关联区域。当然，它的核心是今天成都行政直接管辖区域。既有农耕畜牧文化，也有工商文化，包括中国化、本土化的近现代文明。除了三星堆、金沙等八座"王城"体现的先秦成都城市前身的神秘浪漫（但因为迄今没有发现相关文字，难以进行准确描述，且它们的相互关系也无法言说）震惊世界，成为这座城市乃至中华文明在青铜时代的顶级篇章以外，天府文化特别强调的是，自张仪筑城以来，2300年以上的成都都市文化。它是巴蜀文化开出的花结出的果，是巴蜀文化的浓缩和精彩呈现，是巴蜀文化与中国其他地域文化和世界上的其他文明发生碰撞、交流、融汇的主要代表。这个代表的使命和功能有时是桥梁，有时是引领，有时是兼而有之。其奋斗目标是：传承巴蜀文明，发展天府文化，努力建设世界文化名城。其核心与个性是：创新创造，优雅时尚，乐观包容，友善公益。

"天府文化"的提出和实践，是成都市委站在新的事业起点上，以对历史记忆的豪迈认同、对时代需求的积极回应和对未来发展的卓越追求的姿态，强力助推成渝地区双城经济圈、公园城市示范区、成都都市圈的重要举措，全面体现了成都文化下一步建设、发展的不凡志向，且已经产生强大的传播力、动员力。天府文化建设的目标可以分为对内对外两个指向：对内，形成全市人民的价值共识和共有精神家园，推动文化事业与产业健康发展。对外，让成都成为一座被亲近被仰望的城市。

对简阳影响最大，也使简阳进入并融入成都"东进"战略的，是成渝地区双城经济圈建设、公园城市示范区建设和世界文化名城建设的多重需求。把这样的城市文化规划、文化理想、文化志向、文化行动作为坐标，与成都市其他区（市）县相比较，当今简阳，除了在人口、面积、水面上，依然可以号称"雄州"以外，其他能够彰显现代化、国际化、全球化大都市文明，在城市模式、范型、经验、风韵等方面能反映成都乃至中国、世界顶级物质文明、制度文明、精神文明的成就，数量明显偏少。特别是紧密围绕"创新创造，优雅时尚，乐观包容，友善公益"天府文化总体个性展开的文化资源保护、传承，创造性转化和创新性发展工作，简阳并不是一个"雄州"。但2100余年的建置史以及与成都长期的互动交融，让简阳在人文地理、文化个性等方面的塑造具有深厚的底蕴和鲜明的特质，形成了壮美的历史、至美的人文和优美的风光，无论是从历史的维度还是客观的现实来审视，简阳在天府文化中都具有值得一提的分量，或可成为天府文化中辨识度较高的区域城市，为天府文化的建设与发展作出独特的贡献。

四、努力方向

融入成都后，简阳文化更是成为天府文化密不可分的一部分，因此，要充分借力于简阳文化的挖掘、阐释与传承，迅速提高文化行动的站位、统筹以及文化特色与亮点的打造，努力使简阳在天府文化的

版图上成为名副其实的"天府雄州"。以高新产业和高端服务业为主体的成都东部新区建设、设施世界一流的天府国际机场的建成及其附带产业、事业的展开，简阳市委、市政府对文化建设的高度重视和竭诚努力，正是简阳在文化建设方面奋起直追、迎头赶上，焕发"天府雄州"城市荣光的良好基础；而科学、系统、准确认识简阳最有代表性的八大文化，并将之放在巴蜀文化、天府文化的坐标体系中来擦拭、打造，正是一项十分重要的奠基性工作。

第二节　理论建构与运用

一、衡量城乡文化水准的四个层次理论

任何城市或乡村既有的文化水平，可被分为四个层次：被忽略、被记住、被向往、被仰望。所谓被忽略，是指城市或乡村，因为平庸、落后，无法让人留下正面印象，自然它们不仅不能获取外部资源与发展机会，自己的人、财、物还会流走，这样的地方没有任何振兴的希望。所谓被记住，是指因为具有某些特色或个性，能在过此地的人心中留下正面的印象，换来某种好感，这样的地方具有了一定发展可能，但空间有限。所谓被向往，是指具有比较突出的优良个性与条件，使来过此地的人们，心向往之，产生在此地居住、生活的愿望，张艺谋先生为成都做的"成都，一座来了就不想离开的城市"的广告，展示的就

是这样一个境界，这样的城市，发展会比较顺利。所谓被仰望的城市，是指因为具备某些独有的诸如崇高、伟岸、浪漫、仁慈、温暖、高雅的特质，使外部受众产生仰望感觉的城市。达到被仰望，是世界文化名城的主要标志。因为在全球化的时代谈文化，不可能不带有竞争性，只有处于被仰望水准的城市，不仅它的优秀子孙和其他优质资源不会流失，而且全世界优质的人、财、物，都会自动流向此城此地。因此，它在竞争中将立于不败之地。成都自古是中国的标杆城市之一，在公认的中国是文明礼仪之邦的漫长历史上，至少从汉代起，成都就经常是世界文化名城。伴随中华民族伟大复兴的征程，成都的目标自然是重新成为被仰望的世界文化名城。

简阳城乡的文化建设，可参照此理论，根据目前自身拥有的资源、文化发展水平，有针对性地进行规划和谋篇布局。底线是要使所有社区（村）摆脱被忽略，至少被记住，有条件者形成被向往，条件最优者要迈向被仰望。从历史文化资源的发掘、运用来讲，状元文化、东灌文化以及名人文化中的顶尖部分，要从形成被仰望的城市形象去努力，突出其崇高、庄严、伟岸的精神属性，并进行传播和表达，形成简阳人民文化自豪的主要依据；龙垭文化、名人文化、商道文化，要从形成被向往的城乡形象去发力，突出其在中国有特质、四川有个性、成都有魅力的属性，产生强大、持续的感染性、感动性，形成简阳人民文化自信的深厚基础；而农耕文化、群众文化、非遗文化，应该主要从形成被记忆的城乡形象入手，突出其个性化的浓烈乡愁和文盛工巧、守望相助、急公好义的温暖感与亲和力，助力宜业宜居的幸福简阳的形象塑造。

二、衡量市（村）民文化修养的四个类型理论

城市文化的深厚根基，是市民的文化修养。人的文化修养，可分为四个类型：失律、他律、自律、自励。所谓失律之人，是指自暴自弃者，缺乏做人做事的起码规矩，最有可能违法失德，成为社会负能量；所谓他律者，指只能由法律、法规加以刚性约束的人，法律法规力量不及的时间、地点（比如有红绿灯但没有摄像头的十字路口），这样的地方就会有人闯红灯，成为社会的负能量；所谓自律之人，靠自我约束，服从、服务于集体、社会，一般都是社会的正能量；所谓自励者，是指特别具有奋斗、奉献、牺牲精神的人群，他们是人群中最强大的正能量。我们的文化建设，要让自励者家喻户晓，受到广泛尊敬和追随；让自律者身心放松，受到最多优待；让他律者知其愚暗，得到进步之鞭策、鼓励；让失律者良知复活，否则必遭严惩或鄙视。

改革开放以来，作为曾经的农业大县，简阳开启了逐渐增速的城市化、城镇化、国际化进程，尤其是纳入成都以来，这一进程空前提速。必须清醒地看到，新老市民有不可忽视的精神家园重构、价值共识凝聚问题。面对大部分市民村民，文化建设的目标，应致力于全面消除失律人群（法治治标，文化治本），包容他律人群，壮大自律人群，对少数自励的精英（突出表现在重要历史名人和当下每年简阳产生的各种优秀人才中），应该在城市和社区文化建设中，得到最大的尊敬，事迹得到广泛传播，产生更多的能够代言天府文化、巴蜀文明，甚至中华文化的简阳精英（状元文化、东灌文化、名人文化大有可为），为成都市最终成为举世仰望的世界文化名城，做出点滴成涓并最终汇流成河的简阳贡献。

三、认识、运用成都的生活美学

最近几年，"有一种生活美学叫成都"逐渐家喻户晓，体现了成都人植根传统、因应现实、勾连未来的生活方式的独特魅力。它是成都被向往、被仰望的重要资源，简阳虽然融入成都的时间不长，但长期以来形成的生活美学追求与成都的生活美学内涵可谓一脉相承，但在生活美学的呈现上，还有一定的差距，充分运用简阳文化资源，加以创新性转化和创造性发展，是简阳对标对表、奋起直追，加快融入成都生活美学的应有之义。所谓生活美学，是指怎样的生活方式及其内涵具有美感，使人从内到外拥有并洋溢轻松、愉悦、自在、幸福之美，使人赏心悦目，或能获取关于美的正向思考。概而言之，成都生活美学就是生活的艺术化、艺术的生活化中间形成的人文风情和社会风尚，它是成都优良城市个性中最具有同理心、最具有穿透力和传播价值的"成都故事"和"中国故事"。其灵魂是平民化的人文关切，艺术化的都市风情，使所有人都能迅速放松的空间、景观创制哲学。规划、行动的关键词是平衡、协调——成都始终是一座其主人公能够轻松实现自然与人文、物质与精神、感性与理性、个体与群体、历史与现实、城市与乡村、男性与女性之间多重平衡、协调的城市，不管是这些平衡、协调的多元性，还是这些平衡、协调本身的稳定性，成都均罕有其匹，

并因此缔造了超高的人民生活的幸福指数。连续 13 年，成都在中国大都市幸福指数排名中名列第一，很大程度上依靠其独有的生活美学的支撑。

生活美学追求在简阳，以"简州八景""文盛工巧"和"大道至简，阳光致远""诚诺四方·铭刻简阳"和"城山相映，人水共生"这些物质实体、精神文化表达所体现的崇尚平衡、协调的人文气质为古今标识，农耕与工商、文教平衡，儒释道在此地和谐共生，官民生活崇文尚武并重，以羊肉汤为代表的简阳平民化美食城乡咸宜、雅俗共品、老少同尝。但是我们必须看到，生活美学作为典型的都市文明的高端部分，它在指向性、精致度、辨识度、传播力、同理心上都有较高的要求，简阳与成都的一二圈层城市相比，尚有明显差距。简阳城乡社区文化应注重成都生活美学个性传承与弘扬，将生活美学内涵充分纳入街道、社区文化建设中，扎根本地文化资源，以精致、个性的场景营建和空间打造，以及独具简阳烟火味、文化韵和艺术范的氛围营造为着力点，聚焦城市生活高品质属性打造、品牌建构；注重窗口行业以及购物和消费场所的多种语言使用；形成城乡关系和睦、新老市民亲善、弱势群体受关怀、各个阶层各种个性的人彼此理解、雅俗文艺活动有充足的公共空间预留的和谐共生局面（市民活动空间的环境和程序设计，不仅是精致的，更是人性的、温暖的，有艺术情调的，能带来愉悦和幸福感的）。

四、健全城乡文化优良生态的"河流理论"

纵观人类城市文明史，伟大的长盛不衰的城市一般位于大江大河的入海口，或多条河流交汇的地理空间，除了人类取水用水的需要使然之外，更重要的是这样的地理位置也是生物多样性最丰富多彩的区域。物质提供的丰富多彩不仅是精神世界、精神文明丰富多彩的决定性依据，而且保持生物多样性需要的条件与文化保持以多元多样为根本的活力需要并无二致。我们可以把地域文化圈比喻为这样的河流和海洋、河流与河流交汇的三角洲：浩荡前行不可阻挡的主流，水流充沛各具特色的支流，必不可少的回流，星罗棋布干湿、深浅不同的湿地、沼泽，各种类型的浅滩、树林。主流，在八大文化中状元文化、东灌文化、名人文化是其历史标志；支流相当于在此区域内有正能量有特色的价值选择与生活方式，比如成都这座城市或某个区（市）县长期以来形成的有特色有重要影响的风俗、节庆、非遗（如简阳独有的商道文化、非遗文化）；回流，就是一些人不违背公俗良俗和法律的个性化生存方式，比如独身、丁克、吸烟、小富即安、打麻将、斗地主、玩手机、打游戏、夜店生活；湿地、沼泽和浅滩、树林，是所有人都可能在某个时段、某种状态下需要的空间和生存条件，比如同学会、战友会、同乡会、行业组织、公益组织及活动等（简阳群众文化和农耕文化的普通层面）。城市文化河流理论告诉我们，城市基础的文化建设，当然要顺应国家和地方的文化建设主旋律，但也必须包容、体恤甚至尊重人群的喜怒哀乐，在理解、帮扶、尊重的基础上去谋求逐渐

的优化，永远没有必要以强求、高压、非此即彼的态度和思维去实现
"文化振兴"。因为这个理论的关键，不是比构成这个生态系统的诸要
素谁更重要更优越，而是强调诸要素的互相支撑、互相生成。所以如
果有一个社区文化属于"主流"，当然光荣，但那些属于"支流""回
流""沼泽"的社区并不应处于被歧视的地位，所以，每个社区应根据
自己的资源、条件，做符合规律的事情，服务好在地居民。这个理论，
可以帮助我们理解成都文化包容性的内涵（在中国所有城市中，成都
的文化"河流"提供的文化多样性支撑，无与伦比，但这得另专题论
述），找到各类正常治理下的社区都可以作出独到贡献的根基，以及思
考如何实现这一优良城市个性的创造性转化与创新性发展。

　　总之，上述理论，符合城市优良文化生态的形成和运行规律，有
利于建立文化活动和文化事业评价的科学标准，形成文化事业和文化
产业发展的科学谋划，并在扎实开展体现文化产品、服务供给的公平
正义的常规工作的基础上，集中优质资源，优化顶层设计，点面结合，
逐步打造具有简阳鲜明个性、天府风韵、巴蜀味道、中国气派，并不乏
国际范的城市文化名片。

　　以上的理论，将在后面八大文化的专题论述中有所体现。

第三节　文化与城市发展

一、城市是文化的创造和聚散中心

中国的城市，绝大多数起源于政治统治、军事控制（含抵御外敌入侵和镇压内部叛乱），以及开展最盛大的宗教或祖宗、神明祭祀等文化活动的需要，因此，聚集着、吸附着最有能量的人、财、物。在古代、近代和现当代，自然都是所在区域的文化生存、发展和交流的主要舞台。它吸纳乡村和异域、异国的文化，也在自己有力量和渠道时，对乡村、异域和异国输出自己的文化。在这种吸纳和输出中，"出超"越多，竞争力越强，"入超"越多，竞争力越弱。根据我们的文化竞争力理论，以及符号学和品牌塑造理论，城市竞争力的从弱到强，可以分为被忽略、被记住、被向往、被仰望四个层次。在一般情况下，没有城市愿意被忽略，也没有城市不希望自己被记住、被向往，最好是被仰望。只有价值观和生活方式更有道义感召力、人性温暖度，更使人产生生活幸福感的城市，才可能被仰望、被向往。简阳在历史上多数时期是拥有属县的州府所在地，后来虽降格为普通县，也因为其独特的自然、经济、政治地理和人文传统，是一个拥有较强文化创造和"出超"能力的雄州。融入成都后的简阳，天时、地利、人和，条件更加优越，八大文化的传承弘扬，既有利于简阳在文化软实力上实现较大提

升、城市特质塑造上标识鲜明，也有利于成都实现更大规模的文化"出超"，成为世界文化名城。

二、文化是城市能否生生不息的关键力量

古往今来，任何族群或国家，都不可能在所有方面永远领先，盛衰沉浮在所难免，这是人类社会演变的铁律。城市作为其生存、发展的主要据点，也会有荣辱兴替，甚至完全毁灭。成都平原的所有城市，包括简阳，都至少经历了宋末元初、明末清初原住民几乎全部被消灭的巨大苦难。人类历史上，有些国家、族群、城市，毁灭了就永远消失了，但中华民族、中国的无数城市，都能够在一次次苦难中凤凰涅槃，创造新的辉煌。在拥有两千年以上历史的文明古国中，只有中国有这样的力量。其关键在于，以仁义礼智信和忠孝廉耻为核心的价值观、以诗词歌赋琴棋书画为生活方式的中华文化，在成都、简阳这样的城市的人民中间，代代传承与弘扬；加上能够海纳百川、吐故纳新、进退有据，使中国的城市，生生不息。当今中国的社会主义城市文化，是中华优秀传统文化与时俱进的时代表达，而成都市第十四次党代会加以丰富的"开明开放、创新创造"的城市品格，"奋斗幸福、达观友善"的人文特质，则是成都实现多重重大历史使命，尤其是建设世界文化名城的号角和旗帜。简阳，必须主动汇聚在这一旗帜下，积极探索，将历史文化代表的简阳人民的精、气、神，转变成天府文化的"简阳实践""简阳经验""简阳模式"。这样的简阳，才能更好地造福子孙后代，并成为大成都的亮丽风景和决定性文化力量。

三、优良的文化个性是城市的"唯一不动产"

在以市场经济为杠杆的现代化、全球化浪潮中，衡量一个城市的发展水准，最常用的指标是 GDP 总量和人均 GDP，这样的指标固然重要，但不可过分迷恋，除了各国形成这些数据的统计方法有别，使用的货币只能反映货币兑换关系，掩盖了部分实际购买力的真相以外，各国的税收制度的差别、贫富差距的差别，以及可以供给的商品和服务的种类的差别，都可以使 GDP 总量和人均 GDP 与具体的人的真实生活水平有不小的差别。而且，在解决人的温饱和形成基本体面的生活以后，物质财富的累积和超越常人的炫耀性消费到底能否增加人的幸福指数，能增加多少幸福指数，因人而异，但在中国文化里（包括儒、释、道），炫耀性消费是没有多少价值，甚至是被鄙视的，因为注重物质与精神生活平衡的人，会在拥有温饱或体面的物质生活以后，将人生的重心转向精神生活，由精神生活（与诗词歌赋、琴棋书画、学术教育、收藏鉴赏、造福桑梓、捐赠贫弱等有关）获取生命的精致、温暖、庄重、崇高等感觉。为富不仁被人鄙视，为富行仁、富而好礼才是社会的福音、个体的升华。成都是中国所有大都市中，延续了两千多年这样的平衡的城市之一，天府文化用十六字表达的个性，全部与此有因果关系。世界上所有长盛不衰的城市，均有正能量强大的优良文化个性，在这个资本的力量无所不在的世界上，所有东西几乎都可以转化成商品被买走，只有成为根深蒂固的观念和传统的城市文化，是城市的无价之宝，别的城市顶多只能模仿、借鉴，但无法买走。所

以，简阳文化中蕴含的简阳独有的优良文化基因与个性，必须变成强大的文化软实力，并形成若干中国一流、四川一流的文化品牌，显著地增强简阳人民、甚至成都人民的文化自信心和自豪感。当这一天到来的时候，简阳的优秀人才会普遍以报效祖国、造福家乡为最高荣誉，简阳以外的优势人财物资源，会越来越多自动流向简阳，那时的简阳该是何等辉煌。

简阳城市文化的形成与发展

　　简阳市，位于北纬 30 度这一黄金纬度，拥有地处川中、沱江纵贯、山水多样、立体秀美的自然地理，农耕资源富集、物产丰饶、四川主要商道穿越的经济地理，毗邻成都（历史上大部分时间都是蜀郡、成都府的属县）、常有军队驻扎、战事演绎，四川最重要的官道（包括沱江航运）穿越的政治地理，以及两千多年一以贯之的宗教和文学艺术吸附力、创造力，既崇文也尚武的人文地理格局。简阳，特殊的方位，使它可集聚和演绎儒、释、道的正能量，并在形成既有中华文明共性，也经历了"西学东渐"的洗礼，不乏巴蜀文化、天府文化魅力的优良鲜明的人文个性方面，拥有充沛的动力和资源。

第一节　简阳城市文化的形成

城市文化，是一个城市主流、大众的成型、稳定的价值观和生活方式，如果还具有某些优良禀赋与个性，并得到很好的传承与弘扬，便成为这个城市的"唯一不动产"。中国人爱从天时、地利、人和的视角论述重要人物沉浮、重要事业兴替、重要现象显隐，下面我们就来说说简阳城市文化形成的三个因素。

一、天时

我们认为，简阳城市文化形成的天时，是源远流长的中华文化、巴蜀文化和天府文化对它的深厚滋养，以及历代王朝对于四川形成并努力维持"天府之国"，和成都控驭大西南之首位城市的繁荣富庶，所需的政治、经济、文化、社会乃至生态活力的各种支持与扶持，以及历史上多次以政府作为主角的帮助四川成都恢复、发展、壮大的移民运动、救灾和赋税蠲免行动。出土文物显示，简阳至少在西周时期已经与华夏主体文化有了交流，并有蜀国和秦汉地方军队驻扎或军事活动发生，因此有尚武的传统，但也延续了巴蜀文化、天府文化神秘浪漫的传统。李冰治水、文翁化蜀同样是牛鞞县诞生的依据。在汉朝气势恢宏的开疆拓土需求，和成都已经成为世界级的伟大城市（毫无疑间，汉武帝时期的中国是世界一流强国，其"五都"都是世界级的都市）的绚丽文化辐射的背景之下，牛鞞县逐步形成，这也浓缩、体现了非同凡响的来自国家、地方政府层面的引领性力量。从一开始在行政隶属和城市功能定位上，就服从国家大局，形成了简阳城市文化的一个优良个性。

二、地利

（一）始终拥有面积较大的空间

简阳在历史上经历过牛鞞县、武康郡、阳安郡、简州、简阳县的建置流变，作为郡与州时，常下辖2~3个县。明朝的简州，还包括了龙泉镇巡检司和资阳镇巡检司，唯独清朝的简州，没有下辖县，但包括了龙泉镇巡检司。中华民国建立后，简阳县就是一个单独的县了。即使没有了辖县的清代以来，简阳仍有2500多平方公里的空间，是四川盆地中西部的一个大县，即使后来龙泉驿区和洛带区被划出，仍然保留了2200多平方公里。在较宽广的空间上生存繁衍、创新创造，能更好地辗转腾挪，整合资源，聚合力量，当然更有利于文化资源的生存、文化活动的开展、文化类型的丰富。今日简阳的八大文化，多数都与这空间的辽阔有关。

（二）自然、人文美景多样、交融

地处黄金纬度北纬30度之简阳，境内平原、山地、江河、浅丘、森林齐备，尤其是成都平原东部屏障龙泉山的巍然矗立、绵延不绝和

沱江中游在此的奔腾不息，境内自然美景丰富多样，动植物、农作物资源十分丰富。简州八景、圣德寺白塔、石盘题名塔、禾丰字库塔、众多摩崖石刻，以及历史上数不胜数的儒释道庙宇殿堂和会馆，地方神祇、祖先崇拜景观，再加上众多名人在简阳留下的碑刻、墨宝，与自然山水城乡院落有序交融。20 世纪 70 年代东灌工程完成以后，形成了三岔湖、龙泉湖的辽阔水面，与龙泉山遥相呼应，形成壮美的"两湖一山"佳景。在视觉、心理感受具有丰富美感的环境中生存，当然有利于培养人对真善美的热爱和向往，培养乐观豁达、积极向上的人生态度，甚至更加浓烈、深沉的乡愁与家国情怀。名人文化、状元文化、群众文化，尤其与这样的资源禀赋有关。

（三）地理位置绝佳

简阳之西毗邻成都（在龙泉驿、洛带属于简阳的漫长历史时期，简阳还在平原上与成都直接相连）、向东通过官道和商道（含水路），直接勾连川南、川东的内江、重庆等。新中国成立以来，简阳先后迎来成渝铁路、成渝高速、天府国际机场，回归成都以后，纳入大都市圈的交通网络，不论是对接成都平原各种优质资源，还是连接中国各地以及走向世界，简阳已成为一块被其他市县羡慕的高地。与龙泉山以西的成都下辖区（市）县不同，简阳通过这种优越位置既可以得成都经济文化多方面滋养，也可以获得川东、川南巨邑雄府的丰富信息和人财物流动的正能量，同时对周围世界辐射简阳独特的人文魅力。名人文化、商道文化、非遗文化与此紧密关联。

三、人和

　　古今简阳，农耕条件极其优越，人民朴实勤劳，手工业从业者心灵手巧，从汉至宋，曾经在其土地上生活过的獽、夷、僚等土著民族，经济与文化水准以及社会发育都明显落后于原蜀人与华夏族混居后形成的新族群，文献记载，獽、夷、僚等土著民族后来逐步离开了简阳，但这一过程很长，并没有汉族人欺负、驱赶这些民族的记载。历史上的简阳，只要是和平和非暴政恶政导致的改朝换代时期，总是安土重迁、耕读传家、诗礼传家、文武并重、文化和宗教信仰包容、人民守望相助、热心公益的一块热土。简阳的城市文化，就在与本地农耕文化的水乳交融、与成都府城及其所属的县市官员士大夫和民众的友好交往中形成并与时俱进、推陈出新。除了龙垭文化，其他文化都与简阳古今的人和有密切关联。汉语中讲"政通人和"，其实主要来自官员思想和行动的"政通"与主要来自普通民众基本文化素养的"人和"是互为因果、互相成就的。宋以来，简阳科举有不俗的表现，主要原因之一就是地方官员注重办学和民间教育的培植，与民间源远流长的耕读传家、诗礼传家、科举兴家的风尚形成了良性循环。清代简阳主官普遍重视学校教育，众多书院都得到他们以及地方士绅的鼎力相助，成为简阳走出众多进士、举人、秀才的决定性因素。宋代的情况应该更好，因为笔者研究过宋代成都历任知府，他们几乎无一例外都真诚地关心、扶持以府学为主体、书院为重要支撑的教育活动，所以简阳走出了四个状元。

第二节　简阳城市文化的发展历程

一、简阳城市文化的历史脉络

（一）文化基因与源头

1. 蜀人祖庭，自带神秘浪漫气质

简阳地区，是四川盆地最早有人类活动的地方之一。发现于现重庆市巫山县，距今有204万年的巫山人，属于原来的四川，但该地严格来讲不属于四川盆地。因此，四川盆地的旧石器时期人类遗存，目前只有出土于资阳沱江河谷的"资阳人"和出土于简阳的龙垭文化（距今约2万—3万年），[①] 说明简阳地区的自然地理和经济地理，自古特别适合人类生存、繁衍。在先秦时期，此地属于古蜀国，目前学术界对于古蜀国的族群、政权、疆域盈缩的状况以及它们的聚散离合众说纷纭，莫衷一是，但三星堆、金沙遗址出土的文物，却显示了古蜀国的人民不仅有政教合一的丰富多彩的精神生活和艺术追求，也有以盛大祭祀和浪漫夸张的器物制造、制作体现的罕见的想象力、审美意趣，以及他们对神灵和王权的共同敬畏。这一神秘浪漫的文化基因，使蜀

---

① 鉴于"资阳人"和龙垭文化遗址距离仅40公里，都在沱江附近，有人认为，资阳发现的古人类化石（女性）有可能是洪水从上游的龙垭遗址冲击移动、漂流过去的。因为龙垭遗址出土了丰富的旧石器时代晚期的工具，甚至像吊坠这样的装饰品，还有包括剑齿象象牙在内的被人类狩猎获得的动物化石，而"资阳人"出土地有人类头盖骨，却没有任何古人类活动的痕迹，以及动物骨骼化石。

地尤其是成都地区成为中国早期神话传说、仙化思维最活跃的地区。后来的道教诞生于此地，其高人离开人世后可以羽化成仙的宗教理想，应该是来自对古蜀五祖死后仙遐而去（甚至带着身边臣民）神话传说的借鉴。这一浪漫传统，简阳也是正宗的发源地（龙垭文化出土的装饰性吊坠是旧石器时代发现的罕见的遗存）、传承地之一，在简阳博物馆，西周牛头兽面铜罍和战国多耳有盖铜罍显示着这一地区从西周到战国就有与中原华夏政权的有规格的往来，这是实实在在的富足、优雅的生活，但馆藏汉代石棺中的 3 号棺材让我们看到简阳先民在汉代生动、浪漫的精神世界——其棺后档和左右侧的装饰图案，就有人神交汇，生死相通，人与具有图腾、象征意义的动物（龙、虎、蛇、龟、麟、鸟、马）同情共舞的生动体现，其中还能看到伏羲、女娲崇拜（简阳也有女娲脚印的传说）和人与动物（或者其灵魂）飘逸升遐的神话与传说，它们甚至被带到了幽冥世界陪伴喜欢这种故事和信仰的亡灵。后来简阳的文学艺术繁盛，并成为状元文化、名人文化的深厚根基，与此有源远流长的互动关系。所以讲述简阳城市文化的历史脉络，首先必须从其神秘浪漫的古老基因说起。

2. 李冰治水和文翁化蜀：近水楼台先得月

简阳在秦汉时期属于蜀郡，虽然没有直接享受到李冰治水带来的灌溉之利，但应该受益于治水以后航运更加通畅发达，尤其是受益于成都平原成为沃野千里的天府之国以后，就近辐射给简阳的各种信息与资源，这是那些远离成都平原的普通州县不可比拟的。而文翁化蜀，兴办地方官学并治理湔江，简阳无疑也是近水楼台先得月。总之，李冰治水和文翁化蜀，简阳比大灌区以外的一般州县受惠更多，是后来

它成为天府雄州的最早基因。

3. 军事、治安要地，自古不惧战争，崇尚英雄

至迟在战国时期，四川盆地发生族群、政权冲突成为常见现象。开明王朝在与巴国、秦国的较量以及作为"戎狄之长"平息内部纷争中建立了数量不菲的常备军，有专门的军事、治安管理布局。当时包括了龙泉山在内的今简阳地区，应该至少是一个军事驻扎、管控据点，秦汉尚武开拓，这一局面当延续。在简阳博物馆比较有代表性的文物中，战国和汉代的多种形制的兵器引人注目；牛鞞县设置以后，属于以管控、安抚西南夷为主要功能的犍为郡，均是直接或间接的证据。

秦汉时期，中国境内外多战事。四川盆地在先秦时期留下了众多族群，成都和蜀郡、巴郡还肩负着管控、汉化众多族群的使命（司马相如、唐蒙出使西南夷就是典型），矛盾、冲突在所难免，龙泉山主要隘口具有突出的军事和治安属性，常有驻防的军队和兵丁夫役，因此官府对此区域的治理不可能不加以留意和重视。对战争和军事、军队的关注，对保家卫国、安宁一方英雄的崇尚，一直是简阳的文化基因之一。所以后来的简阳，既崇文也尚武，近代产生那么多将军和抗日名将，其来有自。

4. 曾隶属犍为郡，是国家开拓前进基地，族群和而不同

简阳地区的矿产资源（除了盐以外）相当匮乏，但男耕女织条件甚佳，多样的山水、地貌，使其动植物、农作物品种极为丰富，满足一般生产和生活需求的手工业产品近可以满足本地，稍远可以补充近在咫尺的成都工商业及其市场，并与之交流互鉴。所以当汉朝的成都凭借秦汉交替之际几乎没有大型战乱的破坏，李冰、文翁治水和文翁兴

学化蜀，以及开辟南北方丝绸之路和开拓西南夷之需求迅速增加，成都"列备五都"的时候，简阳作为一个城市（牛鞞县）正式在国家建置中产生（地方官署在今简城镇绛溪河北岸古牛鞞镇）。但接受犍为郡（前130年，汉武帝元光五年，因开西南夷而设置，治所在今贵州遵义市西部，最多时领有包括资中在内的川中南、黔北、滇北十二县，总户数大约10万。牛鞞隶属犍为郡一直延续到东晋穆帝永和年间，即345—356年，跨越了两个多世纪）管辖，这是很有趣但一直被忽略的重要线索，起码可以说明两点：第一，当时靠近成都的牛鞞县应该是汉朝武装力量向南开拓西南夷，向北拱卫成都的军事、政治前线据点。第二，牛鞞县也应该是一个族群成分相对复杂多样的地方，但历史上这里的族群总能够和而不同。证据有，秦灭巴蜀以后，随秦军及其家属而来的两万多人，估计绝大多数都驻扎、生活在成都平原，因为李冰治水以后的成都平原完全能够养活他们（除了可能的小规模军队驻扎龙泉山以外——但迄今尚无任何文献或文物显示这一点）；秦汉交替，四海鼎沸，天下户口减半，但成都平原没有任何大战乱的记载，所以汉高祖面对战火废墟上残存下来衣衫褴褛、嗷嗷待哺的人民，国家无力帮扶，只好下令他们可以"卖子就食蜀汉"。这些人有多少到达了蜀汉，不得而知，但即使到了，多数也肯定是在谋生最容易的膏腴区域，比如汉中平原、成都平原，难以来到龙泉山以西以南的简阳；那么，原来开明王朝遗留下来的众多族群在简阳依然会是人口的多数。族群成分相对复杂多样，应该也是牛鞞划归犍为郡管辖的重要因素，否则，不归近在咫尺的成都管辖，岂非咄咄怪事！隶属犍为郡跨越了200多年，也可以说明上述两个因素一直在发挥重要作用。

5. 因大汉强盛、成都繁荣而生；2000多年，紧密伴随国运和成都城市命运而荣枯

简阳的最早前身牛鞞县，带有后来简阳文化个性的大部分基因。除了上述四个因素的作用以外，应该特别强调它是汉帝国蒸蒸日上、中华文明第一次威震世界，需要设立更多州县来建立文治武功时期的产物；是益州地区的中心成都，依靠秦汉时期相对平静、李冰治水和文翁化蜀、开拓西南夷、开通南北丝绸之路等契机，借助汉朝的崛起，已经成为中国乃至世界特大中心城市，对周边地区进行强有力辐射（简阳的出土文物可以看到成都的巨大影响）和影响（当然这种影响是双向的，当时的牛鞞不可能不对成都产生影响，只不过朝廷把这种影响力设定为开拓、控制、同化西南夷）的结果。此外，在秦汉郡县制下，一个地区要创设一个县，不可能是皇帝和三公九卿突然脑洞大开，便做出决定，而是应该广泛听取各级州郡官员的意见，甚至由州郡官员率先动议，逐级上报、讨论、决策，才可能最终确定。就此而论，牛鞞的设置，应该有驻扎在成都的益州主官加犍为郡官员的建议，汉武帝领导下的朝廷的专门讨论并最终由皇帝拍板的。牛鞞县，应该是大汉帝国开拓进取的浪潮、蜀地官员政治智慧的产物。

由于两汉朝廷的重视，牛鞞县领域面积很大，西魏末年（555）牛鞞县竟然变成了武康、金泉二郡。武康郡下辖阳安县和婆闰县。北周时，武康郡增添了白牟县（县治在今金堂城厢镇），撤销了金泉郡。隋文帝仁寿三年（603）设置简州，隶属益州总管府，管辖阳安、平泉、资阳三县，州府设在阳安。隋炀帝上台，撤销简州，阳安、平泉重新属于蜀郡，资阳县重新属于资州。唐高祖武德三年（620年），重建简州，管理阳安、平泉、金水三县。玄宗天宝元年（742），国力和户口达于极盛，改简州为阳安郡。肃宗乾元元年（758），深陷安史之乱苦难中的唐朝，政治收缩，又改阳安郡为简州。唐朝简州，一直隶属剑南道（757年剑南道分东西川，简州属于西川）。五代时期，皆设简州，管理阳安、平泉、金水三县。宋代，中国文治昌盛，成都和四川也达到有史以来都市文明和区域文化最为璀璨的时期，户口众多。但因经历辽、金、蒙古越来越严重的冲击和蚕食，在南宋，管辖区域逐渐由三个县变成只剩阳安、平泉。元朝地广人稀，政治设计和管理粗陋，地方行政机构除了行中书省，还有路府州县四级。在宋朝原简州阳安郡，设置简州，隶属四川行中书省成都路，下辖灵泉县，原辖阳安、平泉二县并入简州。明朝武宗正德八年（1513）以前，设简县，以后，设简州，均隶属成都府，其中简州所辖还短暂包括了资阳县、乐至县（1514—1522），以及龙泉镇巡检司、资阳镇巡检司。明末清初，四川人口基本灭绝，简阳也不例外，依靠湖广填四川而艰难恢复，简阳地位比起前朝进一步下降，在清朝隶属成都府，不辖县，兼领龙泉镇巡检司。中华民国和新中国前期，简阳地区均设单一简阳县，行政隶属改变较多，1913—1935年，隶属四川省西川道（大致相当于清朝的成都府）；此后至1949年，隶属治所设在资中县的四川省第二行政督察区。新中国成立以后至1985年，一直以普通县隶属于内江专区（内江地区、内江市）。1994年，撤销简阳县，设立简阳市，由省直辖，省政府委托内江市代管。1998年后又归资阳地区、资阳市委托管辖。1959年和1976年，简阳市所属龙泉驿区和洛带区先后划归成都管辖。2016年5月，已经确立为国家中心城市的成都，为谋求更大更好发展，经国务院正式批

复，代管简阳。融入成都，给简阳带来历史上最好的发展机遇，壮丽的宏图正在徐徐展开。

综上梳理，可以归纳出三点：第一，简阳在历史上的盛衰与国运和成都市的命运完全同步。两汉（含其辉煌余响三国）、隋唐、两宋、清末民初、改革开放以后的40余年，是成都发展或显示力量的黄金时期。这些时期，也是简阳因为其独特的正能量而在国家行政管理中地位相对很高或很受重视的时期。这种与国家和成都休戚相关、风雨同舟的关系，孕育出了简阳人民深厚的家国情怀和对于成都的文化归附心理，如清末四川文化巨子傅崇矩，生于简阳，后移居成都，便终身以成都人自居。第二，国家多事或危难之秋，简阳也往往要在归属管辖范围上做出调整。显然，简阳的特殊区位和历史脉络一直在给成都、四川乃至国家层面如何面对、安置简阳提出与时俱进的"难题"。简阳"身份"定位的变动不居，恰恰证明了它有一般县市不具备的扮演多种国家和社会所需角色的潜力，而这背后的根基是简阳文化的多元性、可塑性、很强的适应性。第三，自公元前115年形成郡、州、县建置以来，简阳大部分时间的地位高于普通县，具有准府城的地位和影响力。迄今2137年历史中，直接隶属于成都的时间约1470年，隶属犍为郡的时间465年，隶属资中、内江、资阳共计81年。由于四川和成都经历过宋末元初、明末清初两次人口大灭绝，所以对今天简阳、成都、四川文化影响最大的是明末清初的移民文化。从1644年清朝建立开始计算，简阳隶属于成都府依然占据了275年，隶属于资中、内江、资阳的时间一共只有81年，所以，简阳的文脉和文化主体，属于成都，今后也将是成都最有个性和活力的一部分，可以展望。

二、简阳城市文化的近现代演变

(一)近代简阳的文化

1840 年鸦片战争以来,在奉行丛林法则的西方列强的坚船利炮、基于不平等条约的商业贸易、文化交流的冲击下,中国逐步沦入半殖民地半封建社会的深渊。清朝本身也各种积弊缠身,变革迟缓,终于酿成辛亥革命。中华民国建立,北洋军阀政权和蒋介石国民党政权因为并未代表中国的正确发展方向,痼疾顽症缠身,不可救药,便又有国民革命、中国共产党领导的彻底推翻三座大山压迫的旧中国,建立独立自由新中国的伟大革命。中国各地,均逐步纳入了这一历史进程。作为深处中国内陆,交通和信息发展都相对滞后的成都府所属州县的一部分,与沿江沿海同级别城市乡村相比,除了社会动荡和民生不易,西学东渐,洋产品、洋思潮、洋风尚不时出现并对中上流社会和知识阶层产生越来越多的影响以外,在整体上,对绝大多数民众而言,简阳经济上依然以农耕生活为主体,小规模手工业、民间技艺和活跃的中小规模的商业活动为辅助;主流价值观以传统五常和崇尚耕读、诗礼传家为特征;在政治生活中,乡绅和大族协助政府管理社会,并且导引着民间的认知和风尚;而起自康熙发动的湖广填四川运动形成的五方杂处、会馆林立、守望相助、平等相待、儒释道和各种地方神祇、祖先崇拜互相包容的移民文化,构成简阳城乡的基本文化生态;即使民国时期,因为西化较晚,且前期军阀割据混战(简阳多次成为战场和搜刮重点),后期重心在于解放战争,简阳的传统文化依然保存较为完整。

在忠孝节义和家国情怀、崇文尚武传统以及纷至沓来的新思潮和政治风云的影响下，简阳在近代成都和四川的社会变革、学习近代科技文化、投身辛亥革命和中共领导的革命活动、卷入近代军阀武力纷争、投身伟大的抗日战争、中外文化沟通等方面，涌现了一批杰出、优秀人才，有的具有良好的国际影响力（刘子华、罗淑），有的勇立时代潮头，以革命或改良的形式，留下助力国家进步的功德和气节（夏之时、傅崇矩、吴雪琴、董朗、毛却非、毛克生、彭宝珊），有的投身行伍，参加辛亥革命，也在乱世中卷入过军阀角逐，甚至参与过蒋介石强力推动的"围剿"红军（均被红军击败），毁誉参半，但后来绝大多数都义不容辞投身抗战，建立功勋，成为近代四川的风云人物（刘存厚、陈鼎勋、汪尚方、廖震、陈良基、曾烈等）。除了上述名人在科学研究、文学艺术创作与翻译、社会进步和红色革命、赴汤蹈火于抗日战场的丰功伟绩外，1944年，1.5万多名简阳民工，在县长黄幼甫等人领导下，用不到两个月的时间，主要依靠人工，夜以继日、流血流汗便提前完成的支撑中美空军轰炸日本侵略者使用的平泉机场的故事，也是简阳人民爱国主义和急公好义人文精神的生动体现。

总之，近代简阳的文化形态和文化变迁，都可以在简阳这座城市绵延近2000年的文化基因中找到依据。简阳儿女在迎接近代革命和改良的过程中，文化变革和社会发展比较协调，优秀的人文精神与传统没有迷失，因此能涌现至少十几位对国家、对四川和成都有重大贡献、重要影响的风云人物，相较它不大的经济实力、不高的政治地位来讲，简阳堪称近代四川的文化雄州。这个"雄"的核心，就是家国情怀、崇文尚武并重、敢为天下先等价值观、人生观。

（二）现当代简阳文化

现代中国，革命和建设事业都有一个艰难曲折的探索过程，抗美援朝、抗美援越和"两弹一星"等事业完成了中华民族站起来的历史使命；1978 年掀开帷幕的改革开放，找到了让中华民族富起来的正确道路；而党的十八大以来，共和国在强起来的道路上取得了非凡的成就。基于中华优秀传统文化传承、弘扬的中国的文化自信和文化软实力，空前增长。尤其是成都，通过改革开放，形成了以天府文化为代表的文化志向、文化谋划和文化个性，以健康的经济、活跃的文化、舒适的生活为内涵的"后现代气质"，以及广受赞誉的"城市生活美学"。成都世界文化名城的追求也得到国家的认可，并写进了成渝地区双城经济圈的规划纲要（而重庆没有）。放在这样的发展历程和时代背景下，审视简阳，体现 1949—2022 年城市文化活力与个性、文化传承与变革的主要事件和人物依次有。

1. 主要事件

（1）1950 年，简阳军民团结一心，英勇无畏，以牺牲 163 名教师、学生、政干校工作队员的代价，平息旧政权残余势力掀起的武装暴乱，也是成都红色文化的重要篇章。

（2）热血儿女，踊跃投身抗美援朝。1950—1953 年，发生抗美援朝战争，简阳人民积极响应保家卫国的号召，热血儿女慷慨从军，前赴后继。报名人数超过 1.5 万人，其中妇女 120 名。经过选拔，最后3200 名青年光荣加入中国人民志愿军，至 1953 年 4 月，全县赴朝参战的勇士超过 5000 余人，其中 57 人光荣牺牲，涌现出了薛志高、赖文

禄等许多战斗英雄。在这一伟大的战争中，简阳人民再次表现了他们尚武和崇尚英雄的人文个性，并作出了自己的贡献。

（3）气壮山河的东灌工程与精神。为了造福子孙后代，20世纪70年代初，10万简阳干部群众，流血流汗，历时两年零五个月，打通龙泉山，并建立蓄水灌溉配套工程，开创东灌工程人间奇迹，使都江堰大灌区延伸到简阳，让简阳绝大部分区域告别了缺水的历史，形成了简阳人民引以为豪的"东灌精神"。（见后面专题论述）

（4）2016年以来，简阳重新成为成都管辖的一部分，并快速在各方面融入成都。其中天府国际机场的修建、运行和简阳市西部约三分之一的土地建立成都东部新区所带来的现代化、国际化、全球化物质文化、制度文化、精神文化新观念、新要求，正在简阳掀起一场前所未有的思想和观念以及生产、生活方式的革命，"天府文化"成为简阳的文化归属。市委、市政府与时俱进，全面对接国家、省、市关于建设公园城市示范区、成渝地区双城经济圈、世界文化名城、"三城三都"、大都市圈等发展战略，并寻求简阳的最佳定位和发展路径。

2. 主要人物

（1）首届茅盾文学奖获得者周克芹。周克芹（1936—1990），简阳石桥人。只读过一个相当于中专的成都农校，担任过乡民校、公社农中教师以及大队保管员、会计，简阳县红塔区公所不脱产种子员，1978年被吸收为公社干部，并调县文化馆工作，次年1月入党，3月因为其曾经发表过短篇小说集《石家兄妹》调省文联从事专业创作。这年8月，他写出了长篇小说《许茂和他的女儿们》，该书描写了十年动乱对于农民带来的灾难和他们的抗争与追求，有浓厚的地方色彩和乡土气息，情节曲折起伏，引人入胜。1980—1981年，他新推出的《勿忘草》《山月不知心里事》，连续获得全国优秀短篇小说奖。1982年，他的《许茂和他的女儿们》获得首届茅盾文学奖。1984年迁入成都定居，后来担任过省作协领导，主编过《现代作家》。

（2）全国农业劳动模范张泗州。张泗州（1920—1980），简阳县清风乡人，中共党员。因为是种棉能手和积极主动兴办互助组、初级农业生产合作社，并担任负责人，以及曾经参加第三届中国人民赴朝慰问团到朝鲜慰问志愿军、参加中国农业出国访问团赴东欧两国访问，获得了县、专区、四川省劳模、全国人大代表以及公社社长等众多荣誉和职务。并且长期坚持参加生产劳动，并努力学习摆脱文盲，后来又致力于棉粮品种的引进和培育，并培育繁殖了数十个品种。1968年相继担任过县、地、省三级革命委员会副主任，1969年被免职。作为代表赴京参加党的九大，在九大和十大都被选举为中央候补委员。

（3）两位院士：叶朝晖，1942年生，北大毕业，曾在美国做访问学者，物理学家，武汉光电国家实验室主任，中科院院士。魏复盛，1938年生，毕业于中国科技大学，环境保护专家，历任中国环境监测总站室主任、副站长、总工、全国人大常委会委员、全国环境监测专委会副主任等职，中国工程院院士。

总的来看，新中国成立以来，简阳的文化发展，呈现比较曲折、重心下移、重量级名人减少，但体现群体人文精神的事件和实践增多的格局。与新中国探索社会主义建设的曲折历程有关，也与成都和简阳的关系远近有关，还与简阳近六年面临全新的发展格局有关。70余年的现当代简阳文化史，只有周克芹及其作品获奖、功德震撼人心并引

发海内外关注传播的东灌工程及其精神、回归成都以来简阳逐渐呈现的崭新气象和不可限量的发展前景，堪称无愧于历史的，能够引来"向往""仰望"的重量级文化现象。"天府雄州"正在归来，但任重道远，简阳必须看到自己的差距（与成都其他区市县的差距和国内优秀县市的差距），尤其是融入成都才六年，许多理念和习惯心理都需要澄清甚至重塑，干部群众需要更加广泛、深透的共识、共情，才有可能用好资源、抓住机遇，创造简阳文化新辉煌。八大文化的深度挖掘和提炼，具有不可替代的重要价值。不能洞察过去，焉能看清现实，又怎能展望、谋划好未来？不看护、运用好属于自己的"唯一不动产"，岂不是最大的浪费？

三、人口变迁的影响

纵观简阳的历史文脉及其演进，其文化的盛衰以及个性的传承与丰富，与人口的变迁关系极大。笔者著有《成都传》，里面梳理了历史上九次向成都为中心的四川盆地的大规模移民活动，其中每一次移民对成都的影响与对简阳的影响，都是大同小异的，但也有一定区别。下面试做一论述。

（一）"染秦化"移民

公元前316年，张仪、司马错率领大军灭蜀，并带来数以万计的秦人家属，造成的结果是"染秦化"，毫无疑问是成都进入华夏文明的重要一步。张仪、张若所筑之新成都，严格按照秦国城市的营造法式，进行规范化施工，成都首次版筑（过去是夯筑）城墙，使用了铁工具、砖瓦技术，自然更加有序、更加坚固、更加有统治中心的威严气象。此外，张若在蜀郡、巴郡统治区所筑之郫、临邛、江州、阆中等次区域中心城市，同样是新的技术、新的气象。在此基础上，秦汉时期，"蜀以成都、广都、新都为三都，号名城"，可见已经是一个"城市群"的态势。此次移民，对于历史上简阳（简州）这块与成都毗邻的土地的影响应该是大同小异的。秦国特别崇尚耕战和军功，龙泉山应该有小规模秦军驻扎，这样的价值观念和力量配置态势，对于汉代牛鞞县的城市形制、城乡人民的观念和生活方式应该有重要影响，汉代牛鞞县归入犍为郡而不是蜀郡管辖，并在随后的朝代中延续三百余年，也应该与此次移民影响有关。

（二）秦汉迁徙人口入蜀

秦王嬴政（前259—前210）流放吕不韦（？—前235）及其附属亲朋人群入蜀，完成《吕氏春秋》写作（司马迁《报任少安书》："不韦入蜀，世传《吕览》"），即使按照有的专家的论证此书在入蜀前已经完成写作，这带来的也是携带顶尖思想文化的人群。秦统一后，秦始皇对山东六国遗民中的强势人群（如贵族、巨商大贾）是否效忠秦完全没有信心，决定将他们从原居住地强行迁徙到异地生存，于是"巴蜀道险，秦之迁人皆居蜀"（《史记·项羽本纪》）。如钢铁大王卓王孙、程郑，原为山东（原齐国）富豪。这个人群带来的是先进的技术和管理，以及民间资本。汉高祖初年，令民就食蜀汉，也至少为四川增添了劳动力。

"染秦化"和秦始皇强行迁徙拥有政治、经济、文化能量的人群入居蜀地，商品经济的极大发展，列备强汉五都之一的成都，不仅称雄西南，商品、大赋代言华夏，而且出现了"居给人足，以富相尚"的风气，乘坐高车驷马，穿戴王侯美衣，豪奢夸张地婚丧嫁娶，美酒歌舞游猎伴随家庭和朋友聚会，成为人生成功的标志。这一点，司马相如也未能免俗，他出驷马桥奔向长安时的豪言壮语，成为成都这座城市在汉代表达主流社会信心满满、要通过才华取得功名并享受幸福生活（包括精神生活）的标签之一。

这次移民，从时间来看，也发生在牛鞞县出现之前，它对牛鞞县的影响应该与成都其他区域大同小异，增强了此地官员和人民的大一统意识，进一步融汇了本地族群与来自黄河流域的华夏族群，使之增加命运共同体意识。

（三）巴氏流民入蜀

西晋末年，朝廷内讧，益州刺史赵廞（？—301）失势，即将被调离成都，回首都后前景不妙，他决定借助已经进入四川的巴氏流民（时关中干旱，连年饥荒，六郡汉、氐、羌、賨等各族民众10余万人经汉川流入巴蜀地区就食。当地官府并不欢迎其来蜀）形成自己的势力，抗衡朝廷，于是以政府的名义招引流民领袖李特，使其派三弟李庠带领一支流民军潜入成都，设下了埋伏，合作诱杀了代表朝廷的耿腾。随后赵廞接管了西晋成都官军，杀李庠等以震慑李特，不料激起李特率领流民军从其根据地绵竹反攻成都，击杀赵廞，征服成都。此前流民们已在蜀中过了两年苦日子，积怨已久，遂捕杀官吏，也对成都进行了烧杀和洗劫。随后，朝廷派来征西将军罗尚镇压李特，李特因骄傲轻敌被杀。但罗尚凶恶虐民，成都百姓有歌谣曰："李特尚可，罗尚杀我！"所以李特其弟李流和其子李雄继续战斗。一年后，罗尚败逃关中，李雄称成都王；两年后即公元304年，他建立大成国。李雄的大成国有过保境安民30多年的岁月，因后代淫暴，347年被东晋消灭。这次移民为找到活路进入四川，开始是政局动荡，流民人多势众，地方官有心无力阻止的结果，但进入成都，则是地方官别有用心招引的结果。至于后来的局势演变及其对四川的影响，则很难一言以蔽之，但留下了如何处理少数民族移民入川入蓉的经验教训。

这一次移民活动，在历史上叫五胡乱中华建立的第一个异族政权，是历史上对于川西为主的蜀地的多次移民中，因为族群差异、隔阂太大，引发了大规模战乱，唯一负能量大于正能量的移民活动。对于牛鞞县的影响也应该如此，虽然牛鞞的人口、财产损耗应该小于成都，因为政权、资源的争夺的主战场不在牛鞞不在犍为郡，但乱世的牛鞞经济文化都乏善可陈。

（四）唐二帝避难入蜀

唐代两位君王，唐玄宗（685—762）、唐僖宗（873—888），先后因为安史之乱和黄巢进攻长安逃难到成都，两拨君臣及其附属人口入蜀时都是数以千计。在成都"驻跸"的时间，玄宗年一年（756—757），僖宗四年（881—885）。大批天潢贵胄、翰林文士甚至高僧大德入蜀，虽然是帝国衰落中的痛苦音符，但客观上带来了雅文化的浸溉和融合。至今成都、四川人回忆两位君王来蜀避难，尤其是谈到相

关遗迹大慈寺、宝光寺、天回镇、青羊宫等等，还是眉飞色舞，洋溢着类似李白在《上皇西巡南京歌》中的感情。

而伴随二帝尤其是唐僖宗入蜀之移民多为华夏衣冠，所以对四川影响深远。史载前蜀皇帝王建（847—918）在位期间（903—918），"是时唐衣冠之族，多避难在蜀，帝礼耳用焉，使修举政事，故典章文物有唐之遗风"。今人游览王建长眠的永陵博物馆，看到那曼妙多姿的 24 位美女组成了使用 21 种乐器的小皇朝皇家乐队，便能感受到大唐雅文化在帝王生活中的流风遗韵。

唐朝的移民，对于已经纳入成都（益州、蜀郡、剑南道）管辖的简州来讲，应该也发挥了增添人口和雅文化资源的功能，所以直到唐末和五代前后蜀统治时期，尽管四川盆地经历了数次战乱，包括韦皋建立煊赫武功的耗费，简州管辖三个县以及县治所在地都没有任何改变。韦皋在简阳留下纪功碑，应该是对于简阳的支撑战争的能力，以及简阳在他发动征讨期间又恢复了牛鞞县在犍为郡的功能等因素有关。

（五）大夏政权的"湖广填四川"

元朝是四川历史上的低谷，因为宋元之际，四川军民极其悲壮的抵抗战争长达半个世纪，人口消耗殆尽。元朝虽有 90 年，但因统治残暴，四川人属于四等人制度下地位最低的"南人"，人口增长极为缓慢。据四川大学李世平教授研究，元末四川总人口不到 80 万，其中巴渝地区的重庆路、夔路，只有约 20 万人口。而大夏政权的首都设在重庆，所以明玉珍（1329—1366）在位期间，为了增添国力，除了率领湖北人居多的将士及其家属入川以外，还至少两次在湖北、江西等地招民入川。据统计一共为四川地区增添了约 40 万人口，其中三分之二安置在了人口尤为稀少的巴渝地区。移民中，以湖北籍为最多，又主要以黄州、麻城为主，在统计的 214 姓中就有 112 姓，占移民总数约 52.3 ％，超过半数，奏响了"湖广填四川"的序曲。明朝统一四川后，虽有一部分军事移民后来被调到外地或四川卫所，但仍有许多军事移民留下。这些移民为明清，特别是清代大移民准备了地缘基础。

这次移民，来到川西的数量不多，到简州的应该很稀少（后来洪武年间移入的也仅 30 姓 86 户），当时简州属下也只有一个灵泉县。元朝主要建立在野蛮的武力征服之上，实行愚蠢的四等人制度，政治设计粗陋，皇帝短命无能者多，吏治腐败早，形成四川历史上的一个低谷，经济文化都远比两汉、唐宋落后，这种低迷也制约了大规模的移民发生，简州也一样。

（六）明末清初"湖广填四川"

明末清初，中国士大夫和战乱地区民众经历了"天崩地坼"的江山易主和心理剧变。由于以张献忠为主，其他势力（含清军、李自成、明军、土匪"摇黄贼"、支持吴三桂叛乱的势力等）为辅，基于政治和军事斗争需求，以及发泄各种私愤和变态心理的各种屠杀行为，加上瘟疫和自然灾害，四川人口再一次濒临灭绝，其中成都城池彻底毁灭，人口荡然无存。所以在康熙皇帝（1654—1722）平定吴三桂叛乱后，朝廷组织了从四川周边省区向四川大规模的移民活动，其中成都平原地区又成为移民填充、率先恢复的核心地区。这次移民，政府对劝导

移民入川并加以妥善安置的官员加官晋爵，努力对百姓入川在沿途提供管理、关照，对已经定居落户的百姓任其所能占有田土，并给予生产生活方面的临时性救济和起步阶段的若干年的赋税蠲免，遇上大的天灾人祸也减免赋税。待经济逐步恢复后，四川地区成了中国各地谋生最容易的地区，比如，笔者研究过清代中国几个主要产量区域的大米价格（江浙、湖广、四川），至少100年中间，成都地区的粮食价格都是最低的。

这一次湖广填四川包含了康雍乾三朝，绵延至少120年，来自中国各地18个以上的省的百姓，披星戴月、扶老携幼来到新天地，筚路蓝缕，以启山林建设新家园，他们既在整体上接续了巴蜀的文化传统和精神命脉，又把各地域的优秀文化在四川盆地进行碰撞、交流、融汇，形成了以川菜、川酒、川剧、川话、竹枝词、四川清音等为代表的充满平民情怀和眼光向下的文化价值、审美追求，因为移民都是清一色的平民，他们最早彼此相处的文化基因里没有文化和身份歧视，后来逐渐富贵的人家也很难产生那种基于血缘的文化和身份傲慢，即使有人出现了这种傲慢的苗头，也很难得到广泛的承认和尊重。平民化与儒释道三教在成都、四川的和平相处、相得益彰，进一步强化了巴蜀文化的开放性和包容性。至于成都、四川为什么美女、帅哥成群，也可以在18个省的同胞联姻之中找到生物学、遗传学上的依据。

简阳的情况也与上述几乎完全一致，移民文化影响深远。因为生计比成都平原要艰难一些，但又比四川其他绝大部分州县好一些，且与成都华阳县直接接壤，简阳文化的平民化个性更加突出，耕读传家更加勤奋、主动，这从起自清代的简阳民间风俗和非遗的草根性与淳朴性，以及书院私塾的广泛设立，并且书声琅琅，崇尚科举，可见一斑。客家文化据点（会馆）保存最丰满的洛带，当时也是简阳的一部分。简阳的应第莲池、题名塔与至今尚存的四川地区罕见宏伟、多样的字库塔一起，也诉说着简阳既与成都禀赋相似、命运与共，但也在某些方面（如尚武、勤劳淳朴、看重读书和科举、客家文化集中、女性更多承担家庭内外的责任）具有自己的优良个性。

（七）抗战时期，精英荟萃地

1937 年七七事变爆发，中华民族面对骄狂残忍的日本法西斯的全面卫国战争掀开帷幕。国民政府迁都重庆，中国最重要的工矿企业、学术和文教机构，以大学师生、科学家和工程技术人员、各种文学艺术大师为代表的民族精英来到四川，汇聚成都、重庆，他们中的大部分都在成都、重庆、四川度过了数年艰难时光，得到四川军民同生死、共患难的拥戴和善待。这一时期，是巴蜀文化与国家轴心文化的一次最温暖、最无缝的对接、融汇。抗战胜利后，国共两党都先后高调宣示，感谢四川和四川人民作出的巨大贡献。许多近现代名人后来都对在四川的这段时光充满刻骨铭心的温暖回忆，而成都、四川人民，也因为这段历史而深感骄傲和自豪。今天，屹立在重庆的抗战遗址博物馆、成都大邑的建川博物馆和地处长江边上的宜宾李庄，所记录的四川人心目中的抗战生活以及他们心中崇敬的先烈和英雄，已经成为此地此城的精神地标。而且抗战中与反法西斯各国军人、政要、外交官、新闻人士、学术与文化教育交流人士所建立的国际友谊，也成了人类城市文明的共同财富与遗产。帮助四川特别是重庆、成都大大提高了

国际化的水准。

抗战时期，大量移民的到来，使成都的工商业也有了飞跃发展。据20世纪40年代中期统计，成都市区商店达28 480家，与抗战前相比较，净增加15167家，而且形成了以春熙路为中心，北接总府街、商业场，延续到提督街，南接东大街，一个繁盛的商业闹市区。金融和房地产也呈现空前的活跃，以春熙路为例，抗战中期，地价飙升，暴涨到寸土寸金，一个单间铺面，租金高达数十到一百两黄金。

抗战时期移民入川，对于简阳当然也增添了资源，但那时交通还十分不便的简阳，吸引力还有明显差距，影响远小于成都平原，因为优质的人财物更多集中在了华西坝为主的平原上，和躲避日军轰炸更安全的宜宾李庄等地。不过简阳人民也因为商道（含水路）和驿道的空前繁忙、平泉机场的修建、亲历或亲属朋友在成都传回的各种国际、国内最新资讯，包括成都惨遭日寇多次轰炸、中国空军跌宕起伏的命运，以及宋美龄与简阳大耳羊之间的故事等，得到了这次大移民所产生的丰富正能量，简阳官民的视野、知识、观念获得了一次全方位冲击和提升。

（八）三线建设迎来工业化人潮

三线建设，是指1964—1980年在中国中西部地区的13个省、自治区进行的一场以战备为指导思想的大规模国防、科技、工业和交通基础设施建设。这些区域处于与美苏开战的战略大后方，所以称"三线"。发生背景是中苏交恶，苏联在中苏边境屯兵百万，以及美国不时发出的战争叫嚣与威胁（包括美、苏对中国的多次核讹诈）。

中央政府投入了占同期全国基本建设总投资 40% 的 2052.68 亿元巨资；400 万工人、干部、知识分子、解放军官兵和成千万人次的民工，在毛泽东主席"备战备荒为人民""好人好马上三线"的号召下，跋山涉水，进入大西南、大西北的深山峡谷、大漠荒野，风餐露宿、肩扛人挑，用艰辛、血汗和生命，建起了 1100 多个大中型工矿企业、科研单位和大专院校。在 1964—1980 年期间，国家共审批 1100 多个中大型建设项目。贵州、四川东部山区、四川中部平原地区、汉中、秦岭北麓等地区新建的项目数量多，规模大，迁入工业人口多。其中，四川成都主要接收轻工业与电子工业，绵阳、广元接收核工业与电子工业，重庆为常规兵器制造基地。经过三线建设，成都、重庆、西安、兰州、贵阳、安顺、遵义等一大批古老的城镇，进行了首次的工业化，拉近了与东部城市的差距。数百万建设者在异地他乡献出了青春和汗水，甚至是宝贵的生命，使改革开放在 1978 年撩开序幕时，中国虽然人均收入较低，但却是世界上罕见的具有完整的国民经济体系和国防自主生产体系的国家之一。

在这一历史时期，因接纳数以十万计的来自东部发达城市的科技工作者、工程技术人员和优秀产业工人，接受了他们身上服从国家建设大局的气节、严谨的科学精神、忘我的奋斗意识，以及现代大型企业的管理文化和崇尚极致的大国工匠风范，成都、四川人文个性无疑增添了极为重要的与时代发展接轨的崭新内涵。

简阳虽然没有成为重点地区和城市（也许与它不属于成都有关），但也带来了扎扎实实的好处。《简阳县志》人口志记载，中华人民共和国成立后，1953—1985 年，境内共迁入人口 669262 人（同期迁出

664733 人，基本持平），年均为 20883 人。其中 1958 至 1960 年共迁入 100856 人，年均达到 33619 人，为一个迁入高峰，尤以 1958 年为最，达到 50967 人。1975—1977 年共迁入 75290 人，年均 25096 人，为又一个高峰期。50 年代迁入者，主要是军队和南下干部、省内调简干部，以及因婚姻或投亲来简阳者。60 年代中后期，国家加强西南三线建设，境内先后迁入一批工矿、企业人口。关于流出人口的原因，主要是婚姻、就业、支边、升学、参军等。《简阳县志》工业志记载，1965 年后至 70 年代中，境内国营工业大增，地属以上"三线"厂内迁，陆续新建投产，一共八家，到 1985 年，还拥有干部职工 10268 人，产品销售收入 10965.2 万元，占全县独立核算国营工业企业的 56.2%；提供税收 910.9 万元，占全县独立核算国营工业企业的 55.44%，他们不仅有力支撑了地方经济，带动了简阳县举办国有企业的积极性，更为重要的是，他们把新中国现代工业文明的气息、观念、风貌展示给了简阳人民。此外，如果没有这批三线建设工厂提供的科技、知识、技能密集人口（含其家属、子弟）的供给，以及明显改善简阳的经济生活和精神生活，简阳人口流进和流出的诸多指标，都会差得多，简阳的城市和区域形象，也会落后得多。

（九）改革开放幸福之都吸引大批新移民

1978 年，由四川广安人邓小平（1904—1997）作为总设计师的中国改革开放揭开了帷幕，迄今为止，实现着中国的伟大腾飞与和平崛起。成都和四川也实现了历史性的跨越。1993 年，重庆市成为中央直辖市，原川东属于巴文化圈的一半空间和大部分经济文化资源划归重庆，新四川的历史叙事也从此开始。

不管怎样，成都作为老四川、新四川的首位城市的地位没有改变，只是它与重庆市这对巴蜀文化的双子星座的行政地位和各自的使命呈现了新的格局。总的来看，外地外省乃至国际友人作为移民在这一时期入川的主要目标是成都，省内的区域之间的移民目的地也绝大多数都是成都（尤其是重庆直辖以后）。成都吸引移民的主要魅力有：它有得天独厚的自然、人文环境，自己独具魅力的"生活美学"和自然天成的后现代气质；它是连续 12 年中国幸福指数最高的城市；它的城乡统筹、城市规划、基础设施建设、极其方便的交通通信、硬实力与软实力的同步增长、以"三城三都"建设为抓手构筑世界文化名城为目标的愿景、它的敞开胸怀吸引四方英贤天下才俊的诸种政策和措施都是不容忽视的核心竞争力。而"传承巴蜀文明，发展天府文化"的扎实行动，正在为它源源不断地注入植根历史、观照现实、引领未来的新动能，成都、四川，必将在竞争全国、全球优秀移民的道路上，成为领跑城市之一。

多少有些遗憾，改革开放这 44 年，简阳在前 38 年不隶属于成都，因此得到的人口红利比成都其他区（市）县少，因高端、优质人口的持续流入增添的经济和文化活力自然也有些滞后，比如与国内国际一流城市竞争所需的现代化、国际化视野，做景观、场景、品牌要高端精致的传播意识，视人才和效率为发展灵魂的观念，法治和市民行为规范意识，营商环境的优化，高品质地保存城市文脉、气韵的城乡统筹与融合，以"天府文化"为统领，发现并优化城市独有的生活美学等，都存在这样或那样的不足。行政归属成都，发展纳入成都，和精神上

完全融入成都，但又要把"天府雄州"的文化个性树立起来，建立充分的文化自信和文化自豪，已经成为简阳市委、市政府和全市人民的共识与行动。精准的城市定位，远大的发展前景，清晰的发展路径，宜业宜居的城市生态，也是简阳重新实现人口迁徙与自身发展的良性互动的信心与保障。

最后，归纳一下自己的理论思考。一般来讲，有利于文化发展的人口变迁态势是：人口总量增多比总量减少好，因为这意味着其物质文明、制度文明、精神文明乃至生态文明形成的人类幸福生活的承载能力强；涵容的族群越多越好，因为这意味着此城此地文化开明包容性强，并且尊重个性；平均受过教育的年限越长、级别越高越好，因为这意味着可能、可以从事文化活动的人的基数大、消费文化产品与服务的市场潜力大；平均年龄相对越年轻越好，因为文化不仅要推陈，更要出新，文化不仅是事业，也是产业，后者更需要年轻人的朝气和勇敢；流进流出越自由越好，因为这意味着文化基因的远缘、多元杂交成为可能，后代一定更强，新果一定更甜；新旧居民、不同阶层之间的居民歧视越少越好，因为固化的阶层隔阂，以及支撑歧视的自以为是或傲慢，从来都是以德服人、"以文化人"的敌人；男女两性比例越接近越好，这样的城市，因为人的基本欲望得不到满足、从而乖张暴戾甚至变态的人最少，而基于阴阳平衡而产生的具有最广泛人类共情、通常乐感压倒苦感的宗教哲学、文学艺术活动才会自然地枝繁叶茂，人民才会普遍从官方、民间、个体组织、呈现的各类精神生活、文学艺术中发现、品味美和幸福。此外，能够吸附外部文化艺术重要人物前来旅游观光、停留驻足，甚至因为喜欢、欣赏、留恋而留下文学艺术作品加以赞美的人的多少，更能反映此地此城的文化，到底有没有魅力、有多大魅力。从最后这个指标来看，简阳因为其秀美多样的山水、状元和名人较多（包含此地产生的名人；以此地为活动舞台的名人；以及留下了赞美此地此城的诗词歌赋、书画墨宝，乃至影视作品的名人三类。其遗迹应该尽可能保护、恢复或重建），三教和移民文化景观林立，特色美食（如简阳"餐饮九绝"）和风俗节庆（如简阳的非遗活动，正在倾力打造的几个集商贸、观光、娱乐、地方风物展示为一体的节庆）的个性魅力等，加上连接川西与川东的官道、商道纵贯简阳，是相当出众的，所谓"蜀都东来第一州""入蜀最宜游简郡""成都东大门"绝非虚誉，而是历史上许多文人雅士的集体记忆，其中薛涛留下的《酬郭简州寄柑子》《江月楼》最为有名。美丽的女诗人收到简阳姓郭的长官寄来的美味柑橘引发的心中愉悦，和她亲临简州游玩，并登上的简阳名胜江月楼看到的美景，产生的可与江南比美的赞叹，都是唐朝魅力、幸福简阳的生动记录。

简阳城市特色文化内涵

第一节 龙垭文化

一、龙垭遗址的发掘

2010 年 4 月底，简阳市简城镇龙垭村村民建房时发现两根象牙门齿，长者约 3.15 米。在随后进行的实地调查中，发现遗址中伴出有人工打制的石制品，初步推定为一处旧石器时代遗址。2010 年 7 月至 9 月，四川省文物考古研究院联合简阳市文物管理所，对该遗址进行了抢救性发掘，实际发掘面积 87 平方米。遗址地处沱江二级支流康家河的一级缓坡状阶地上，高程约 398 米。当前地表为果树林和应季作物。发掘过程中严格按照田野考古规程正北向布方，自上而下、由晚及早逐层清理发掘。至埋藏动物化石和石制品的文化层后，按 1×1 平方米打格分方，并按 10

厘米一层水平向下发掘，准确记录标本出土坐标，测绘部分标本埋藏现状，并采用水筛法采集微小标本，采集部分早期土样。龙垭遗址地层堆积自上而下分为5层，其中第四层为旧石器时代文化堆积层。龙垭遗址主要出土动物骨骼化石、石制品及装饰品等。发掘区内出土哺乳动物骨骼、牙齿、角化石标本近180余件，另有数千计的动物骨骼化石碎块，这些化石不少于6个属、15个种，主要有东方剑齿象、中国犀、鹿、牛、羊、猪、獾、竹鼠。初步整理骨骼化石（据下颌骨）可知东方剑齿象个体至少有3头。部分骨骼表面有大小不一的凹痕，可能为砸击、刮削痕迹。龙垭遗址出土砾石3000余件，其中石制品700余件，大部分选用材质较好的石英砂岩的砾石打制，总体体现出南方砾石工业的传统特征。出土石制品主要有石核、石片、砍砸器、锛形器、刮削器、尖状器和石球等。

龙垭遗址还出土三件装饰品，其中，一件选用动物骨骼，两件选用哺乳动物臼齿。穿孔技术为双向对钻的方式，两端孔径略大于中间部位，孔径约1.5~2毫米。动物骨骼的挂饰钻孔位于骨骼中部偏薄位置，牙齿挂饰钻孔位于齿根，钻孔前对牙齿修整、打薄，以利于钻孔。龙垭遗址旧石器时代人类活动的文化层不能分层，埋藏堆积中不见河湖相的水平层理。大量石制品风化、磨蚀程度轻微，动物骨骼化石散布发掘区，并无固定方向排列迹象。推测该遗址石制品及动物骨骼化石等遗存埋藏前可能未经长时间暴露或远距离搬运。

龙垭遗址石制品以大型砾石石器工业为主，与东方剑齿象-大熊猫动物群的多种动物化石伴出，同时发现钻孔技术，其年代可能处于旧石器时代晚期。龙垭遗址位于沱江流域，其下游30余公里的黄鳝溪曾发现著名的"资阳人"，二者文化面貌、性质较为一致。此次发掘为探索沱江流域早期人类文化增添了新的资料，同时，结合古代地质地貌的科学发掘也有助于总结出丘陵地区早期文化的调查方法。发掘后期，四川省文博院邀请中国科学院古脊椎动物与古人类研究所、四川大学、成都文物考古研究所等单位相关学者召开了一次专家论证会，并到遗址发掘现场参观。与会专家一致认为，"龙垭遗址是在中国西南新发现的一处重要的旧石器时代晚期遗址，该遗址地层清晰，出土遗物丰富，对研究古人类在该地区生存、演化的历史和探讨四川盆地的环境变迁具有重大的科学研究价值"。

二、龙垭文化的历史价值和对简阳的意义

（1）提供了四川盆地在旧石器时代后期，远古人类的生产工具、生活用品、伴生的动植物，以及当时四川盆地的气候比今天温暖的丰富信息。这是迄今独一无二的珍贵资源。由于先于它发现的断代相当的"资阳人"只有一个头盖骨，缺乏其他证据，而且两者的发现地点仅仅相差40公里，因此，"资阳人"为龙垭人死后被洪水冲到资阳所在地的可能不能完全排除。至少两者共同证明了四川盆地是中国各地最早有人类生存繁衍的地区之一。

（2）提供了关于古蜀文明建构者——最显赫的考古发掘当然是三星堆、金沙遗址显示的人类青铜时代的活动证据——是来自川西高原还是来自盆地内部土著，或者是两者融合、联合形成的族群的有证据的新可能。

（3）巴蜀文化的神秘浪漫、强大的审美情趣与能力最早的源头在哪里？龙垭文化的装饰品提供了最早的实物证据。

三、人文精神归纳

龙垭文化，是 30 年来最重要的旧石器时代遗址，是具有多方面唯一性、独特性的"文化不动产"，证明此地在远古便最适合人类生存繁衍，当时的人们已经有了艺术审美追求，甚至原始的宗教信仰，证明了简阳地区是四川盆地先民最早的发祥、活动区域之一。中华文化看重"慎终追远"，习近平总书记十分强调的中华民族共同体意识也与此相关。此外龙垭文化距离"资阳人"出土地仅 40 公里（在河流上游），而且时间略早。因此它至少可以归纳出的文化内涵可以表达为：蜀祖故里，艺术原乡，神人和谐，万物并育。

这样的总结和表达，可以在中华文化多元一体，巴蜀族群来历溯源等历史语境中，确立简阳独一无二的天府之国的族群和文化艺术祖庭形象。这一具有神秘浪漫属性的文化资源的传承弘扬，将有力增强简阳"被记住""被向往"的优良文化属性。

第二节　农耕文化

一、成都、简阳农耕文化的起源与禀赋

笔者与马英杰博士合著有《走近天府农耕文明》（四川大学出版社

2021年7月版）一书，书中对于天府文化视野下的农耕文明有一个系统的梳理与论证。所谓农耕文化，在百度百科和360词条里面的解释是："农耕文化，是人们在长期农业生产中形成的一种风俗文化，它是世界上最早的文化之一，也是对人类影响最大的文化之一。农耕文明集合了各民俗文化为一体，形成了独特文化内容和特征，其主体包括国家管理理念、人际交往理念以及语言，戏剧，民歌，风俗及各类祭祀活动等，是世界上存在最为广泛的文化集成。农耕文明决定了汉族文化的特征。"其实这是比较空泛，难以理解、把握和论述的定义，在笔者看来，农耕文化就是基于男耕女织为主体的经济生活而形成的具有稳定性、连续性的价值观和生活方式，及其伴生、耦合的宗教信仰和风俗习惯。

考古发掘和大量文献可以证明，成都平原及其周边地区是中国农耕文明的发祥地之一。她独一无二的自然地理条件、历代先民通过"立德、立功、立言"所塑造的稳定延续的人文性格，保证了其农耕文明的长盛不衰，即使遭遇剧烈的天灾人祸，也能很快修复并继续新的创造与发展。而简阳，因为地理与行政隶属与成都在历史上的紧密关联，也是这一过程和传统的参与者、建构者之一。

天府文化四个方面的优秀禀赋能够长期延续的广阔土壤和深厚根基，正是其不同凡响的农耕文明。特别是其最为突出的个性——乐观包容特质，更是与其"优越秀冠"的农耕生活，水乳交融、相得益彰，并在近代以来工业文明和现代化、全球化浪潮冲击中得以继续传承。中华优秀传统文化的家国一体情怀；忠孝廉耻和仁义礼智信为代表的核心价值体系；以及儒释道三位一体的精神家园；风雨同舟、休戚与共、患难相扶的命运共同体意识；敬畏天理、敬畏神明、敬畏自然、敬

畏尊长、敬畏圣贤的风俗习惯，主要奠基、植根于人类最成熟、稳定、连续的农耕文化。而天府农耕文明是其中重要而独特的组成部分。谭继和先生认为："都广之野"是中国农业的一个起源地，它以治水为特征，以江源文明为标志，孕育和发展出"优越秀冠"的天府农业文明，这是西蜀文化的第一个特征，也是最主要的特征。谭继和先生指出，古蜀农业文明的起源是从岷山河谷，包括成都平原、临邛（今邛崃）、江原（今崇州）、南安（今乐山）这一三角地带开始的。国学大师蒙文通在《巴蜀史的问题》一文中曾专门加以论证。他认为"中国农业在古代是从三个地区独立发展起来的，一个是关中，一个是黄河下游，在长江流域则是从蜀开始的"。他主张"农业是从江源入成都平原的，江源、临邛，正是岷山河谷，蜀的文化可能从这里开始"。岷山河谷就是"广都之野"，成都平原就是它的中心，这里是蜀文化即江源农业文明的起源地。其起源的次第，从都江堰治水开始，次发展到临邛和江原，再发展到温江和双流（古广都，在历史上，牛鞞、简州、简阳一直与其接壤）。温江"因雪水自此始温"而得名，表明最早的优质农业是在温江出现的，因岷山雪水到温江等成都平原腹心地带，才更适宜于灌溉。正因为这里是农业起源地，才出现了《山海经》记载的周人农祖后稷葬于都广之野的传说和蜀人农祖杜宇与朱利相会于江原（今崇州）结为夫妇的传说。西蜀农业起源时代是同大禹、鳖灵、李冰相继治水的文化联系在一起的。在这个基础上才发展出特色鲜明、优越秀冠的天府农业文明。所以，西蜀出现了农耕时代特别悠长、农耕文化特别鲜明的面貌，它成为西蜀文脉基本性质及其展现面貌的决定性因素。直到近现代进入工业社会后，农耕文明这一决定性因素还对西蜀城乡文明与生态文明，直到西蜀人心理状态、生活方式、思维方式和社会习俗起着根深蒂固的作用。笔者认为，简阳一直参与或分享其润泽的天府农耕文明的优秀禀赋与个性，除了治水的智慧和丰功伟绩（在历史上，简阳享受过李冰治理岷江、文翁治理沱江上游带来的巨大效益；20世纪简阳人民气壮山河完成的东灌工程，则把自己直接纳入了都江堰大灌区这一人间农耕乐土）外，内涵还应该包括：耕读传家蔚然成风，奠定自古文宗出西蜀之深厚根基（简阳的状元和文豪可以证明它是天府文化这一领域的领头雁之一）；孕育出成都在人类丝绸文明和丝绸之路历史上不可取代的重要地位（牛鞞县服务于开拓、融合西南夷，而此事业是南方丝绸之路得以形成、维持的根本保障）；川西林盘和生机勃勃的场镇，成为维系成都普通百姓在和平年代拥有的很高幸福指数以及今后实现乡村振兴战略的优异资源（简阳的林盘具有独特的浅丘特色，与龙泉山以西的成都区市县的林盘具有明显的差异化之美）；孕育出以教化、学术、文艺为主要功德的名门望族和以重视、投身家乡各项公益事业、乐于为家乡父老排忧解难为特征的乡贤文化，连接官民城乡，引领、化育、造福天府（这一点，以宋代简州"刘氏三溪"和清代众多耕读传家、诗礼传家、科举兴家、慈善扬家的家族和乡贤、民间义士为代表，简阳也与成都其他市县可以并驾齐驱）；是道教诞生、发展在成都的深厚土壤，大大削减了对"三农"的古今歧视（简阳道教据点多，地方文献多有百姓捐资修建、复建道教庙宇之记录）；使本地"男尊女卑"观念很弱，女性受到尊重，涌现众多诗文技艺名满天下的才女和敢作敢为不让须眉之巾帼英豪（简阳有女娲崇拜；罗淑站立时代前沿留下名作并得到巴金尊重、传扬；抗美援朝征

兵,有120名妇女报名;东灌工程,简阳妇女以顶半边天的精神,踊跃参与,花季女青年同样承担、完成最艰险的任务;而有客家文化支撑的简阳妇女的勤劳和心灵手巧,在四川都是很突出的景观);强烈的家国情怀与统一意识,成为中国历史上度过多次重大灾难的可靠战略后方和和平年代的"中国后花园"(突出表现在宋末简州刺史李大全英勇抗元壮烈殉国,留下"忠国岐山""化碧祠"等古迹和名垂青史;涌现众多喋血沙场的抗日将领;1.5万名民众流血流汗提前完成抗战所需平泉机场;抗美援朝踊跃从军;积极适应新中国建设布局,行政隶属、区划发生多次改变;积极致力于城山相映、人水共生的公园城市建设等);各宗其主、特点鲜明的地方神祇、先贤崇拜(突出表现在川主崇拜和移民会馆代表的多种精神信仰和风俗习惯的和谐共处、美美与共);缔造了集田园之都、花卉之都、丝绸之都、音乐之都、诗歌之都、书香之都、美食之都、休闲之都于一体的城市舒适浪漫情调(这八都,简阳大部分都有历史底蕴,值得给自己定好位,有所为有所不为,积极参与,突出个性与特色)。

今天的成都和简阳,继承着这"八都"的属性与魅力。缔造这"八都"属性的行业、产业,几乎都离不开农村、农民、农业的健康发展和创新创造。振兴乡村,大量机遇就在其中。

总而言之,两千多年来,可用"优越秀冠"代指的成都、简阳的天府农耕文明的上述内涵所包含、携带的正能量无一不是成都乐观包容人文性格的有力支撑。虽然近代以来,尤其是改革开放以来,回归成都以来,简阳的主要经济支撑按在GDP总量中所占份额的标准来衡量,已经不是农业,而是让位于屹立潮头努力追赶的各类以现代工业文明及其制度、理念为底色的制造、"智造"行业，但是，简阳仍然具有鲜明的"小城市带大农村"的发展特色，这并不能改变两千年以上农耕文明为主所积淀所优选形成的天府文化的独特个性，而且伴随天府农耕文明与时俱进的创造性转化和创新性发展，与第二、第三产业的良性衔接，必将有力削弱以西方的制度、观念为基本坐标的现代工业文明，必然伴随、携带的个人主义、实用主义、机会主义、工具理性、消费主义对城市既有精神家园和人文传统的冲击和破坏，尤其是防止物欲的坐大，商品和货币拜物教的称雄，人际关系的冷漠化，贫富差距的拉大等弊端，因此保住、增长成都自改革开放以来自然天成的后现代气质——即这座城市同时具备健康的经济、活跃的文化、舒适的生活，从而始终是中国乃至世界普通公民幸福感出类拔萃的城市。保持清醒认识，做好顶层设计，拿出有力行动，自然和人文资源富集的简阳，宜业宜居的城市发展目标，就一定可以与新农村建设和城乡融合的事业一起，比翼齐飞。

二、简阳农耕文化的归纳

四川盆地尤其是成都平原的自然环境与经济、人文地理，决定了它拥有"优越秀冠"的农耕文明。位于沱江两岸，人民勤劳智慧，且西邻成都中心城区、东连重庆的简阳，以男耕女织为标志的农耕活动，条件优越，数千年的积淀，孕育了勤劳诚朴、耕读传家、爱乡爱国的文化传统，产生众多的物质与精神财富，支撑浓烈的乡愁和家国情怀。是天府农耕文明的重要代表，其历史积淀和当代表达，至少是简阳"被记住""被向往"的深厚土壤。

第三节　状元文化

一、状元文化及其价值

状元，是隋唐有了用科举考试选拔官员的制度以来，在朝廷（通常是礼部）主持的会试、皇帝亲临并钦点的殿试中脱颖而出，名列第一者的荣誉称号。千百年来，它是无数学子求学路上希望登临的巅峰，是走入仕途，实现名扬天下、光耀门楣、显耀家乡、忠君报国的最佳功名，是传统中国人普遍认可的四大幸福（久旱逢甘霖，他乡遇故知，洞房花烛夜，金榜题名时）中的极品幸福。虽然科举制度有一些弊端，但统计数据告诉我们，古代科举制度不仅明显利大于弊，与"大一统"观念、伦理道德、教育制度、学术和文学艺术取向实现了高度耦合、互相促进，而且对比同时期的世界其他国家的相关领域，它无疑是世界上最公正公平，也最有保障的优秀人才选拔制度，因此被深入了解中国文化的西方学者称为中国的第五大发明，西方近代以来的文官选拔制度，很大程度上就是学习借鉴中国古代科举考试制度的结果。我国现行的公务员"逢进必考"、考试程序要尽可能公平公正，同样是这一历史文化遗产的当代传承。因此，所谓的状元文化，就是围绕状元的产生、使用而形成的以尊师重教、崇尚学术、礼敬诗文、公平竞争、追求卓越等为核心内涵的价值观念及其需要的生活方式。

科举考试制度是对依靠血统、血缘可以世袭垄断高官显爵或在社会观念中垄断高等出身的"门阀士族制度"的全盘否定，并具有防止阶层固化，使各个阶层都有可能实现升降流动，大大增强社会活力和国家内部凝聚力的重大功效。宋代以降，中国形成了"士农工商"四个阶层，虽然可以升降流动，但"士"（主要是指读书人，尤其是取得了秀才、举人、进士出身的读书人）成为最受尊重、最有影响力的人群和阶层，这促使耕读传家、诗礼传家、科举兴家、功名荣家成为基层社会的普遍现象，实际上是传统中国最人性、最温暖、最体现文明礼义之邦气质的人文景象。而中国各地，几乎无一例外，都把本地本城在历史上涌现出的状元及其数量，以及产生他们这样一个使家乡父老和后代子孙为之骄傲和自豪的人群的原因视为文化建设的最佳资源。状元的数量也成为该地该城学术和文学艺术繁荣程度的主要标志之一。

二、简阳状元文化的成因与体现

（一）共性成因及体现

简阳从汉武帝元鼎二年（前115年）牛鞞县诞生开始，共计有2137年的城市和乡村发展史，其中约1470年，直接隶属于成都府或办公机构设在成都的军政机构。如果主要以科举考试的成就来衡量的话，它在五代，尤其是两宋，迎来了自己的发展高峰。而这与四川在历史上的兴衰沉浮完全一致。笔者著有《宋代四川人才辈出的文化机理》一书，其中有一个基本结论，就是宋代的四川，为何能够人才井喷（仅

是一个成都府学，就培养出了进士上千人，号称甲冠天下），辉映华夏，感化异邦，光照东亚儒家文化圈，最重要的原因是巴蜀文化的气质，与赵宋开创并坚持始终的以不以言治罪、不杀士大夫、崇尚文治（包括体现公平正义的科举制度的空前完善、不允许宰辅官员子弟当状元）的国家气质，实现了历史上的最佳耦合，形成了巴蜀地区人才通过科举考试制度和国家应对众多内忧外患形成的洗礼萃选（宋代三进士身上表现十分明显）脱颖而出立德立功立言的最佳生态环境。此外，宋代君王统治成都，有前期对待蜀人轻狂傲慢引发包括王小波、李顺起义在内的多次起义和兵变的沉痛教训，所以从选择张咏治蜀开始，皇帝和宰相在选择四川和成都的行政长官时，均不敢怠慢，而是精心挑选，所以莅临成都的长官，不仅几乎没有贪污腐败、无德无能之辈，而且多数长官都十分关心、扶持地方教育，并胸怀宽广做伯乐，积极发现、奖掖、推荐蜀地中青年俊才雅士。

文翁化蜀以来的成都，是中国尊师重教、崇尚学术、崇尚诗文艺术风气最为浓烈的城市之一，五代后蜀，是中国半个多世纪乱世中的一方相对的净土和文化、教育、艺术高地，著名的"孟蜀石经"和宋朝开国后《开宝藏》等旷世大典在成都完成雕版，都证明后蜀的深厚文化基础与实力（这是后蜀简阳产生状元王归璞的基础）；而两宋，天府之国的经济和物质技术（包括造纸术、印刷术、图书出版发行）又能为这些价值追求的实现提供有力支撑，出现三个状元，也属于必然。①

---

① 南宋时期国土更加逼仄，首都东移临安（今杭州），成都和四川对于国家的分量更加重要，朝廷为了体恤四川学子前往临安参加会试的艰难，专门为川、陕设立类省试，第一名准首都会试，第三名推恩（即享受相当于第三名的功名），并可以进一步赴京参加殿试。其余赐同进士出身。

（二）个性因素及其体现

1. 宋代前期起义、兵变罹祸较少

北宋统一四川，后蜀孟昶迅速选择了投降，花蕊夫人后来曾感叹"君王城头竖降旗，妾在深宫那得知？十四万人齐解甲，宁无一个是男儿！"北宋前期，因为北宋王朝文化心理上对蜀地的傲慢，长时期将掳掠的孟蜀财富运往开封，加上骄兵悍将的胡作非为，以及五代以来主户、客户积累的矛盾，贫富差距，先后爆发了声势浩大，朝廷必须派出大兵才能镇压的全师雄兵变，王小波、李顺起义，王钧兵变，战火所及之地，自然难免会造成许多破坏。而这些战事、灾祸几乎没有对简州所在区域造成严重破坏，简州在这个时期经济文化得到了良好的恢复发展。

2. 隶属成都、连接川南川东的区位

北宋的简州，下辖三个县（南宋时有所萎缩），直接连接成都平原和川中南的梓州，通过水路大道，还能方便直通川东，这样的地理位置，使简阳比普通县更能顺利获得成都路包括府学、交子、印刷术、十二月市、若干学术教育科举大家族时代繁昌代表的都市带中小城市和广大乡村圈（宋代眉州属于成都路，以及后来的成都府，所以"三苏"也是简阳人民觉得身边的顶级名人兼榜样）的文明资源，接受其高度崇文气息的熏染，但简州地域的经济文化条件又肯定比成都平原地区艰苦一些，所以简州的读书人自然更加勤奋和刻苦，这反而使之兼得益州路和梓州路优质资源和勤奋耕读的优势，这从三位状元的为人风格中也有明显反映。

这一个性的分析也有助于今日简阳思考，如何在大成都中传承弘

扬自己的文教个性，培养既得成都先进区市县的都市文明、生活美学中的国际视野、效率观念、精致意识、城乡统筹、社区治理之经验并加以运用，又继续保持简阳人民的淳朴、勤奋、坚韧、文武并重的自身传统与个性，从而不论是与原内江、资阳的兄弟县市比，还是与原成都一二圈层的区市县相比，都有自己独特的竞争力和活力，这将是简阳（甚至包括成都东部新区）未来文化传承发展和文化软实力打造，应该思考谋划的重要议题。而状元文化形成原因与体现的分析，可以呈现历史的镜鉴。

3. 简州四状元形成的文化高光

简阳历史上共出现四位状元，分别是王归璞、许将、张孝祥、许奕，如此状元数量从全国的县级层面来看，都是可圈可点的。由此可见，简州四状元的相继出现，为状元文化的形成与积淀，带来了高光时刻。研究简阳状元文化，更应以此为重点和切入口来分析其内核与外延。

王归璞，是简州历史上第一个状元，据《十国春秋·后蜀·本传》载："简州人，少聪颖、善属文。广政中（公元938—965年）状元及第，后不知所终。"乾隆《简州志》及嘉庆《四川通志·选举篇》载："归璞，唐进士，朝代年份无考。"

许将，是简州历史上第二个状元，据民国《简阳县志》载："宋仁宗嘉祐八年（公元1063年）癸卯科廷试第一。官学士。"其官至龙图阁直学士、知成都府，后做尚书右丞，资政殿学士、知定州，移扬州，又移大名府，入为礼部尚书，后进门下侍郎，累官金紫光禄大夫，资政殿大学士、知河南府等。

张孝祥，是简州历史上第三个状元，据民国《简阳县志》载："宋高宗绍兴二十四年（公元 1154 年）甲戌科廷试第一，管至学士。"其是南宋时著名爱国词人，其词风格豪迈，在中国文学史上占有一席之地，著有《于湖集》《于湖词》。

许奕，是简州历史上第四个状元，据民国《简阳县志》载："宋宁宗庆元五年（公元 1199 年）己未科廷试第一。"曾担任剑南东川节度判官、校书郎兼吴兴郡王府教授、著作郎、起居舍人、吏部侍郎兼修玉牒官、遂宁知府、潼川知府等职务。

三、简阳状元文化的精神内核与彰显

（一）精神内核

用科举考试选拔人才和官员，是中华文明打破血缘和身份垄断，用公平正义的方式选贤举能的伟大制度文明。中国各地所产状元的数量，始终是衡量该地历史上文教水准的最重要标志之一。中国历史上有姓名记载的状元不超过 674 人，而中国今天有 2000 多个县，也就是说平均 3~4 个县，才可能产生一个状元。而简阳历史上，涌现了 4 个状元，这在四川和除了陕西以外的中国西部各省的州县中是很罕见的，是十分珍贵并至少在川西具有唯一性的文化资源。而且 4 个状元的活动，都是历史上国家和社会的正能量。简阳的状元文化，是一种公平竞争、追求卓越的奋斗精神，诗文立身、智慧报国的优雅风貌。尤其能够激发简阳儿女的文化自信与自豪，着力传承、弘扬简阳这一最珍贵历史文化遗产，使之成为简阳"被记住""被仰望"的城市禀赋。

（二）如何表达

陈寅恪先生有一段名言："华夏民族之文化，历数千载之演进，而造极于赵宋之世"。四川的历史文化也是如此。两宋的成都，因为经济繁荣，文教昌明，并最后才经历蒙古的战争摧残，府学质量中国第一，长时间成为中国各地参加进士考试竞争中的佼佼者。而简阳作为成都府路的属县，竟然创造了为大宋输送许将（仁宗嘉祐八年，即 1063 年状元）、张孝祥（高宗绍兴二十四年，即 1154 年状元）、许奕（1170—1219，宁宗庆元五年，即 1199 年状元）三个状元的奇迹。就笔者视野所及，这在四川省甚至整个中国西南地区的历史上，其他县尚无出其右者。所以评价简阳的状元文化，可以用"中华文明巅峰时期的巴蜀文化皇冠上的明珠""宋代四川文教冠冕""两宋成都的辉煌代言"等语言来表述与彰显。

第四节　名人文化

一、简阳名人文化资源梳理

因为自然地理、人文地理、经济地理、政治地理较为优越，以及在历史上大部分时间都是成都直辖的四川盆地腹心区域，加之历史演进中的一些因缘巧合，简阳的名人文化资源[①]与同级别的县市相比，是位列四川前茅、成都地区中上游水平的。全面加以梳理，简阳的名人文化资源有以下主要类型和特点。

（一）主要类型

1. 一大家族

宋代简州，以"刘氏三溪"（"前溪"刘泾；"东溪"刘伯熊；"后溪"刘光祖）为代表的"七世九进士"教育、学术大家族，以显著的正能量，活跃在大宋政治、学术、文学艺术的顶级殿堂中，显示宋代除了三大状元以外，简阳（当时建置叫简州阳安郡）保持了持续的教育学术繁盛、人文荟萃、科举显赫，人才辈出，是当时不仅在成都府路所属同级别同幅员州县里，文教科举最为璀璨的领先区域之一，而且在全中国的文化、教育、科举地图上，也是光芒四射、不可忽略的雄州巨邑。乐于与三刘为同道、为师友、为良朋的两宋众多泰山北斗，包括王安石（刘泾的伯乐和举荐者）、苏轼、苏辙兄弟（刘泾过从甚密、诗词唱和的朋友）、黄庭坚（刘泾挚友）、赵汝愚（贤相，高度评价刘伯熊的道德学术）、朱熹（敬重刘伯雄的道德文章，书信中尊刘伯熊为"前辈"）、魏了翁、真德秀（刘光祖终身同道兼挚友，其墓志铭也由真德秀撰写）。可见他们的道德文章在宋代的重要影响力和强大正能量。而刘光祖的贤内助李氏，不仅帮助他把四个儿子中的三个栽培成了进

[①] 一般认定地域、城市的历史名人（比如两批四川十大历史名人），标准有：出身于此地；在此地生活、活动过一段时间，并在此地有立德立功立言的重大建树；籍贯在此，且父辈出生于此地此城（这一条有争议，但一直也被基本认可）。

士，而且待人接物十分仁厚。这样善良的家族，焉能不和睦安宁、子孙繁昌！事实上，在历史上，简阳成为魅力十足（被向往甚至被仰望）的"雄州"，很大程度上靠这个家族及其遗留的活动遗迹，加上明清时期仰慕他们的家乡官民建立的纪念性的景观（最重要的是清代晚期简州知州颜守彝主持修建的三溪祠①）。宋代拥有进士身份，但博学多识、淡泊名利的地理学家王象之（1163—1230）在其考究精详的《舆地纪胜·简州》中留下的诗句"入蜀最宜游简郡，寻山须是访刘家"成为历史上夸赞、推荐简阳人文魅力最客观最真挚，影响力最大的"公益广告"。

2. 三大英烈

在简阳历史上，为了国家民族的正义事业，敢于成仁取义的英烈很多，不过就其分量来讲，有三人尤其值得纪念。宋末元初率领简州军民坚持抗元、英勇战死的简州刺史李大全，不仅正史有作为忠烈记载，而且为了纪念他，简阳还曾有"忠国岐山""化碧祠"等古迹。薛志高（1930—1952，简阳贾家场五里村人）在抗美援朝战争上甘岭战役中英勇杀敌，负重伤依然参与进攻，壮烈牺牲，记特等功一次，荣获志愿军二级战斗英雄称号；赖文禄（1931—1952，简阳平泉镇人），时所在班负责坚守82号阵地之194高地。1952年9月23日，穷凶极恶的"联合国军"，向他们的阵地倾泻了上万发炮弹，七辆坦克和一个营向他们发起进攻，他们只有一个班，却打退敌人十余次冲锋，最后他孤身一人又打退敌人五次冲锋，其军帽上有7个洞（此军帽被中国人民革命军事博物馆收藏），后来与突破炮火前来增援的2名战士一起，

---

① 此祠如能照原貌修复就太好了。

继续坚守到次日才被撤换下来。朝鲜政府颁给他国际勋章，志愿军总部给他记一等功，中央军委授予他二级英雄称号。

3. 四大状元

即五代孟蜀的王归璞，宋代的许将、张孝祥、许奕。即使只计算正统中国王朝（宋）的 3 个，这也是中国西南地区罕见的，且 3 人全部是历史上清廉爱民、忠君报国、才华横溢的士大夫。比如许将以其非凡的气质和才华（包括射箭）赴辽朝解决辽朝发起的纠纷时，不仅赢得辽朝君臣敬重，而且引起辽朝都城万民空巷，"争看南朝状元"的事件，是两宋朝廷多屈辱妥协的外交活动中最使人怀念的风景。笔者通读过《宋史》《辽史》《金史》《续资治通鉴长编》《建炎以来系年要录》等巨著，深知两宋时期的中国历史，不能完全站在汉人的立场来研判，当时的宋朝，战争经常不占上风，但文化上一直是辽、金、夏、元朝野暗中学习、模仿的榜样，是他们的老师，这种文化软实力，是民族艰难大融合最深沉的决定性力量，也是宋代名人文化中最有价值的类型。而许将无疑既维护了北宋的尊严，也辐射了北宋的文化力量，其效果，在军事没有优势的外交中达到了登峰造极的地步。这一点，过去关注、评价是严重不够的。关于 4 个状元的生平事迹，蒋向东、陈学明、陈水章先生所精心编写的《简州名人》（中国文史出版社 2006 年 12 月版）和王宏斌同志编委会主任编写的《天府雄州　幸福简阳》（四川大学出版社 2013 年 10 月版）两书已经有很好的介绍和归纳，本书不予赘述。但其中有两人作为文豪类型时，将择要介绍其相关生平。

4. 八个文豪

（1）雍陶（805—?），字国钧，成都人，唐文宗大和八年（834）

进士，历任御史、国子监毛诗博士，854年出任简州刺史，后来隐居庐山而终。喜游历，足迹遍布大半个中国。为人个性鲜明，习惯诗酒自娱，史载其律绝最好，亦善赋，是唐朝后期重要的山水诗人。其生平行迹在《云溪友议》卷上、《唐诗纪事》卷56、《唐才子传》卷7中均有记载。虽然其所著十卷诗集失传，今人仅能从《全唐诗》卷518中看见一卷，但他在唐朝后期的山水诗人中的一流地位是没有问题的。重要的是他为简阳横跨东大路上的"情尽桥"改名"折柳桥"并赋诗诉怀，从而留下简阳一段文豪与交通互动的浪漫佳话，感动了很多后人，连现代建筑大师茅以升先生都关注到了这座桥，尤其是雍陶的更名诉怀诗，可见雍陶及其折柳桥名人名桥的故事，历史上是简阳使人向往、仰望的一个点。

（2）许将（1037—1111），简州人，徙居河北，自幼聪颖，号小神童，民间流传有小许将在家乡与民间老伯对对联的故事。仁宗嘉祐八年（1063）高中状元，历任地方判官、通判，朝廷集贤校理、同知礼院、右正言、知制诰，熙宁七年（公元1074年）出使辽朝，依靠博闻强记、谈吐自若，驳回契丹的无理要求，并以比试箭法一箭中靶，赢得敬重。回国后广受赞誉，任过翰林学士权知开封府、会试主考官、兵部侍郎、知成都府、吏部尚书、尚书左丞、中书侍郎，期间也因卷入新旧党之争，反对"新"派凶狠的打击报复和迫害而沉浮。许将不仅是出色的政治家、外交家，也是顶级文豪。史载他工于诗词，尤喜作赋。他高中状元后，欧阳修读其赋，谓曰："君辞气似沂公，未可量也。"沂公乃王曾的尊称。王曾（978—1038），字孝先，青州益都（今山东省青州市）人。北宋名相、诗人。王曾少年孤苦，善作文辞。咸平年间，王曾连中三元，即发解试、省试、殿试皆第一，后两次拜相，封沂国公。他在宋朝士大夫和文人中有崇高声望。许将于元丰八年（1085）以龙图阁直学士知成都府，一干就是三年，其间与名士们在西园（当时的成都名园）有很多酬唱之作，今人能看到的计有 10 首。许将还为家乡简州写有《观澜亭》诗，立意高远、气势雄浑、情感豪迈，是简州八景之一的"四崖泛月"的重要文化底蕴。许将的词如今只能见到的只有两首《惜黄花·雁声晚断》《临江仙》，都是笔力雄健、开阖自如、情景交融的佳作。

（3）张孝祥（1132—1170），南宋简州人，绍兴二十四年（1154）高中状元，历任秘书郎、著作郎、集英殿修撰、中书舍人和多地知府、提点刑狱、安抚使等职。一生疾恶如仇、忠君爱国，反对秦桧，力挺岳飞，主张北伐，所以多遭打压，几次沉浮，最后以显谟阁直学士致仕。才气纵横，诗、词、文、书法俱佳。他的状元差点被秦桧弄掉，但殿试时，他的廷对不仅万言雄文，一挥而就，而且字写得极好，史载喜欢书法的高宗见他字画遒劲，卓然颜鲁，"疑为谪仙，亲擢首选"。在文学史上，张孝祥是南宋公认的最有代表性和影响力的爱国诗人之一。

（4）刘泾（1043—1100），简州阳安人，神宗熙宁六年（1073）进士，调成都府户曹参军。次年，王安石爱其才，授提举修撰经义所检讨。元丰（1078—1085）中，授太学博士。元祐元年（1086）遭御史王岩叟（此人也是状元出身，才华横溢，但属于反对变法、清算变法很激进的旧派，是协助司马光实施"元祐更化"的悍将）弹劾，以"不

协众议"贬谪，知咸阳县，后任过通判成都、知坊州等职。①在北宋后期混乱的政局里，刘泾作为政治家并没有重大影响力，但作为文豪，却是当之无愧的。史载他"早登苏子瞻之门"，与苏轼、苏辙过从甚密，"笃志于学"，是一位"以文知名"的学者，被编入当朝《国朝二百家名臣文粹》和《宋史·文苑传》，现存《东坡全集》里有三篇苏轼与刘泾的唱和之作，一篇苏轼应答刘泾的散文；而苏辙的诗集《栾城集》中有四篇他和刘泾唱和的作品。刘泾的书画技艺也非同凡俗，除了自己搜集有大量古书画以外，他擅画林松竹石，与当时名人米芾及长安人薛绍彭并称米薛刘："三公风神萧散，盖一流人也。"与米芾友善，米芾在其著作《书史》《画史》《宝晋英光集》中多次提到他。此外他还著有《西汉发挥》《成都刻石总目》等史学、文献学书籍。

（5）刘光祖（1142—1222），字修德，号后溪，简州阳安人，孝宗乾道五年（1169）进士，在地方曾任剑南东川节度推官、襄阳、江陵、潼川（今四川三台）、遂宁知府，在朝廷历任太学正、校书郎、皇太子宫小学教授、秘书郎、军器少监、殿中侍御史、司农少卿、中书舍人、起居舍人兼侍讲（皇帝读书的辅导老师），最后以显谟阁直学士（从三品）致仕。任御史时"极言道学朋党之弊，摧奸击强，不少顾避"，号称"铁面御史"，当然也遭遇过政敌的打压。他对于南宋后期逐步减少、停止对于朱熹代表的道学的打压作出了显著的贡献，所以受到赵汝愚（朱熹的支持者）和朱熹本人的高度评价。而他的学术和文学艺术造诣很高，著述宏富，经学、散文、诗词并举，《全宋诗》卷2611录其诗8首，

---

① 在历史学界，关于王安石变法本身及其引发的宋代士大夫的较量和纷争，是非曲直极难评判。迄今也没有被广泛接受的结论。

《全宋词》第三册录其词 21 首，《全宋文》卷 6313 收其文 6 卷。文学史家评论其词庄重、凄丽；其文不事雕琢而气韵浑厚，以质直为贵；真德秀论其诗"尤清婉"，为张栻激赏。其墓地在简阳养马河荷花村，规模宏大，当地百姓称"官坟沟"，可惜毁于"文革"。

（6）罗淑（1903—1938），其虽英年早逝，但其《生人妻》和爱国、抗战主题的文章已经足以让她位列同时代最优秀女作家的行列，得到了巴金等众多大文豪的关注、爱护，足见罗淑在中国文学史，尤其是女性文学史上应有光荣的一席之地。

（7）周克芹（1936—1990），简阳石桥人，出身贫苦，只读过成都农校，但热爱家乡，痴情文学创作。两次获得全国优秀短篇小说奖，长篇乡土小说《许茂和他的女儿们》获得首届茅盾文学奖。他继承弘扬了艾芜、沙汀等著名作家的乡土文学精神，留下了家乡人民真实生动而感人的生产生活画卷，拥有现代中国一流作家的地位。担任过四川省作家协会党组副书记、常务副主席，是简阳、成都、四川的骄傲。

（8）李鸣生（1956—2022），简阳人，当代著名作家，三届"鲁迅文学奖"（1996；2000；2010）得主，中国报告文学学会副会长，《中国作家》首席纪实作家，被文学界誉为"中国航天文学第一人""继徐迟之后中国第二个写科技题材的佼佼者"，被网民赞誉为"最有良知的作家"。其作品"航天七部曲"，影响及于海内外。三部获奖作品分别为《走出地球村》《中国 863》《震中在人心》。

5. 十个奇才

（1）李淳风（602—670），唐朝伟大的天文学家，他是土生土长的简州人，死后也葬于故乡。他的一生，精通当时朝野均认为最神秘深

奥的天文历算阴阳之学，并有许多让人惊奇的发明创造。比如，他20多岁以参与指导修订《戊寅元历》引起太宗关注，而进入太史局任职；制造出当时世界上最先进的浑天黄道仪；撰写《法象志》7卷，系统总结历代浑天仪之得失；升任太常博士、太史丞后，撰写《晋书》《五代史》最难的天文、律历、行、志部分，后人评价在所有正史天文志中以《晋书·天文志》最佳，他也因此获得男爵；李淳风还超越《戊寅元历》，制定出更加先进的《麟德历》；在关于他的众多神奇故事中，他与太宗打赌，并成功地预测了日食出现的准确时辰最为著名。他还是了不起的数学家，为古代数学经典做注释，丰富了中国古代数学文献。唐高宗龙朔两年（662），他被授予秘阁郎中（即太史令）之职，以至终老。李淳风还利用自己作为占星学家的威望，阻止了太宗听闻有谶书预言"唐中弱，有女武代王"，而想诛杀所有有嫌疑者的滥杀欲望。李淳风对于"风鉴堪舆"也属于神秘难测的顶尖人物，他留下的《乙巳占》《推背图》《百决图》《中国科学技术史》就是证明。也许今人面对李淳风，就会想起什么叫玄学。李淳风还是人类历史上第一个给风定级的奇人，他把风从小到大定为8级。400多年以后，英国航海家蒲福在其基础上，将风的定级扩展为13级。英国科学技术史巨匠李约瑟（1900—1995）对李淳风有科学史上的最高评价，比如他认为《晋书·天文志》是天文学知识的宝库；他在其皇皇巨著《中国科学技术史》第3卷中称赞李淳风是"整个中国历史上最伟大的数学著作注释家"。李淳风，是一个可以让自己的故乡、祖国被仰望的巨星。

（2）德山宣鉴（782—865），唐代顶尖高僧，其影响及于古今海内外。他是汉传佛教历史上第一个敢于"呵佛骂祖"，破除偶像崇拜带来的个体走向觉悟的枷锁，发明"德山棒"对初学、愚顽弟子行"当头棒喝"加以警醒、开悟，在当时僧俗两届都感到惊世骇俗（在历史上，这种对权威、偶像的质疑、挑战精神，刺激并引起反弹的人绝非个别，包括了清朝的雍正皇帝，他曾经下令将德山宣鉴从高僧名录中除名！）的佛教改革者。他是禅宗云门宗、法眼宗的祖师和佛门中"人文精神"的最早提出者。他的一生，留下了许多经典故事。如初信北禅渐悟，在成都"初讲金刚经，名冠成都"，但他却要跋涉万里，出川挑战主张顿悟的南禅，结果在湖南澧阳斗法，最终被崇信大法师以黑夜点灯、吹灯送行感悟，得到崇信心印，遂心服口服，烧掉自己从简州带来的曾经自鸣得意的《青龙书抄》（如今湖南常德乾明寺还有纪念此事的焚经坛），变成坚定的顿悟派。他接下来又辞别崇信，去与南岳系沩山灵佑法师（按辈分属于宣鉴的师叔）切磋斗法，终于占有上风，沩山预言了他必然走向呵佛骂祖。历史上的宣鉴，虽然个性鲜明，但其德行至纯，学人无不敬仰，归服者众，所以他的第三代弟子得以创立南禅中有名的云门、法眼两宗，并一直传承至今，信众遍及海内外（尤其是日、韩、越南）。基于各种因素，德山宣鉴出川后，主要活动据点在湖南常德（今天的常德，早已经将宣鉴作为他们的佛教文化名片加以传播、打造），再也没有回过四川，但他是简阳人，并且在简阳、成都形成、展示了佛学根基与信仰，并禀赋巴蜀文化、天府文化的鲜明个性（见前面的论述）走出四川，成为中国佛学、佛教历史上创新变革的里程碑式的高僧。他出家的古卧龙寺在简阳，实在应该做一点文章。

（3）石经寺楚山绍琦禅师。石经寺在简州（今四川省成都市简阳市）西北六十里，原属简阳久隆场乡，今归成都市龙泉驿区茶店镇，在

成都市东南七十七里，为成都市南郊一大佛教名胜游览地。据传石经寺始建于东汉末年（220），蜀汉时为大将赵云家庙。根据民国《简阳县志》记载，石经寺原名天成寺，坐落在龙泉山脉中段天成山南麓。明代正统年间（1436—1449），浙江楚山禅师挂锡于此近三十载。楚山为当时有名的和尚，来蜀后，时与蜀定王和成都权贵往还，诗酒唱和，颇受礼遇赏识。蜀定王还曾出金增修天成寺。成化九年（1473），楚山在天成寺后栖幻庵坐化。众僧遂将尸骸移供山洞中，装塑成菩萨，号为楚山祖师，供善男信女奉拜。楚山肉身在"文革"中被毁。楚山和尚著有《楚山语录》和诗稿传世。天成寺倚傍龙泉山脉天成山南麓，依山而建七层大殿。进山门为天王殿，左为念佛堂，右为五观堂。沿宽直石梯而上，为大雄宝殿，系明蜀王派工修建，构造甚为雄壮。殿中壁画彩绘佛像，生动逼真。左侧为阎王殿。由大雄殿右侧，登阔石阶三百余级，到达后殿。再上，为观音殿、祖师殿、燃灯殿。祖师殿右侧有总务室、衣钵寮、方丈室、退院寮、花园、客堂和宿舍。中华人民共和国成立前，全寺院房舍共有三百余间。整座寺庙，依山势构筑，雄奇挺拔，处于群山环抱之中，树木葱郁，风物秀丽，实为川西一处极佳的佛教旅游避暑胜地。明末张献忠入蜀，起义军纪律严明，所过之地保护寺庙。因见天成寺庙宇巍峨雄峙，更加注意保护。后来寺僧却编造出张献忠欲举火焚寺，"三举火三熄，遂骇散去"的神话。于是迷信楚山祖师的人更多，附近州县来寺求神拜佛者，络绎不绝。清乾隆三十二年（1767），简州知州宋思仁到天成寺游赏，既爱风景清幽，更仰楚山道德学识，于是送石刊《金刚经》一部，刻在三十二块巨石碑上，竖立庙中。此后，天成寺遂改名为石经寺。寺中僧众又传出神话，说是宋州牧家中老太太患眼疾，向楚山祖师爷许愿，治好了眼病，才送的这一部石刻《金刚经》。借以炫耀楚山祖师的"灵验"，广为招徕俗众。这部石刻经书，历经战乱，到解放时，已仅存一块石碑，被寺内视为"镇山之宝"。清末状元骆成骧有《石经山云歌》，诗云："朝云带雨飞上山，千峰万壑云雨间，人随云雨相往还。暮云挟月凝不流，空山六月疑高秋，人与云月相淹留。山云可攀不可束，山月可携不可掬，山人可亲不可渎。伟哉楚山真气多，远祖如来近达摩，洞观尘世如风波。一身屹作须弥柱，四海归来此山处，山与楚山同今古。有时绮语戒不定，偶随猿鹤斗清韵；寥天寂寂闻钟磬，明师传灯灯转明；儒佛一家同化城，四山风雨读书声……"

（4）"疯子画家"吴昂（1801—？），渝州（今重庆）人，博闻强记、学识渊博，工书画，尤擅长残书，也擅风水。性格倔强，不求名利。大约在道光十年（1830），只身离家出游到简州，得到知县欢迎善待，他与石盘铺方肇春关系很好，遂从县署移居于该地万寿宫，虽然经济上穷困，但却安之若素，经常与乡间文人学士诗酒唱和，与百姓乃至乞丐可以絮语终日，唯独与权贵见面无语。日常独居，或连日不餐，或数日沉睡，或嬉戏逗趣，所以被人目为"疯子"，他也不与计较。而一旦作画，则连日累时，不成不止，成则拊掌欢呼雀跃。其画虽多，一般人不容易得到，只有一些知心朋友可以有机会获得。知心朋友的接济，他也接受，但却不以作品与达官贵人交接。从现存的作品（画上多有题诗）来看，吴昂是个性鲜明、志趣旷达、倡导耕读，具有清奇轩昂风格的画家，以山水画、花卉画等为主。在简阳，还有关于他的身世可能是太平天国洪秀全手下幕僚、避祸来简隐居示人以疯癫，以及他建议修建了当地著名景观题名塔、铁灯杆，以带来财水不流走、文气不

泄漏、山水秀美永驻等益处的传说。吴昂并不见于四川的重要人物才可能收录的名人词典（包括笔者担任副主编的最新的《成都历史文化大词典》），与他的个性、生活方式与层级、作品传播较窄等因素有关，但至少，他是地方城市文化中的一个对于巴蜀文化、天府文化特质有鲜明体现的"奇人"。

（5）地方"拳王"余发斋（1854—1946），石盘铺人，祖上余飞（绰号"赛燕飞"）顺治年间从湖广移民到简阳，喜好武术，性格豪爽，曾偶遇一位高僧，并收留一位从河南躲避豪强欺负而来的宋大师于家中，并学到他们在武术上的绝活。他将僧、宋、余以及南北拳融会贯通，创立了"余门拳"。传到余发斋，已经是第十四代。1918年，四川靖国军总司令熊克武的贴身保镖李国超在青羊宫摆擂，被过关斩将的余发斋击败。1928年，其长子余鼎山打败了大力士陈牛，遂受聘任教重庆国术馆，弟子众多。1930年，余鼎山参加重庆市市长潘文华主持的"武壮士考试大会"，荣膺壮士称号者15人，余门弟子占了12人。中华人民共和国成立后，余门拳后人余绍华（余发斋的侄孙）受聘担任过成都体育学院武术教练，两次参加全国性比赛，进入中国武术名人辞典。后来，随子孙走向各地，余门拳的传播中心移出了简阳（川东最多）。2010年，简阳武术馆成立了余门拳研究会，2016年，余门拳入选成都市非遗项目。其后人在政府和社会支持下，正在简阳逐渐恢复这一携带着华佗"五禽戏"基因，形成于明代中叶，清代在简阳率先光大，具有手法多变、短手寸劲、套路丰富等特点的拳种及其"武德""仁术""养气"合一的武术文化。

（6）开成都近代文明风气之先的傅崇矩（1875—1917），字樵村，简阳石盘人。出身于举人家庭，自幼性喜杂收博蓄。随父举家迁往成都，超爱成都，所以终身以成都人自居。曾就读于尊经书院，深受维新变法思想影响，立志匡世济民，尤其致力于科技传播开启民智、以举办报业开启市民视野，他还有创办黄包车行、发行彩票等诸多"四川第一"的实践。秉性善良的他没办法不交到伪善的官员和损友，终至实业委顿、黯然神伤。晚年，他将精力主要集中于为家乡"立言"，10 余年中，他汇集出版了规模宏大的《傅氏丛书》，提供了大量四川进步所需珍贵信息，其中尤以 31 万字的《成都通览》最功在近代，利及千秋，分四百多个栏目，详细介绍了清末民初成都的方方面面，被称为当时成都社会的"百科全书"。傅崇矩因此成为那个时代成都最伟大的文化巨子和乡贤之一。今日的简阳，已经恢复成为成都的一部分，所以以他的事迹和思想努力进行文创和各种形式的传播，构建城市的文化自信、自觉与自豪，将是文化建设的当然义务。

（7）传奇名医郑子壬（1878—1973），简阳武庙乡人，因幼年多病，曾拜活佛学佛，后随名医郑相臣学医。还学过藏医，并在西藏贡嘎山萨迦寺出家受戒。1915 年赴京参加文官考试，通过后有一段在沈阳和成都担任法官、军队军法处长的短暂经历，多数时间从事军医工作。1935 年，在成都国医院任教授。他是一个意志力和志向非凡的人，为了学佛、学医，曾 8 次入藏，两次去印度，足迹遍及中国各省。十分聪颖，通晓梵文、藏文，对于文字学、文章学也很有造诣。他把中医藏医之"以毒攻毒"发挥得淋漓尽致，其虎狼配方常常令人胆寒，但却能够去疑难顽疾，包括名将刘湘也接受过他的虎狼之方的成功治疗。他还能够调制多种丹药，过程、方法十分神秘，并成功治愈当时四川著

名的获得过全国短跑和接力赛冠军的女运动员汪孝军的骨结核病。此病即使今日医学界，也是一道难题。

（8）扬名华人圈的草书笔圣杨永宪（1838—1956），绰号"杨草仙"，简阳江源杨家河人，当过乡村教师，后到安徽当师爷，最后辗转沈阳、日本、上海、南洋等地，逝世于新加坡，享年 118 岁，仅是其高寿，就足以令人称奇。在家庭、职业选择等方面，个性刚愎倔强，走上卖字为生的道路，到达南洋时，其妻与之断绝了联系。他书法打开市场后，收入不菲，在日本时遇上火山爆发，平民伤亡惨重，他捐资 20 万相助。以至于他回到上海时，家人生活有时还需友人接济。他的草书艺术，风格有些奇崛怪异，但却以其非凡个性，受到了很高评价，有媒体甚至誉其为"三千年来草书笔圣第一人"，可见其欣赏者的热捧。他的思想、言论、人格、文章、艺术种种皆有特长，"占有文明进步主权，可谓华国之国粹"。可见声望之高。他每次下笔以前，还有一番纵跃运动，"如国术家砍大刀、舞长剑、挥铜锤铁棒，轻便异常"；可以"左右两手，双管齐下，俄而先左后右，俄而先右后左，万年顿舒，一气贯成。"观者无不大呼过瘾，击掌赞叹。他的字因此曾估价高达每个字 1 万至 2 万元。91 岁时他在台湾表演并展陈自己的作品，获得热烈追捧，所书草书梅花体，被当时日本名流评为"中华草圣之第一"。此外，杨永宪还是一位古体诗和现代诗都有造诣的优秀诗人，对于中华文化在儒家文化圈内外扩大影响力，有自己的独到贡献。

（9）用易学推测太阳系新星的天文学家刘子华（1899—1992），简阳洛带人①，幼年当过学徒，读过私塾，从其姑父（简阳中学英语教师）学习英语，1918 年，考取留法勤工俭学预备班，一年后以第三名的成绩获得赴法旅费资助而到达巴黎，参加过早期留法中国共产党人的革命活动。1923 年考入巴黎大学（预科），1926 年就读医学院。1932 年，在国际大学生联合会就国际联盟问题举行的征文比赛中，他的论文一举夺魁，获得"特别荣誉奖"。随后有人请他讲解《易经》，西方人觉得它很神秘。刘子华将其研究转向天体物理学。从 1937—1939 年，住在最廉价公寓、因为付不起取暖费，经常被寒冷折磨的他，以巨大的努力，完成了博士论文《八卦宇宙论与现代天文——一颗新星的预测》并提交答辩。这篇论文学跨古今中西，内容深奥，由几个教授分别审读，令教授们惊叹，1940 年 6 月，法西斯战火已经烧到法国，为了躲避空袭，刘子华在公墓里学习和研究。11 月他获得了博士学位。在解决出版资金时，这篇论文获得了著名科学家约里奥居里（居里夫人的丈夫）领导的科研机构和法国外交部的支持。按照惯例，书上应该有作者照片，但刘子华坚持要求附上其母亲的照片，结果，经过巴黎大学特许，其博士论文形成的科学著作前面，印上了一张中国农村妇女的照片。1943 年，论文获得法国最高学位——国家博士称号。这是赴法勤工俭学学生首次获此殊荣。巴黎大学邀请刘子华战后在该校任教，但 1945 年，国民政府号召海外华人归国，刘子华回到了祖国。回国后，国民党要求他参政，以壮自己统治的声势，他不喜欢政治而不配合，

---

① 龙泉驿区（含洛带）历史上长期属于简州、简阳，今日简阳，可以理直气壮地把分家以前的名人，作为自己的历史文化资源，但开发利用时，简阳市与龙泉驿区应该加强沟通协调，努力实现双赢和更好的布局，防止陷入非此即彼之争。

加上他的学说在充斥着崇洋情节的国内学界被视为邪说，刘子华陷入没有工作的窘境，生机维艰。中华人民共和国成立后虽然任过四川省政府参事，但还经历过磨难，改革开放后他的博士论文及其贡献才得到公允评价。

（10）智保青城山遗产的道教领袖傅圆天（1925—1997），简阳久隆人，出身贫寒，体弱多病，只上过短暂私塾，1946年遵母命在汶川县黄龙观出家，师从全真道龙门派道长张永平，从此终身献给了道教。1955年到青城山道观，先后被推举为上清宫宗家、青城山道教协会会长、成都市道教协会会长。1986年，被选为中国道教协会副会长。1988年7月，傅圆天创办了"青城山道教学校"。1992年3月，在中国道教协会第五届全国代表会议上，傅圆天大师当选为会长，并兼任中国道教学院院长。同时，他还担任全国政协常委。傅圆天一生勤劳朴素，从不搞特殊化。他待人诚恳，平易近人，和蔼可亲。他的为人风范，可以看成"大道至简、阳光致远"的最佳诠释之一。

傅圆天最具传奇色彩的智慧突出体现在"文革"中，当红卫兵气势汹汹上山，即将在道观"破四旧"的时候，他和易心莹大师率道众，将道观内外文物，全部用纸张裱糊覆盖，上面写满领袖语录以及当时最"革命"的口号。红卫兵到来，只好悻悻离去。随后，他和易心莹大师率道众把文物搬到上清宫，掩藏起来，每天亲自奉养。平时，为了防止其他盗贼惦记文物，他白天率道众下地劳动，晚上则安排人巡逻不敢有丝毫大意。"文革"期间，青城山的文物幸存状况非常好，全靠他和易心莹大师的勇敢机智。此外，为了解决混乱状态下道众们的生计，稳住队伍，他一边组织道士们种植茶叶，以茶换粮，还不辞辛劳，利用道家秘方——猕猴桃素酒配方，数百次的勾兑实验，制作出了"道家洞天乳酒"，并建厂生产。后来被人借助政治力量介入搞垮。改革开放后，重建了"洞天乳酒厂"，并成为青城山的旅游商品之一。这些故事都是具有传奇色彩的。

此外，傅圆天在带头做公益慈善和捐赠方面也有崇高风范，比如，1993 年，他就代表青城山一次向希望工程捐款 100 万元。

6.12 个将帅。据蒋向东、陈学明、陈水章先生所编之《简州名人》和简阳集体编写的《天府雄州　幸福简阳》一书所载，在历史上曾经对国家、四川发生过重要影响，具有程度不等的历史正能量和纪念价值的将帅，至少有以下 12 人。

简雍，三国时期，深得刘备尊重的蜀汉昭德将军。

韦皋（741—805），京兆（今陕西西安）人，字成武，唐朝中期的杰出人物，在平定安史之乱和平定军阀朱泚称帝之乱中建立奇勋，被封为大将军，并于贞元元年（785）被委任为成都府尹、剑南西川节度使，在蜀地 21 年，成为威震西南的杰出军事家、政治家。

关于韦皋作为简阳名人，可能会引起争议，但他基本符合我们前面交代的地域历史名人的标准。他长期是唐朝剑南西川节度使，主要历史贡献是收服、联络南诏、东蛮，对付吐蕃，保障唐朝西南平安，取得煊赫武功。韦皋多次派兵抵御吐蕃，牵制其主力，还在一定程度上保障了西北边防。又数度出师，屡次收复失地，史称其"凡破吐蕃四十八万，禽杀节度、都督、城主、笼官千五百，斩首五万余级，获牛羊二十五万，收器械六百三十万，其功烈为西南剧"。除了军功，作为西南军政首长，在政治上，韦皋也是恩威并用，比较得人心的。德

宗封他为南康君王，已经位极人臣，所以后世又以韦南康尊称他①。而简阳，因为是其建立武功的重要基地与支撑，此地官员和人民也做出了重要贡献，所以唐德宗在韦皋去世之年，决定"宜刻金石，用表忠心"，亲自口授诏谕，由太子（后来的唐顺宗）亲自书写了纪功碑内容（1200余字），然后派充当监军使的心腹太监李先寿奉旨宣读后，由眉州、简州地方长官组织刊刻的。②因为有此碑体现的韦皋与简阳的特殊互动，且迄今成都、四川对于韦皋作为历史文化名人资源的重视和运用都很落后，所以简阳当然可以把他作为自己的历史名人。据简阳专家蒋向东、陈学明、陈水章所著《简州名人》综合史料考证，韦皋征讨吐蕃时，曾率清化军长期在简州驻扎、训练，因此简州是他建功立业的重要阵地，应该没有问题。史载韦皋著有《开复西南夷事状》（已佚），他把简阳应该是当成了汉朝开拓西南夷时的牛鞞县。

夏之时（1887—1950），四川合江人，曾东渡日本学习军事，参加同盟会，回国后在成都新军中任职，并从事革命活动。1911年保路运动发生后，11月5日，本为普通军官却被公推为革命军总司令，率领龙泉驿驻军，打响了四川辛亥革命第一枪。起义后，率军抵达重庆，担任过重庆蜀军政府副都督。后来还担任过孙中山的靖国招讨军司令、川西护法军总司令等职。解甲归田后，他还在成都创立了锦江公学。1950年在家乡合江县被误杀，1987年平反昭雪。

① 关于韦皋晚年有权臣之行，虽然属实，但比起他的功勋来，不可相提并论。此外，他由亲近到反对王叔文、柳宗元集团，甚至参与了逼顺宗让位宪宗的恩怨、功过，很难进行简单褒贬。

② 此外，韦皋的纪功碑，在蜀中还有两处，分别位于资州（今资中）和叙州（今宜宾），前者为韦皋从孙韦铤担任资州长官时所立，后者是叙州刺史张九宗立，时为元和五年（810），这两个碑的重要性不及眉州、简州二碑。今天，其他三碑已经消失，唯有简阳，保留着此碑，保留着简阳这块热土与这位英雄紧密关联的历史证据。

刘存厚（1885—1960），简阳三岔镇兴隆场人。曾留学日本陆军士官学校，参加同盟会，参加护国战争，参加军阀角逐，庇护过吴佩孚，1933 年曾奉蒋介石命令，任四川"剿共"军第六路总指挥，与红军交手，被打得大败，而被蒋介石免职，后 16 年寓居成都。1949 年得到老同学阎锡山帮助，逃到并终老台湾。

田颂尧（1888—1975），简阳县龙泉驿人，毕业于保定陆军军官学校。曾任川军 21 师旅长、师长，北洋政府陆军上将、国民革命军第 29 军军长，参加过军阀战争，被红军击败过，后来参加 1949 年刘、邓、潘起义有功，任省政府参事，晚年热心家乡教育事业，有积极贡献。

陈良基（1890—1952），简阳平息乡人。抗日战争中，在长沙保卫战中建立功勋的国军中将师长。"中国人民抗日战争胜利 60 周年纪念章"获得者。

黄隐（1890—1969），简阳县龙泉驿人，保定陆军军官学校第一期毕业，川军儒将。曾任国民党中将军长、四川江防司令，近代成都建市以后首任市长。1949 年在成都起义，1950 年后，任原成都军区副司令。

廖震（1890—1949），简阳三岔镇人。就读于四川军官速成学堂，在川军中供职，并逐步崭露头角。反共和抗日行动都很突出，最高担任国民党第 44 军军长。"中国人民抗日战争胜利 60 周年纪念章"获得者。

陈鼎勋（1893—1973），简阳义和乡三岔坝人，曾参与四川军阀角逐，但后来抗日功勋卓著，晚年回归并造福桑梓。"中国人民抗日战争胜利 60 周年纪念章"获得者。

董朗（1894—1932），简阳县平安乡人。黄埔一期学员，南昌起义重要军事指挥员之一、海陆丰革命根据地创建人之一，曾任红四军参谋长（军长贺龙）。不幸死于王明"左"倾清洗的红军著名将领，1954年被追认为革命烈士。

汪匣锋（1899—1953），简阳白石坝人。刘存厚的侄子，并在其麾下逐渐升职，1932年升旅长。随刘存厚进攻红军，所部被彻底击溃，乘夜只身逃脱。在抗日战争中任师长，与日寇多次血战，后获得"青天白日勋章"，升为47军中将军长，解放战争中被俘。"中国人民抗日战争胜利60周年纪念章"获得者。

曾烈（1901—1945），简阳石钟滩人。毕业于成都讲武堂，毕业后加入川军。1937年以20军（军长王瓒绪）某旅参谋长（少将）出川抗日（他的家乡简阳平窝乡乡亲为他唱大戏3天"欢送曾参谋长出川抗日"），参与了安庆保卫战和随枣会战，尤其是参与指挥了1943年底给日军沉重打击，共计歼敌2.9万余人，并成功收复城池的"常德战役"（这是正面战场最威震敌胆的战役之一）。"中国人民抗日战争胜利60周年纪念章"获得者。

一个普通县，竟然涌现了这么多在国家和四川历史上不可忽略的将领，在四川是很罕见的。

上述类型的名人，就是简阳人文个性、城市精神和优秀传统文化的主要代表。当然，"名人"主要是指其在世时和离世后有很大的名声，不等于他们都是完人，尤其是十二个将帅这个类型，在变动不居、波诡云谲的近代历史上，他们中有的人像当时旧政权下的几乎所有高级军官一样，有参与军阀混战、"反共"、搜刮民众等历史遗憾，但中国文化包容迷途知返，赞赏弃暗投明，欢迎落叶归根，尤其是把在保家卫国战争中建立功勋看得十分重要和光荣，所以笔者作了这样一个总结。

当然，作为历史上名副其实的雄州巨邑，简阳乃人文渊薮，人才辈出，还有诸如近代以徐鹤轩（1882—1957）、李霜如（1873—1959）、吴雪琴（1872—1952）等人为代表的竭诚终身报效、服务家乡，造福家乡人民并作出贡献和表率的三个乡贤；曾参加抗战击落日机，在解放战争中决定弃暗投明，作为登陆舰舰长率领官兵起义，不幸被国民党特务机构破获而牺牲的革命烈士毛却非；中华人民共和国成立初期在征粮和平息剧烈匪患中英勇捐躯的烈士中的佼佼者；为新中国科技事业做出重要贡献的简阳籍两院院士叶朝晖、魏复盛等，值得今人关注、后人铭记。

二、名人文化的价值归纳

中国儒家主流文化主张"人过留名，雁过留声"，以立德立功立言为终极标准，确定人是否能够青史留名。历史名人在社会历史发展进程中起着重要的推动作用，其影响不仅在于其所创造的丰功伟绩，更宝贵的是所留下的物质与精神遗产，成为影响后人的巨大财富。在他们身上，所体现的中华优秀传统文化以仁义礼智信、忠孝廉耻为代表的崇高价值追求，和杀身成仁、舍生取义体现的庄严、伟岸的精神气节，以及爱我家乡、造福桑梓表达的温暖情感，是简阳形成高端文化形象的珍贵资源。可以凝练为：功德立志，仁义立身，福泽立名。其

中的大多数，都可以成为简阳被记住、被向往、被仰望的永恒历史资源和精神力量。

第五节　东灌文化

一、气壮山河的伟大工程

在简阳近现代历史上，有一伟大壮举必须牢记在心，值得歌颂千秋，这就是东灌工程。东灌工程自 1970 年春动工，至 1980 年主体工程建成，简阳全县共计有 102000 多名干部、民工参加建设，至 1985 年，灌溉总面积达 1151.56 平方公里，耕地 83.07 万亩，占简阳耕地面积的 53.58%，惠及农户 17.51 万户、68.98 万人。引水工程共分为四个阶段进行：第一阶段为龙泉山引水工程，包括引水总干渠、龙泉山隧洞、张家岩水库和南、北干渠，自 1969 年 8 月筹备，1970 年 2 月动工，1973 年 8 月完成；第二阶段为配套工程，包括江源、简资、养马三条干渠和支、斗农渠开挖，自 1972 年 11 月开始，1957 年春建成；第三阶段为三岔水库工程，包括南干渠改造扩建、低南干渠开挖，自 1973 年 9 月筹备，1975 年 3 月动工，1978 年 2 月竣工；第四阶段为石盘水库工程，自 1976 年 10 月筹备，1977 年 8 月动工，1980 年 10 月竣工。

自从李冰治水、文翁治水成功，尽得防洪、灌溉、航运之利以来，成都平原迅速取代关中平原，成为一般年代水旱从人、不知饥馑的举世公认的"天府之国"。历代先民不断增加配套工程，使其受益面积不断扩张，简阳在龙泉山以西的村镇的一部分也纳入其中。但是，简阳的主体因为南北纵向绵延逶迤 200 公里的龙泉山的阻隔，只能望水兴叹。尤其是 1959 年龙泉驿并入成都并单独设区以后，简阳基本上与都江堰大灌区没有了水利上的关联。新中国成立后，简阳脱离了成都而归内江专区管辖，这当然是服从国家建设大举的安排，但毕竟在"地利"上有所萎缩，特别是在"文革"的冲击下，简阳人口自然增长较快，但生产发展缓慢，自然灾害尤其是旱灾（简阳地处川西夏旱和川东伏旱过渡地带，受两旱双重困扰，素有"十年一大旱，三年两头旱，冬干春旱年年见"的说法）的危害日益凸显，促使简阳的干部群众产生并迅速论证、申报、动员、组织、开工建设一个以打通龙泉山，并立即建设配套工程，让都江堰的水永续造福简阳的水利工程，时间在 20 世纪 70 年代初，10 万简阳人民在政治局势不佳，科技支撑孱弱、资金设备十分紧张的背景下，以披荆斩棘、战天斗地的牺牲精神，人力为主，流血流汗两年多，成功凿穿龙泉山并对接，引来大灌区的奔腾激流，通过配套工程，把 70 万亩土地变成水旱无忧的良田美壤，奠定简阳"一山两湖"的壮美山河。《天府雄州　幸福简阳》写道：1970 年 2 月，工程的首场攻坚战"龙泉山引水隧道"开始了。为了完成如此庞大的工程，3 万多名人民公社社员，自带干粮和锄头、扁担、箢箕等工具，浩浩荡荡地开进了荒山野岭，他们不懂技术，就四处拜师傅，边干边学；缺少机械，就靠人工搬运，人多力量大。同时，全县人民积极响应，工农兵学商齐动员，小脚老太用提兜提河沙，敬老院老人拿出节省的肉票，中小学师生捡豆子石、编箢箕，医生送医疗，理发师去理发，剧团、

电影队去演出，商店、邮局、书店搬到工地……暂时不能受益的河东农民，也义无反顾，投工出力。经过两年零五个月的艰苦奋战，终于克服了重重困难，打通了长 6432 米、高 3.4 米，宽 4.3 米的穿山引水隧洞……人们称之为幸福水。紧接着，简阳人民再接再厉，大干快上，相继修起了张家岩水库、三岔湖水库、石盘水库（龙泉湖）……一个集引水、储蓄、灌溉为一体的大型水利工程，巍然出现在简阳大地上……100 余万亩农田得到灌溉，水稻由亩产 549 斤提高到 1028 斤，棉花亩产由 88 斤提高到 142 斤……缺水的历史从此一去不复返。

不管是在中国，还是在其他国家，类似物质技术状态下，类似的代价，完成的类似水利工程，还没有第二个。如果算上配套工程，百万简阳人民同心协力，举全县之力，历时十年，累计总投入十万人（包括数千女民兵），8700 万个劳动日，119 人牺牲，1739 人伤残，这些数字背后的力量，是意志和信念、智慧和血汗的集成，中间涌现了很多干群、工农、技术人员和民工同心同德、甘苦与共、加班加点的动人故事。期间上至中央、省市相关领导，下至普通民众，形成了可歌可泣，体现集体主义、大公无私品质的无数动人画卷。工程逐渐建成、完善后，成为中国水利事业的诸多丰碑，国内外参观、考察、学习、交流的队伍络绎不绝，为成都和内江也带来了独有的骄傲与荣光。

东灌文化是为了家乡获得更好的发展，迎着巨大的困难和艰险，主动作为，省、地、县领导和专业部门上下同心，成都提供技术和运输支持，简阳工农兵众志成城，气吞山河、血汗浇筑的奋斗文化、英雄文化，其中还有一道亮丽的风景线，那就是作为简阳客家文化再升级的巾帼不让须眉的地域文化个性。东灌工程，简阳妇女以顶半边天的精神，踊跃参与，水利工程常年队伍中，妇女占 15% 以上，她们战斗在勘探、设计、施工、试验、钻探、机电、打隧洞、拉驾车所有工程环节，留下了许多震撼人心的英雄故事：

养马工区灵仙工程队"女子攀登掘进排"20 多人，初学开电转，转机震动全身发麻，手背红肿，有的被漏电烧伤，下班后筋疲力尽，还举石头练臂力，同男民工开展革命竞赛。

1975 年三岔水库工地，石板工区红旗工程队"铁姑娘班"，为工程树立起第一个女子架车工和女子炮工的旗帜。

镇金工区清风工程队女子炮工班，为了主坝的回填需要，在马鞍山土料场点起煤油灯打炮眼，一个通宵打出一个 5.3 米深的大炮眼，连战几个通宵……

当年参与工程的干部群众，有的已经故去，绝大多数都已是古稀、耄耋老人，但读他们的回忆录，或聊到共同的记忆，几乎都是动情的话语和自豪。魏明伦所著的《简阳赋》也对"东灌"工程进行了恢宏书写："林县红旗渠，简阳龙泉山。外省遥遥相隔，内涵紧紧相连。红旗前呼，龙泉后应。前引漳河水，后引都江浪。秉承李冰治水，效法愚公移山。肇始于浩劫寒冬，竣工于改革暖春。阻力重重，起步难立项；雄心勃勃，拓荒自攻坚。土法上马，铁臂降龙。羊圈下榻，鸭棚扎营。油灯照明挖隧道，竹管通风排瓦斯。钢钎打开百里洞，箢篼挑走亿吨泥。历时十年八月，上阵万马千军。若干无畏勇士，多少无名英雄。鏖战汗雨淋漓，捷报泉水叮咚。尾声凯歌嘹亮，插曲悲歌壮烈。民工遇难，血染枫叶；技师捐躯，泪洒雪花。剪彩犹思挂彩事，饮水不忘引水人。受益者，苍生；造福者，功臣。壮哉！龙泉意志，简阳精神也！"

对于中青年的简阳人及其子孙后代，不能让他们忘记"东灌"这个伟大工程的艰辛与卓越，简阳的文创和文化旅游、乡土教育，城乡景观和纪念工程打造，在天府文化的版图上和党史国史教育的场域内，创造新亮点，简阳大有可为。

二、精神文化价值归纳

我们认为，东灌工程体现的，是简阳人民在困难的条件（"文革"动荡、旱灾频发、不属于成都）下，迎难而上，为了实现美好生活而不惧艰险、自力更生、众志成城、愚公移山的坚韧品性。它是简阳群众文化的最高境界，是简阳可以传之千秋的优良文化个性、文化潜力的最好说明。

习近平总书记在庆祝改革开放 40 周年大会上所强调的："我们这么大一个国家，就应该有雄心壮志。"东灌工程，是大禹、鳖灵、李冰、文翁等先贤，接续创造四川以都江堰水利工程和大灌区为代表的，为了造福子孙后代，不怕任何艰难险阻，以科学的方法、精心的谋划和组织，汇聚干部和人民的吃苦耐劳、英勇无畏精神，众志成城解决重大水利问题的伟大实践，以这样的方式把大灌区扩展到龙泉山以东，灌溉上百万亩良田，李冰、文翁天上之灵有知，都将流下感动的热泪。作为长达十年的群团行动展示一种以奉献、牺牲为核心的集体价值观与精气神，很难有其他工程能够像简阳东灌工程一样，在和平年代，如此震撼人心，引发集体感动。着眼当下，简阳又迎来了新的机遇与发展。必须清醒地看到，新简阳与成都其他区（市）县比，建设发展条件存在不少软肋，要跟上成都市的发展节奏，并扬长避短作出自己独特的贡献，不仅需要战略眼光，科学谋划，还特别需要赓续、弘扬简阳人民自力更生、众志成城、愚公移山的精神，将建设新简阳的雄心壮志付诸现实。它可以使简阳在"被记住""被仰望"方面熠熠生辉。

第六节　非遗文化

一、简阳非遗文化形成的原因

所谓非遗文化，是指各族人民世代相传、并视其为文化遗产组成部分的各种传统文化的表现形式，以及与传统文化表现形式相关的实物和场所。一般来讲，经过申报或抢救，被政府正式认定并要求加以保护传承者，都是优秀传统文化的重要组成部分。改革开放以来，从国家到地方，其保护、传承，甚至与时俱进的发展，已经成为城市或乡村文化建设的重要任务。与"物质文化遗产"相比，它通常是一种有特定内涵、寓意、价值的技艺、方法、仪轨或空间形态，既可以表达精神、艺术追求，也可以表达人们喜爱或企望的一种生活方式与生活旨趣。中华文化博大精深，开放包容，且版图辽阔，族群众多，各地都有既具有中华文化共性，更不乏个性的非遗及其文化。自古人民勤劳聪慧，地方文化活跃，各种人才辈出，"文盛工巧"的简阳尤其如此。不过由于明末清初四川城市和乡村的普遍残毁，原住民几乎完全消失，

今天能够看到并有价值的非遗，几乎都是十几个省的移民在清代康熙以来"五方杂处"、在生产、生活、贸易以及各种交往交流中重新形成命运和空间共同体的过程中形成，然后在100多年的近代化、现代化、全球化浪潮席卷的城乡演变过程中接受选择和淘汰，所保留至今的。

（一）属于巴蜀文化、天府文化的共性因素

1. 平民化

今日简阳人民的祖先，绝大多数来自起于康熙三十三年（1694），由政府支持，绵延100多年的"湖广填四川"移民运动，全国十几个省的普通平民，经历千里跋涉之苦，族群碰撞之艰，并在数十年中，依靠坚韧不拔之意志，战胜成群结队的虎、狼和乱兵悍匪之侵袭，在政府的优容、体恤、帮扶，以及移民们彼此帮扶和守望相助下形成的平民文化，是非遗的主要土壤。很少有居高临下的名门望族，和强横的"上流社会"对非遗从业者及其技艺本身的歧视，简阳也不例外。

2. 草根性

清代的四川和成都，有一个伴随百年移民运动的艰难恢复历程。移民普遍都是十分勤劳的人群，在战乱停息，虎狼之患逐渐消弭后，加上政府在赋税徭役方面的优免和照顾，人民逐渐摆脱饥寒，呈现兴旺景象，粮食价格曾经为近百年全国主要产粮区最低，形成川粮济楚的格局，城乡普遍重建、重振，耕读传家、诗礼传家的家族开始出现，奠定学术、文教恢复的基础。但天府之国人口的增长速度，在全中国也无与伦比，乾隆后期已经人满为患，经济发展达到极限，转而出现因为人口过剩，而产生的越来越多的游民，逐渐沉积的吏治积弊、民族

与阶级、社会矛盾交织，社会出现严重的白莲教、咽噜子、袍哥问题，所以清代四川和成都，普通百姓和基层社会，从思想观念到生活方式，始终保持了明显的草根性——在非遗活动中，表现为因陋就简、随乡伴村、自发多样、传承传播较为随性。在工艺技术和风格风韵上主要表达、适应最廉价的消费能力和底层民众的嗜好、旨趣。这也决定了简阳的非遗文化主要属于群众文化，而非名人文化、商道文化等。

（二）属于简阳自身演变的个性因素

1. 客家文化的影响

简阳近代旷世奇才、伟大先贤傅崇矩所撰写的清末民初《成都通览》记载："现今之成都人，原籍皆外省人。"他还有一个各省移民所占比例的详细介绍。据统计，客家移民是仅次于湖广移民的一大族群，在当时四川总人口中占33%。[①] 而清代及清末民初以来的简阳，是中国西部客家文化的主要据点，特别是以洛带为中心的区域，更是客家文化的主要据点。客家文化有敬祖宗、重礼教、重耕读、善协作、敢打拼等突出优点，尤其是女性十分勤劳和有担当，不论是家庭养育还是赚钱，她们都比一般族群的妇女更有担当。

2. 绵延的尚武之风

简阳近代的军事、战争、兵匪活动相对较多，促使民风中的重文尚武并重的传统延续下去。

3. 交通进步受益最多

简阳的地理方位，决定了随着成渝之间各类近现代交通工具的联

---

① 客家入川 -2020《天府广记》第 12 期. 成都政协

通，其均是率先的受益者，非遗人才、技艺、资源、文化的内外交流更加便捷，在成渝两大经济圈中的纽带作用更明显，这对于非遗的传承、发展、与时俱进带来越来越明显的助益。

二、简阳主要的非遗

经过最近十年来，政府相关部门和传承人的共同努力，简阳有 10 项非遗已经进入成都市非遗项目名录（其中第五批 8 项、第六批 2 项），包括黑水寺故事、张氏古琴制作技艺、石桥挂面制作技艺、沱江船工号子、九莲灯、余门拳、张氏土陶制作技艺、羊肉汤传统制作技艺、六神曲、李氏华安堂膏药。体现了简阳人民对丰富多彩幸福生活的不懈追求，能工巧匠的勤劳聪慧，以及造福桑梓的仁义精神。从公园城市人文融入、成都生活美学发扬光大的简阳特色与简阳贡献来讲，都是进行文创和开展活动，甚至产业化发展的珍贵资源。

根据笔者的认知，这 10 项非遗，按照其自身属性和发展前景，以及可能融入或影响的人群的大小，羊肉汤传统制作技艺、张氏古琴制作技艺、余门拳、九莲灯最值得传承弘扬，所以下面试做专题论述。

（一）羊肉汤及其美食系列

成都是亚洲第一座由联合国教科文组织授牌的"世界美食之都"，川菜是其充足的底气。川菜有一道上得了府邸，下得了陋室，但主要体现平民需求的美味——羊肉汤。

简阳人民亲近羊的历史源远流长，龙垭文化就有大量的羊化石出土。古蜀先民蜀山氏，属于古羌族，羌族崇拜羊，图腾和代表信仰的饰物多为羊。简阳山水、平原、河谷兼顾，适合羊的生长，其本地有生命力旺盛的"火疙瘩羊"。抗战期间，因为宋美龄女士喜欢喝牛羊奶，遂利用战时的盟国关系，从美国引进了数十头著名山羊品种努比羊。战后宋离开四川，这些羊在转移的过程中流散到山区，与"火疙瘩羊"进行杂交，产生了适应力强，体格高大，生长周期短，肉质细嫩，腥膻味低的大耳羊优良新品种，成为简阳群众喜欢的美食。将民间羊肉汤发展成为一道高度平民化、既有共性，也不乏个性，并与时俱进至21世纪，在平民饮食格调（主要适应普通民众消费水平和习惯，重口味，重价廉物美，重新鲜，而不过于重就餐环境、就餐服务、就餐档次）不变的基础上，衍生出系列美味和菜肴、筵席，适应各种消费层次、类型的川菜品种，凸显出简阳人民对生活的热爱，对美味的推陈出新的热情，对乡土和乡愁的留恋。羊肉汤及其系列里，集合了众多来自十八个省移民的烹调智慧，兼顾了儒家、道家共同的注重生命体验、生存质量和身心健康的深厚养生文化诉求，融汇了中医膳食中治未病的生命哲理，尤其是坚持在民间、乡土、美味、实惠、食材优良等传统特色的基础上，谋求与时俱进，实现饮食文化和美食产业化、品牌化的协同共进，相得益彰。对于经济、民生的正能量稳定而不断增长，比如，在2013年，简阳常年出栏山羊150万只左右，其中大耳商品羊20万~50万只，并外调销往成都、重庆、贵州、云南、湖南等地。

　　一般非遗，核心技艺主要以家庭内部父、子、孙代代相传，或特定的师徒关系实现传承。此外，一般非遗，关涉、福泽的人群都相当有限，但简阳人民在普通的饮食生活中创制的，从20世纪80年代才"火

爆"起来的，贫富、老少咸宜的美食羊肉汤，却具有以下五个特点：第一，为了更好传播，著名门店都公布了部分菜品所用原材料、制作程序、方法等属于"商业机密"的"菜谱"，这体现了简阳人民的淳朴、善良，也体现了他们的自信。第二，简阳受客家文化影响深厚，客家文化的特点是妇女特别勤劳聪慧、敢于承担包括增加家庭收入在内的各种责任，所以，简阳的羊肉汤名店主持人多为女性，或夫妻贡献完全平分秋色地共同打拼、创业，而且，有的名店，家庭传授关键技艺时，传男也传女。这特别体现了天府文化的一个优良品格：尊重妇女与妇女敢作敢为互相促进、相得益彰。第三，至"土"与至"洋"的完美结合，体现美食文化国际交流的重要性。火疙瘩羊和努比羊，是基因杂交最成功的土洋结合（简阳后来还有英国优质羊品种的引入）；宋美龄引进的羊，变成的美食，最后成为简阳、成都草根平民的价廉物美的最爱（迄今，简阳"西部第一汤"的地位基本形成，至少笔者认识的成都、四川人基本都是认可的），这些，都是生动有趣，但又富有启迪的美食文化故事。第四，简阳羊肉汤非遗技艺和饮食文化传承，一直有两条线路：家庭内部的代际传承；以徒弟必须人品、心性可靠为依据的师徒传承，后者不限徒弟来自何地，学成以后是否回原籍去创业。如简阳羊肉汤世家胡贵光、自立门店的高徒李含江，都是以这样开放的心胸来面对技艺传承的。在简阳家喻户晓的李含江（已经去世）带出师的徒弟有28人，其中浙江、福建等地来的有8个，这些高足回到家乡，对于简阳及其美食的大名、影响传播，意义不言而喻。第五，简阳羊肉汤，以其仁厚、亲民、开放、与时俱进的文化格调，从一种小吃性质的"汤"，已经变成了川菜里的一朵成长迅速的奇葩，衍生出了这样一个对于经济、民生、起于乡愁又高于乡愁、连接城乡的福泽的人群越来越大的存在——比如，经过羊肉汤大师们的不断努力，以简阳羊肉为主料的菜品，早已超过了150多个；羊肉的做法，已经发展至炖炒爆煎蒸煮烫烤炸干等十种工艺。简阳的优质羊养殖，已经成为简阳的一个重要特色产业。起于羊肉汤的节庆，已经成为公园城市建设的简阳风景。羊肉汤为灵魂为滥觞的民间美食，已经成为一个独立的菜系。价格从三五十元一盆汤到上千元一桌的全羊席，真的是传承着川菜（及四川饮食文化）的精髓和核心竞争力：来自全中国的勤劳聪慧的普通民众，在清初四川地广人稀、土地足够供应需求的背景下，在不得不积极携手，共同应对食人猛兽、兵匪、贫困的过程中，一边同舟共济、守望相助地发展经济，互相联姻，构建社会，一边利用天府之国极其丰富而价格低廉的食材，融汇全中国普通民众的烹调技艺，生产、制作、贩卖出适合自己的以味美价廉为主要特征的万千美食。天府文化、巴蜀文化儒、释、道和谐共生、相得益彰的文化生态（近代还包括了耶、回），拒绝把人格式化，包容异端和个性的胸怀，以及看重身心健康、生命和生活真实品质的价值观，衣食住行都可以通过在细节上增添情趣（艺术化）来提高人生幸福指数的生活美学，都在羊肉汤这一川菜奇葩、简阳非遗的崛起中得到了生动诠释。简阳市也一直在为它进一步成长为参天大树和城市名片而努力。

（二）张氏古琴制作技艺

成都自古就是中国的音乐之都，其前身三星堆和金沙两座城池体现的青铜文化、玉石文化、金器制作的精细和高妙，所有文物及其出

土的蚕丝都证明其极为神秘浪漫的文化和艺术气质，那些盛大的祭祀或发号施令活动没有音乐是不可想象的。三星堆、金沙遗址均直接出土了大型乐器石磬（其中金沙的更大），配合文献记载的开明十二世的爱美人胜过爱江山留下的乐歌等信息，成都作为音乐之都至少有 2500—3000 年的历史。在古代音乐活动中，七弦古琴无疑是乐器之王，历史上存留至今、身价最高的古琴，是唐朝成都至少绵延了一个多世纪的制琴大师辈出的雷氏家族，所制作的极品雷琴"九霄环佩"。无疑是中国古典乐器的巅峰制作与遗存。

无独有偶，历史上多数时期都属于成都，与成都悲欢、兴亡与共的简阳，如今也有一个从 15 岁开始学习古琴制作的已经 35 岁的传承人张勇，所代表的传承了 3 代（其父辈在北京民族乐器厂从事乐器制作与修理），古琴制作技艺高超，大国工匠精神始终不坠，因此产品身价不菲，并能够被成都主要的文化活动场所采用的张氏古琴（位于简阳市江源镇。其古琴被用于杜甫草堂、峨眉山、都江堰等各处大琴馆），并且受到了众多媒体的广泛报道和专业机构的认可、赞誉。2015 年 9 月，他的作品"传统手工艺古琴"参加了"看四川——民间文艺创作工程优秀作品展"，在数千件作品中进入前十，获"优秀作品奖"。

根据相关介绍，张氏古琴制作技艺（行内叫"斫琴"），具有以下特点。

严格的大国工匠精神——在程序和工艺上，坚持标准，精益求精，每把琴需要 3~4 个月时间、九十道工序才能完成。

强烈的品牌意识——面对供不应求的市场，宁缺毋滥，坚决保住品牌之信誉。

海纳百川、有容乃大的传承意识——据网上"文化简阳"专页介绍，张氏古琴第一代叫张永四，自学制作古琴，在"文革"中因地主出身，被终止制琴，改当了石匠。其后将制琴技艺传给了四个儿子。其中张以全（张勇父亲）最有天赋，他先后向北京、洛阳、西安等地名师学习，其古琴的音域、音质因此堪称一绝。张勇15岁起随父亲在外学习制作古琴，后回到成都，受到四川古琴制作大师曾成伟栽培，并在18岁便小有名气，逐渐自成风格。后来受到南京成功亮、台湾葛殊聪、李孔元等名家好评，显然也是对他的鼓励。显然，非遗技艺，不仅要延续好自己的绝活（比如张勇的技艺最早肯定来自祖父、父亲的熏陶或指点，他也始终坚持手工完成绝大部分工序），而且要学习、借鉴众家之优长，才能避免抱残守缺和落后于时代需求。正是因为如此，张勇先后学习、取经于广陵派曹珑，2005年回简阳创立"张氏古琴"。如今，已经成为简阳城市的一张非遗名片，在助力成都的音乐之都建设中，前途无可限量。

（三）余门拳

简阳是一个既崇文也尚武的地方，所以近代以来走出了众多将领和英雄。它的非遗文化中，有一个在四川地区具有鲜明移民文化特色，融合中华众多门派之精粹，已经传承十多代的民间武术流派——余家拳。前述名人文化部分，地方"拳王"余发斋条目里，已经有对余家拳的介绍，此处不赘言。

简阳本地对于这一非遗的传承和弘扬，有忧亦有喜。所谓有忧，是指半个多世纪以来，余家拳主要在川南自贡、内江，重庆、涪陵、万

州、达州等地传播，弟子数万，仅在重庆市，就有8000余人传习余家拳，参加各级武术比赛，获奖百余项。而在简阳，则相对后继乏人，21世纪初调查，全市只有十余人传习，令人唏嘘。所谓有喜，是指近十余年来，简阳有识之士发现了余家拳"墙内开花墙外香"问题，政府也开始重视，经过努力，先后在资阳市、成都市被列入非遗名录，并采取其他措施，如进行调研，找准解决之道；成立相关研究会；举办省内外余家拳联谊、交流活动；媒体关注报道，进行各种帮扶，局面正在改善。余家拳要想在简阳发扬光大，除了上述努力应该继续坚持外，还应该鼓励其传承走出余氏后裔，拳术的开发或变革、传播，努力适应成都都市化进程，尤其是抓住利用以武术教学与研究为特色亮点的成都体育学院迁址简阳（后划入成都东部新区管辖）的大好契机，借助东简一体发展区域合作深入推进，进一步推进校地加强协作，吸引人才回归，同时应学习借鉴川南、川东余家拳蓬勃开展的经验和做法，吸引更多青少年习练余家拳，传承弘扬简阳这一重要非遗文化。

（四）九莲灯

在清代四川，地方官及其学校倡导、传播以理学为核心的主流文化，其影响包括了士农工商各个阶层。正是因为如此，巴蜀文化、天府文化保持了与中华轴心文化的共性。但在实际生活应用层面，理学影响的主要人群是士大夫和读书人（而且第一目标通常是通过科举考试）。对于人数占据绝对主体的广大民众而言，他们更多地受家风家训和在地风土、人情、民俗的熏陶，也就是说，寻求并体现生活的意义，"士"主要从"礼"，而民主要从"俗"。前者的仪式感、程序性、装饰度都更强更高，后者则无疑更加简洁、质朴、真实。从这个更加广阔、真实的大众层面来讲，以"湖广填四川"的 18 个省移民为主开创的，具有极强的包容性和突出的平民化特征的巴蜀文化和天府文化，在民间信仰和习俗上，体现为各种神祇皆有自己的信众，各类民俗皆有自己的传承地域和人群，当这些人群因为通婚、生产、贸易、节庆逐渐融汇成共同标签为"四川人""成都人""简阳人"的"老乡"以后，他们原先各自信奉的神祇，各自遵从的风俗习惯，也就必然走向嫁接、组装、融合了。支撑这种嫁接、组装、融合的天府文化因素包括：儒、释、道的和谐共生和相得益彰；民间文学艺术（含神话传说）多姿多彩；远离首都和平民化的社会风尚，使这里的民俗表达也最能体现儒家的"和而不同"。在上述背景下，天府文化区域有丰富的小众、小地域的物质或非物质文化遗产传承至今，简阳石桥的九莲灯就是这样的一朵民俗小花。

九莲灯是一种集合了神、巫、佛、道、傩诸种文化意蕴，驱邪祈福，表达民众对于平安、幸福生活之向往，具有一定难度，视觉、听觉冲击力很强的表演艺术。最初是屠户们为了驱灾避难进行的许愿、还愿配套活动，后来逐渐演变为兼具健身、娱乐效果的表演艺术。作为一种民俗活动，一般在城市守护神城隍出驾巡游这天进行，只见九位男子头缠丝巾，上身赤裸，下穿短裤，脚蹬草鞋，前额、两乳、前腹左右、后背左右各挂一盏，两只手臂各挂两盏油灯；九人呈一路纵队，前八人每人用两根龙头木杖支撑双臂龙头，上挂彩色灯笼；最后一人双手高举长竹竿一根，其上交叉固定几个竹块，竹竿顶端和竹块共挂彩色灯笼九个，叫"坐督灯"。表演者一路边走边唱，其词不外消灾免难、逢凶化吉之类。加上锣鼓撞击，围观者众，场面颇为壮观。2012 年 10 月，央视《远

方的家，北纬 30 度》拍摄组在石桥中学内对其进行了采访拍摄。

九莲灯表演，神秘、朴实、粗放，并带有原始祭祀、祈祷气息，展现多元融合的移民文化、宗教文化、民俗文化、乡土文化。其对于简阳子孙和外地游客，具有帮助人们认识、理解巴蜀文化、天府文化先民，筚路蓝缕、以启山林的生活与奋斗历程，不怕艰辛、感动神明，追求平安幸福生活的坚强意志，以及在艰难和并不富足的情况下也能收获快乐的人文性格。

在成都市建设公园城市，必须人文植入的过程中，九莲灯这一简阳独有的非遗，必须保护、传承。就表演来讲，可以适度地与时俱进，在保留其基本形式、内涵和风格的前提下，可以在增添综合性美感上做文章，另外，九莲灯更适合在系列民俗展演活动中作为一个亮点出现，比单独出现肯定效果更好。至少，它可以成为简阳被人"记住"的理由。在文化河流生态中，它至少是一条别致的小支流。

（五）舌画和指墨画

所谓舌画和指墨，即以舌头、手指代笔作画，其效果特殊，别具一格。舌画公认的始祖是清末祖籍河北大兴县的黄二南，而指墨画的历史则可追溯到唐朝美术界公认的始祖张璪。简阳教师闵克耳，师从江南黄二南和西北刘濑云两位舌画艺人。闵克耳及其传人汪一德一直坚持研究、创造，创作了大量的艺术作品，如今在简阳规划馆中展陈着其作品。

舌画和指墨画是一种集大雅与大俗于一身的绘画方式，其在艺术领域的开拓性与创造性，体现了简阳人民从生活的日常中提炼美好的创造能力和创新精神。虽然舌画和指墨画不属于主流画派，但其鲜明的地方个性，成为简阳被人"记住"的个性和特质。因此，在舌画和指墨画的传承与发展过程中，可以尝试着平衡雅与俗之间的关系，让这一非物质文化遗产登上大雅之堂，让市民共同的精神价值追求在有序的传承中得以彰显，并成为城市鲜明文化属性的重要组成部分。在简阳的文艺活动中，亦可适当增加舌画和指墨画的出场频次，让这个非主流的艺术门类，成为独具特色的存在而被广泛认可和记住。

（六）石桥挂面制作技艺

石桥挂面，又称高架挂面，创始于宋代，盛行于元代，延续至今有九百多年历史。石桥挂面用料精良考究，条细如丝，外圆中空，色白味美，煮不浑汤，隔夜回锅仍如鲜面。石桥挂面系手工制作，制作工艺讲究，需经揉面、搓条、抹油、补粉、进槽发酵、拉制、上棍、上架、提面等二十多道工序，因此关于其制作过程，坊间还流传着一首顺口溜："自从'离夫'以后，朝日'打扮擦油'，结交'两个光棍'，周身'摆弄风流'，只说'天长日久'，谁知'刀截两头'。"

石桥挂面制作技艺历史悠久，集中体现了简阳人民千百年来勤劳聪慧的精神品质，彰显了简阳人民精益求精、专注创新的工匠精神。石桥挂面制作技艺的观赏性、参与性，石桥挂面与日常生活的紧密性、关联性，有利于在文旅产业和餐饮行业的发展中重新唤醒这一非物质文化遗产的荣光。融入日常的非物质文化遗产，最能引起人们的情感共鸣，自觉参与到传承与发展这一过程中来，共同成为简阳文化具有记忆点的存在。纵向来看，石桥挂面制作技艺具有悠久的历史，值得

被铭记；横向来看，在全国众多传统挂面制作技艺中，也个性突出、特色鲜明，值得被传承。因此，可学习借鉴全国其他传统挂面传承和弘扬的经验，将这一非遗文化融入简阳人的生活日常，塑造成为具有记忆点的文化特质。

三、简阳非遗文化内涵归纳

文献记载简阳物产富饶，人民勤劳聪慧，因此"文盛工巧"，拥有丰富的非物质文化遗产。最有代表性的羊肉汤、余门拳、九莲灯、舌画和指墨画等本土创造，体现了简阳人民因地制宜、精益求精的美食向往；文武并重、功德兼修的武术理想；消灾免难、逢凶化吉的平安生活愿望；以及因陋就简、美化生活的朴素艺术旨趣。在整体上，可以进一步凝练为"乡土本色，川蜀原味，天府记忆"。传承上述非遗文化，能感受到简阳别具一格的风土人情，形成城市"被记住"甚至"被向往"的独有画卷。

第七节　商道文化

一、商道文化的产生

四川盆地，在近现代交通工具来到以前，在经济生活中，是一个以内循环为主、外循环为辅的地理单元。虽然与世界上多数国家比，这个单元已经足够大，但放在中国的经济版图上，以"蜀道难，难于上青天"代表的古代出入盆地的巨大不便和代价，还是一直维持着大多数人财物不可能走出去参与外部世界的经济文化直接交流的状态。所以，不甘受限的远古的祖先很早就披荆斩棘、跋山涉水，战胜瘴毒猛兽，开创了南方丝绸之路，书写了中国各地最早的、今天有实物（三星堆、金沙文物；新疆尼雅出土之汉代蜀锦护臂"五星出东方利中国"）和文献（《史记》有载，张骞出使西域，在大夏，即今阿富汗市场上看到了来自蜀地的中国商品蜀布和邛杖）为可靠依据的，四川盆地先民最早代表中华文明与南亚、西亚交流；成都是南方丝绸之路的起点城市，四川是北方、海上丝绸之路重要、高端参与者的人类经济、文化史最早的华章。在四川盆地内，从秦汉开始的巴、蜀二地的首府成都和重庆，无疑是决定性的经济枢纽，人财物的主要聚散地，各种经济文化创新创造活力的策源地，最优质、大宗商品的产生、聚散地，外地、外国、异族巨商大贾、文人、墨客的主要居留、访问、旅行地。比较而言，多数时期，尤其是元明清行省制度诞生以后，成都又是四川唯一的政治、经济、文化中心（只有明玉珍据蜀和抗战时期、三线建设以后有短暂例外），地处成都东部门户位置，历史上多数时期均直辖于成都，成渝主要陆路、水路交通线都汇聚于此，历史上多有驻军和专门治安机构（比如专门设置的巡检司）维持平安的简阳，便成为除了成渝以外，拥有绝佳的商业贸易位置的"雄州"巨邑，其陆路、水路通道在和平年代商业贸易的活跃、繁盛，对于简阳人文个性的形成和丰富，一直提供着源源不断的活力，使简阳除了有优良的农耕文明以外，还

有可以刺激、推动本地商品化农业和手工业发展的持续动力，直接或从事、受惠于商业贸易的人群也比一般州县多，简阳水路的码头文化也比一般州县活跃，重农，但不歧视工商业，避免了传统中国许多城乡都有的"重农抑商"，尊士重农轻商的社会风气，使简阳进入近代化以来具备快速与近现代产业衔接的经济与人文土壤。

特别是拥有 2000 多年历史的石桥古镇，曾是连接川西、川中、川东和川南各地的水陆交通枢纽和物资集散地，自清末到新中国成立初期一直是简阳全境的商业中心和政治中心，并逐渐发展成为川中金融中心、水运码头和商贸中心。据《石桥镇志》记载："全国有13 家银行在此设立分行，镇上有 6 大会馆、9 大码头、100 多家茶铺，米、糖、烟、酒、盐、棉、油、山货等'八大商'的商户达 300 余户，靠停石桥码头的大小船只多达千余只。"盛极一时的石桥古镇，代表着简阳活跃的商贸往来，也沉淀着简阳顺势而为的商道文化。从历史的维度来审视简阳的商道文化，石桥古镇曾经繁华的商业盛景不可回避，甚至要作为一个时期的关键段落加以阐释。可以这样讲，石桥古镇的出现，为简阳商道文化的有序传承，架起了一座桥梁，鲜明了一抹底色。

此外，成都的东大路，是成都沟通川东方向的必经之路，最早在蜀汉成型，在唐宋时期已经比较繁华了。至明清，开始普及驿道，东大路就是从锦官驿至龙泉驿再到阳安驿的正线，人员和消息往来最便捷，经过的地方有：得胜场、沙河堡、簧门铺、大面铺、界牌铺、龙泉驿、山泉铺、柳沟铺、南山铺、石盘铺、赤水铺、九曲铺等。而这些驿站有一大半在简阳境内，人员和消息的往来，也让东大路作为商道繁荣起来，带来了商贸的日益频繁。在东大路的遗迹中，依稀还可以想象当年人员往来的喧哗与商贸往来的繁华，还镌刻着简阳商道文化中值得一提的鲜明部分。从东大路出发，如今的简阳早已进入航空、高铁、地铁并行的时代，成为人流、物流、资金流、信息流汇聚的世界级"黄金口岸"，必将带来更加频繁、更高层次的商贸往来，商道文化的内涵也因此而不断丰富，外延也因此而不断拓展。

二、商道文化的内涵与时代价值

2000 多年来，对于巴蜀地区的政治、经济和文化活动来讲，由自然地理、经济地理、政治地理诸要素决定的四川盆地的交通要道，连接成都和重庆的这条道路无疑最为重要，而简阳的区位决定了它在此条道路上的重要地位，形成了独具特色、浓墨重彩的商道文化，汇集了驿站、场镇和移民等精神物质财富，体现的是勤恳、诚信、开放、包容的人文精神。传承弘扬商道文化，打造有特色的景观、活动，可以强力助推简阳成为成渝地区双城经济圈建设中的经济高地、文化重镇，形成省内外、国内外交流合作的金字桥梁。商道，也是简阳乡愁的一部分。这一文化个性的打造，可以增强简阳"被记住"的优良禀赋。

三、简阳商道文化的个性

除了巴蜀文化、天府文化所属市县的一般商道文化的共性以外，简阳因为有蜀都东部第一门户；常有军队或专门治安力量驻扎；历史

上相当长时期兼有以成都为总部的控制、安抚广大西南夷地区的军事基地的使命；山水美景类型多样等特点，其商道文化的研判，可以关注几点。

第一，对于南方丝绸之路开创、维持的贡献。南方丝绸之路是一条最早的巨大的国际商道，其开拓并稳定下来，首先建立在对于西南夷的有效统治（在历史上，有明清改土归流以前的以间接控制的土司制度为主和之后的以朝廷直接委派官员治理——并在一些关键节点适度驻有军队——为主两种形态）上。从前述牛鞞县的归属和韦皋功业与简州的关系来看，简阳在历史上对于南方丝绸之路的建立作出了自己的贡献。至于有没有一条从成都、重庆经过简阳南下而形成的南方丝绸之路的线路，尚待出土文物来证明，但简阳在军事上能够通西南夷，就存在这种可能性。

第二，四川（尤其是成都）是中国最长盛不衰的文学艺术高地，本人在《成都传》里论述了成都是中国诗歌第一城，简阳作为枢纽的成渝商道同时也是文道、艺道，这种重合、交织和相得益彰，农耕文明与工商业文明以及文人雅士代表的宗教或人文信仰、诗词歌赋情趣的和谐共生，因为具有明显的流动性作为支撑，与成、渝或其他雄州巨邑作为城市文明固定景观的呈现，的确有自己的风雅。在新简阳的打造中，可以在两湖一山、城市中央公园、天府绿道、全新交通网络中的文化景观布局中加以考虑与运用。

第三，简阳历史因盐而生，牛鞞县因境内有牛鞞盐井得名，阳安县因境内有阳明盐井得名。在简阳两千多年的历史长河中，简阳商道的主体是盐道，商道文化的主流是盐业文化。简阳制盐业已有两千多年历史。西汉元鼎二年（公元前 115 年）境内始发现牛鞞盐井、阳明盐井。隋代有阳明盐井和牛鞞等 4 井。唐代有阳明盐井，牛鞞等 4 井，以及上军井、下军井。南宋淳熙七年（1180 年），简州煮盐 19 井，产量 13.5 万公斤。蜀中盐课最盛者莫如简州，最多时岁课 48 万余绢。明代洪武年间，岁办上流等 9 井盐课，司盐 95.98 万公斤；弘治年间，上流等井岁司盐 139.7 万公斤。此外，永乐四年（1406 年），简县资阳乡旧有竹筒井重开煎盐，岁得盐 0.5 万余公斤。清顺治十七八年（1660—1661），开始招灶民开凿竹筒小井 18 眼。雍正八年（1730）有 93 井。乾隆年间，渐次分为 4 厂：海济厂井、兰永厂井、田厂井、姜王厂井，此外尚有老君井，境内盐井迭增为 182 井。乾隆五十一年（1786）为 533 井。煎盐灶 54 座，煎盐锅 84 口，温水锅 139 口。清初实行按户计口授盐行引。乾隆元年（1736），改嘉定议撤之州判移驻简州石桥井，专门负责盐引截验，至清末，简州州判前后任共有九十一人。当时简州水引溯沱江经五凤溪销成都，陆引翻龙泉山经龙泉驿销成都，并在简州龙泉驿设巡检司衙门，《四川盐法志》："简州龙泉驿巡检专司巡缉私盐。"光绪三十年，开办官运配销，境内岁产盐 7000 余票，简州票约重五六百斤。民国初年，县内盐灶户统计 32 户，有盐井 260 余眼，其中海井计 60 余井。全县年产花粑盐 100 余万公斤。民国元年撤销井课，每票以 630 斤为准，粑盐两斤为 1 斤，每斤纳税 6 文；花盐 3 斤为 1 斤，每斤纳税 5 文。1915 年，全县合厂每月产盐约 20 万公斤，税收每月约 6000 元，海井居其半。1945 年后，境内有盐井 270 余眼。1947 年，有灶户 39 家，分布石桥火井湾、射洪坝、外四、麻柳林、伍皇庙、石钟、赤水白家湾、老君井、资阳双河

场等处。合计资金 11 400 万元。有盐工 889 人，年产盐 191.16 万公斤。1949 年，产盐 206.25 万公斤。1950 年，全县有盐业 34 户，生产用牛 322 只，全县产盐 149.45 万公斤。1951 年，有私营盐井灶户 29 户，分布简城、石桥附近，及外四、石钟、五皇洞、麻柳林、海井、老君井等地。资方人员 45 人，职员 35 人，工人 833 人。当年产盐 336.60 万公斤。1951 年 6 月，根据中央人民政府政务院"逐渐裁减小盐场，裁减一批成本高、条件差、产量小的小井小灶"的决定，简阳盐场开始废场，工人转务他业。漫长的盐业历史，诞生了灿烂的盐业文化，形成了商道文化的主体。

第八节　群众文化

一、简阳群众文化的形成基础

当我们把前面七大文化梳理清楚以后，简阳群众文化产生的基础已经有诸多介绍，比如农耕文化、非遗文化、商道文化、东灌文化，都既是群众文化在某些方面、某些层面的集中体现，也是不断与时俱进的群众文化，实现蜕变的，面向现实和未来的新的基础和资源。概括起来，除了上述四大文化以外，形成今天简阳群众文化的基础主要有。

不断增添、优化的城乡文化建设的基础设施；党建引领下的城乡街道、社区的常规与特色文化活动的开展；参与、举办市内外、国内外文化、体育、艺术交流活动产生的开阔胸怀和视野。

历史上以仁义礼智信、忠孝廉耻为代表的核心价值，通过家庭教育（含家风家训）、社会景观与风俗、民间私塾和书院、乡贤传递的正能量，向善、向美的氛围及其传承；当今社会，以社会主义核心价值观和天府文化为内涵，通过家庭教育、普及性的学校教育、城乡景观打造、活动开展、先进人物评选表彰、天府文化行动等形成向善、向美、向雅风尚；尤其是在简阳"回归"成都以后，迎来全新的发展机遇和挑战，全市城乡广大群众在文化自信心、自豪感、使命感得以提升的背景下，简阳人民从国家核心价值观体认、天府文化传承，到逐渐以主人翁心态迎接成渝地区双城经济圈建设、公园城市建设、三城三都建设、世界文化名城建设、大都市圈建设的重大使命，所呈现的新观念、新思维、新精神、新气象。

最近六年来，城市已经意识到"文明是城市的灵魂，是城市的第一品牌"，制定、执行了《简阳市创建全国文明城市三年工作规划》，深入实施"五大提升工程"。在丰富多彩的实践中，包括"四川好人""感动雄州"道德模范和"身边好人"评选活动；2021年1月举办第十七届羊肉美食文化旅游季，期间接待游客约170万人次，收入4.5亿元；举办声势可观的龙舟文化节；"东来印象"开始承接比赛；用好文创项目扶持金，支持文创街区和文创空间建设；"互联网＋"7类新媒体建设；"边远乡镇行"文艺演出活动；"百姓舞台"广场大家乐以及广场舞比赛；草莓采摘节、桃花观赏节、九莲灯巡游、春节广场文化周活动、民间艺术表演深入人心；《樱桃红了》《祥哥的情节》《见闻札记》在省市获奖；文明单位业务培训；组织中青年文艺骨干赴市外进行培训、观摩、采

风、交流、展演活动；与省曲艺研究院共建"简阳曲艺支教班"；开展
文明单位、村、社区、服务窗口评选表彰；创作简阳城市形象宣传标识
"诚诺四方·铭刻简阳"并推广应用；对不文明现象的曝光和责令整改；
营造公平诚信的市场环境；营造健康向上的人文环境；营造有利于青少
年健康成长的社会文化环境；利用国庆等时间节点，开展网上祭英烈，
童心向党向国旗敬礼活动；建设覆盖城乡的道德讲堂，深入推进"文明
餐桌""文明交流"等群众关注度高、带动力强、社会影响大的文明礼
仪规范系列主题活动；文艺界开展的多主题、接地气的采风创作活动和
文艺惠民活动；积极开展非公经济人士教育培训，尤其是注重对于民营
企业家的中央、省市重要会议精神传达，政治方向上正确引导，树立正
确理想信念；打造国际化、高品质的文旅景区、项目，推出一批山地运
动、养生度假、生态休闲旅游精品；加强文化小康建设，保护弘扬乡村
优秀传统文化，推进村镇文化基础设施标准化建设；在乡村振兴中，立
足自然、产业、文化基础，把中华传统文化元素如家风、汉服、宗祠等
融入经营，打造景观与空间；积极编撰出版《遇见天府雄州》《简阳有
个周克芹》，定期推出《简阳文艺》；成功举办"简阳市歌入围歌曲集
中展演，推广传唱市歌《简阳》；升级打造四季主题旅游活动，推动"一
乡一节""一镇（街道）一活动"特色化、品质化；线上线下融合，开
启文化活动（文艺演出、公益展览、公益讲座）新模式；积极推进天府
文化进校园活动；借力大运会，策划推出"送简阳羊肉汤上大运"系列
宣传活动，选出羊肉汤十大品牌；邀请巴蜀文化名家袁庭栋以短视频方
式讲述简阳大耳羊、刘子华；确定"简阳不简单"宣传主题，拉近成都、
全国、全球与简阳的心理距离；支持"海底捞"发起冬至简阳全球派送

羊肉汤活动，吸引了全球 30 万人参与……在这些积极探索中，形成的大量有益经验和做法，与学习借鉴其他同级别优秀城市的先进理念、实践经验相结合，再辅之以对简阳八大文化深度挖掘形成的最新研判，在成都市第十四次党代会关于天府文化传承创新和建设世界文化名城的相关要求引领下，一定可以实现简阳群众文化，从内容到形式，到精品力作打造的新的境界，使"文化惠民"在简阳呈现别样幸福、别样精彩。

不过，我们也要看到简阳群众文化的一些短板和不足，诸如形式创新多，但内容紧密结合简阳的优质资源并呈现简阳的优良个性者少；城市群众文化活动追求精致和优雅的水平还远远不够；深受群众欢迎并具有传播、借鉴价值的精品力作尚少（文创作品获奖整体偏少）；群众文化、文明素质还明显参差不齐；基于对简阳文化的家喻户晓，而形成的简阳人的身份认同，以及在此基础上作为简阳市民的自信心、自豪感还需要提升。

二、简阳群众文化的优良个性

2000 多年来，简阳人民依靠自己勤劳的双手，打造了属于自己的幸福生活，形成了爱国爱家、守望相助、淳朴厚道、崇文尚雅的文化个性，成为简阳基本的文化底色和文化土壤。对其内涵和典型事例的挖掘整理，并结合简阳新的定位和使命丰富、增添其内涵，创造互联网时代新的群众文化，将是简阳人民提升、优化自身素质，增强文化生活获得感、幸福感的重要一环。对外，群众文化建设也是增强简阳"被记住""被向往"甚至"被仰望"优良个性的基础工程。

Jianyang Code

of

Tianfu Culture

Written by: Tan Ping

Translated by: Peng Yunxi

New Exploration of Deepening Research on Sichuan Culture

Jianyang, known as Juyi Xiongzhou(powerful region) since ancient times, belongs to part of Chengdu for most of the time. In 2016, it returned to Chengdu administratively, ushering in new development opportunities. In the context of the major missions entrusted by the state to Chengdu, such as the construction of the "Chengdu-Chongqing double-city economic circle", the construction of a world-famous cultural city, and the construction of a park city demonstration area, Jianyang is also facing the task of accelerating the pace with the times in all aspects. Based on the cultural territory and cultural pursuit of Sichuan and Chengdu, it has become an important work for Jianyang to sort out, inherit and carry forward its own cultural personality and charm. The book *"Jianyang Code of Tianfu Culture"*, carefully written by Professor Tan Ping, Dean of the Tianfu Culture Research Institute of Chengdu University, is a fruitful exploration in this field. After reading the manuscript, I have the following feelings.

1. To deepen the study of the culture of Sichuan, Chengdu and Jianyang, we should focus on the case study of the regional culture of representative and typical counties and cities. Such research, which focuses on the medium and micro perspectives, reveals the vitality of local China from multiple perspectives, and meets the needs of the pursuit of modernization with Chinese characteristics and the charm of Sichuan. It is obviously self-evident that such research has the irreplaceable value of traditional and grand narrative historical writings. In addition, it not only can help the cultural construction in urban and rural areas achieve better results, and realize the people's growing sense of gain, satisfaction and happiness of having cultural life and consuming cultural and tourism products, but also can draw inferences from one instance, bring beneficial enlightenment to the cities and counties in the brotherhood, better introduce and express itself in cultural exchanges with similar urban and rural areas at home and abroad, and tell Jianyang, Chengdu, Sichuan, and even the China story well. It is also because of this pursuit that the writing techniques of this book pays attention to explaining the profound in simple terms, and adopts bilingual presentation in Chinese and English, as well as beautiful picture matching, which highlight its uniqueness.

2. The study of county cultural personality is extremely difficult, but we should face the difficulties and promote the county culture of vast Sichuan to not only has the common features of Bashu culture and Tianfu culture, but also show its unique and excellent personality, and form a hundred flowers bloom full of vitality. To analyze the difficulties, first of all, the changes of living and development environment in the cities, districts and counties of Sichuan Basin, ethnic composition and changes, historical opportunities, and major problems faced in current development are very similar. In addition,

historical data and other relevant documents are pretty limited. For various reasons, high-level scholars have little accumulation of this kind of research with medium and micro perspectives. The same is true of the precise sorting, summary and presentation of Jianyang's historical and cultural personality. In particular, it is very valuable to make efforts to connect such sorting and presenting with the cultural pursuit of today's Jianyang, Chengdu and Sichuan, and to put forward some academically reliable, forward-looking and enlightening views and suggestions that stand in a higher historical position. This academic paradigm between theory and application should be advocated in the cause of serving the inheritance of local culture.

The planning and layout of this manuscript is concise, the content is logical and coherent, and the details are appropriate. Its original four-level theory of studying and judging the level of urban culture and the river theory of urban cultural ecology are enlightening. The vivid interpretation of the connotation of Confucianism, Buddhism and Taoism, and the discussions of using it to examine Jianyang's Tianfu cultural resources; The discussions of the logical relationship among Jianyang culture, Bashu culture and Tianfu culture; As well as the interpretation of the connotation and value of the eight most distinctive cultures in Jianyang, all show the author's deep thinking about the exploration of cultural resources in Chengdu and Sichuan and how to realize their transformation of creative value and innovative development, show his heart to take root in Sichuan as a Sichuan native, and to help and promote the Tianfu culture to bloom gorgeous flowers in Jianyang.

Scholarship is not only wisdom, but also the crystallization of emotion. The culture of Jianyang are rich in connotation, and have a unique personality, it is worth to be sorted out, summarized and expressed. This "little" book has undoubtedly made a good start and is at the forefront of the times. It is worth encouraging. The author studied as an undergraduate in the History Department of Sichuan University from 1978 to 1982 and as a graduate in the History Department of Sichuan University from 1985 to 1988. During both periods, he was my student. I am pleased to see that he has been trying to use scientific research to help the development and progress of cultural undertakings in Chengdu and Sichuan. Hereby, this is the preface.

Doctoral supervisor of the School of History and
Culture of Sichuan University, Ran Guangrong
September 27th, 2022

Ran Guangrong: He was born in December 1938 in Chongqing, Sichuan. In 1959, he graduated from the Department of History of Sichuan University with a bachelor's degree, and in 1962, he graduated from the Department of History of Sichuan University with a master's degree in pre-Qin history. He stayed in the department to work. He was appointed as an associate professor in 1983, promoted to professor in 1987, and served as a doctoral supervisor starting in 1995. From 1984 to 1993, he served as the deputy director of the Department of History and the deputy director of the Institute of History. From 1994 to 1998, he served as the director of the Institute of History. In 1993, he started receiving the State Council special allowance. From 1993 on, he served as a counselor of the People's Government of Sichuan Province. From 1998 to now, he has served as a member of the Standing Committee of the Provincial People's Congress and its Special Committee of Education, Science, Culture and Health. In 2000, he served as an academic member of the Institute of Western Development of Sichuan University.

Overview of Research on Jianyang Culture

By Tan Ping

Jianyang is a dazzling pearl of Bashu culture and Tianfu culture. After thousands of years of accumulation and development, it has gradually formed a rich and distinctive local culture. The excavation of Longya Site traces the history of human activities in Jianyang back to 30,000 years ago, which greatly adds to the profound sense of Jianyang's history. It is of great significance and necessity to study Jianyang culture.

After Jianyang was integrated into Chengdu, it ushered in a new development opportunity. Jianyang cadres and masses began a new historical journey. Facing the reality and the future, Jianyang has an important position, significant influence and historical mission that cannot be ignored. Its significance can be found in the construction of Chengdu Chongqing double city economic circle, the "one trunk and multiple branches" development strategy of Sichuan Province, the strategy of the collaborative and integrated development of cities like Chengdu, Deyang, Meishan and Ziyang. The importance of Jianyang can also be found in the need of comprehensively building a park city demonstration area, Chengdu metropolitan area, and a world famous cultural city that practices the new development concept. President Xi Pointed out that excellent Chinese traditional culture is the outstanding advantage of the Chinese nation. Cultural confidence is a more fundamental, broader and deeper confidence. Therefore, deepening the excavation and interpretation of the excellent traditional culture represented by the "Dongguan Culture" will help promote the summary, refinement, inheritance and innovation of Jianyang's culture, enhance the city's cultural soft power, and promote the further "rise" of the central city in the eastern region of Chengdu with distinctive characteristics and vitality.

It is not easy to introduce Jianyang's cultural character to readers at home and abroad. First, one should correctly apply the concept of "culture". In different dictionaries around the world, there are more than 200 kinds of literal explanations of the word "culture". Its accurate understanding and application are the theoretical basis for Jianyang's cultural interpretation. The so-called culture means "humanities and civilization" or "humanistic education" in Chinese. The former emphasizes its resource and career attributes, which is a noun, while the latter emphasizes that the value of culture must be embodied in the optimization of people's quality, which is a verb. Most scholars agree that culture includes three levels: material, system and spirit. It especially emphasizes human spiritual activities with values and lifestyles as the core connotation. Only it can go through the ancient and modern times and lead or support future development of human society. Good culture has the driving force to keep people away from the false, the evil and the ugly and move towards the true, the good and the beautiful. The cultural genes that must be inherited and carried forward are mainly embodied in the lives of celebrities, major events with strong positive energy, and classics. Jianyang's eight major cultures not only include important relics and spiritual consensus formed in the historical developments and sediments for a long time, such as Longya culture, farming culture, commercial road culture, top scholar culture, celebrity culture, intangible cultural heritage culture, but also include the selection of collective values and the refinement and summary of lifestyles of modern and contemporary Jianyang people, such as Donggu-an culture, mass culture, etc. Putting Jianyang's eight major cultures in such coordinates to analyze, elaborate and judge is not only conducive to finding the coordinates of the eight major cultures from the cultural category, but also conducive to highlighting the urban characteristics of the eight major cultures from a realistic perspective.

Second, one should choose the right perspective. In the context of urbanization, modernization, and globalization, in addition to cooperation and accommodation, the concept of competition is much emphasized when culture is discussed. The cultural construction level of a city can sort out its own progress and development through vertical comparison, and can only see its own gap through horizontal comparison, so as to find its own position, and strive to highlight the city's personality and shape its characteristics. The cultural level of the city, of course, is reflected in the sense of security, sense of gain, happiness, self-confidence and pride of local people. More importantly, it is reflected in the comparison of other cities which have similar situation, in that whether the inflow of high-quality people and properties are more than the outflow of them. The attractiveness of a city to external high-quality people and properties can be divided into four levels according to its comprehensive image: being ignored, remembered, yearned for and looked up to. The cities that are ignored by the related parties due to its lack of competitive advantages cannot attract high-quality people and properties from outside. Moreover, their own high-quality people and properties will also "escape" in large quantities, leaving no opportunities for development. Cities that are remembered because of their good personalities will be much better, but their attraction will be limited, unless their competitors leave worse impressions than them. The desired city often has many good personalities, which can be successfully expressed and disseminated, so it will be in an advantageous position in attracting high-quality people and properties. Being looked up to is the highest level of city's competitiveness for high-quality people and properties, and also the core connotation of "World Cultural City". As a city, because of its lofty, grand, solemn, elegant, inclusive and other qualities of values and lifestyle, and after being recognized so by many, the world's high-quality people and properties will automatically converge to it, and such a city will be invincible. The level of the city in these four levels is directly proportional to the level of the local people's sense of cultural gain, happiness, self-confidence and pride. Chengdu aims not only to be desired, but also to be looked up to as a world-famous cultural city. As the first prefecture from the east of Chengdu, Jianyang must sort out the rich connotation and contemporary value of its historical and cultural resources, place them respectively on the map of Tianfu culture, Bashu culture and Chinese culture, find out its own coordinates and positioning, establish its own cultural development strategy both down-to-earth and ambitious, choose a development path suitable for itself, gather and make good use of comparative advantage resources, realize the steady improvement of cultural soft power and the gradual enhancement of cultural competitiveness.

2022.9.27

Tan Ping, born in 1961, professor. His native place is Wusheng, Sichuan University. He graduated from both the undergraduate and graduate schools of Sichuan University and then has been working in Chengdu University. He has successively served as the publicity director of the university and the dean of the School of Literature, Journalism and Communication. He is mainly engaged in the research and teaching of ancient history of China, Ba-Shu culture and Tianfu culture. Has won eight provincial and municipal government research and teaching achievement awards alone or ranked first, with over ten monographs (many translated into English and Spanish), two large-scale literary works, and nearly a hundred papers. He is also the president of the Promotion Association of Chengdu Tianfu Culture Inheritance and Development, the president of Tianfu Culture Research Institute, the academic member of Sichuan Research Institute of Sichuan Academy of Social Sciences, the vice presidents of Sichuan Li Bing and Yang Shen Research Associations, and the director of the academic committee of Wu Zetian Research Association.

Table of Content

CHAPTER I

_____

INTRODUCTION

On the 9.6 million square kilometers colorful and diversified cultural map of China, it is not easy to vividly introduce the regional cultural charm of a county-level city, based on reflection and research. We should not only clarify the common features of Chinese civilization and Bashu culture, but also point out its cultural personality that can keep pace with the times. If one aims at helping the city understanding its history, responding to reality, taking the lead in its future aspiration, he will face more severe challenges. This first depends on the vision and orientation chosen by introducers. Jianyang must be measured on the main coordinates of Chinese civilization and its regional branch, Bashu culture, and the typical urban cultural expressing — Tianfu culture, so as to form a scientific and rigorous overall judgment. Second, it is better for researchers and introducers to have unique theories, so that they can easily generate new enlightening judgments and conclusions on the familiar and common historical materials and others, rather than reassembling the existing facts and research judgments, or the new bottle is still filled with

"Lao bai gan". Third, how to plan a layout is also crucial. Han Yu said that in writing, "old words must be removed". No one is willing to read cliches, and no one is willing to accept the long and tedious "chicken soup". Therefore, we must take the principle of being skillful, concise and vivid to optimize the details of materials and discussions as much as possible.

Section I Understanding Jianyang Culture on the Cultural Map

1. Question raising

As we all know, the Chinese civilization is the only ancient civilization on the earth that has never been interrupted. It has experienced countless natural and man-made disasters, joys and sorrows, and is still full of vigor today. Under the strong stimulation and impact of Western civilization, which pursues the law of the jungle, the Chinese civilization experienced the Phoenix nirvana and rebirth. President Xi repeatedly stressed that inheriting and carrying forward the excellent traditional Chinese culture is our root and soul, and cultural self-confidence is the most important source of confidence and strength. As a spiritual home, Chinese culture is jointly constructed by Confucianism, Buddhism and Taoism, with Confucianism as the main and Buddhism and Taoism as the auxiliary. When studying the historical origin and contemporary expression of Jianyang's culture, we found that in Jianyang's culture, Confucianism, Buddhism and Taoism are like sources of living water, and their practices are also presented wonderfully. Therefore, to study and explain Jianyang's culture, we should first deeply understand the Chinese culture jointly constructed by Confucianism, Buddhism and Taoism, and accurately understand its rich value and connotations. Only in this way can the protection and utilization of cultural heritage (including cultural relics) and cultural landscape move people's hearts, form consensus and establish identity. Inheriting and carrying forward Jianyang's historical culture is a cultural choice to build Jianyang's urban characteristics under the Chinese cultural coordinate system, and a "Chengdu story" and "China story" that help form a broad consensus on urban development and optimize the way of life of the masses. It is of great significance and far-reaching influence.

2. Understanding Confucianism, Buddhism and Taoism is the basis for understanding Jianyang culture

If all cultures (or civilizations) want to keep pace with the times and be alive, in the impact and competition with other cultures (or civilizations), they must answer the three questions most intelligently: the relationship between man and nature, the relationship between man and man, and the relationship between man and himself. Chinese culture just shows great advantages in this point. It belongs to Confucianism, Buddhism and Taoism, or the ancestors and sages that were well versed in them. The Chinese culture has built us a cultural system and spiritual home that can advance and retreat and has the capacity and function of being inclusive, being open and confident, and exhaling the old and inhaling the new. It can be said that this is unique in human history.

The Confucian culture, symbolized by Confucius and Mencius, is the warmest, most humane and wisest theory in the world on how to deal with the relationship between people (including the plural, ethnic groups and ethnic groups, countries and countries). The "Great Harmony" world described by Confucius in the Book of Rites is the earliest origination of the consciousness of a community of shared future for mankind; "All the people of the world are brothers," said Zi Xia, a disciple of Confucius, in The Analects of Confucius, is the earliest anti racism consciousness of mankind; "Gentlemen are harmonious but different" is the earliest declaration to abandon cultural arrogance and prejudice; "The emperor has no relatives, only virtue is auxiliary" and "come with both culture and virtue", point to the noble demeanor of a civilized and ceremonial country. The world's great powers and powerful countries must convince people with virtue and reason (not the law of the jungle). It is precisely because of holding up such values and communication psychology that China has always been one of the countries with almost the vastest territory on Earth for more than 2000 years. Today's 56 ethnic groups can love each other, live in harmony, and return to the center of the world stage 40 years after the reform and opening up of China. The "peaceful rise" is unstoppable. Tianfu Chengdu, including Jianyang, has established a wide-ranging and benign integration within China and with other parts of the world by relying on the grand strategies of "the Belt and Road Initiative", the construction of Chengdu Chongqing dual city economic circle, and the park city demonstration area, and has realized great historic changes. The core values of Confucianism are benevolence, righteousness, propriety, wisdom, trust, loyalty, filial piety, and integrity, which are all good advice for dealing with interpersonal relations. Benevolent people love others and speak of fraternity; Wise people are benevolent and rational. Benevolent people love others, they are philanthropic. These concepts represent the core values of Confucianism, which have established the positive energy among interpersonal communication from all aspects and levels. They have become rich historical nourishment and historical foundations of today's socialist core values. In Jianyang's celebrity culture, top scholar culture, Dongguan culture, and farming culture, we can experience the distinct influence of the Confucian spirit.

In order to better interpret Jianyang's culture from the perspective of the spiritual home of Confucianism, I have also established a systematic statement that the powerful positive energy of Confucianism is: the emotional world with love and loyalty as its core; Values with benevolence, righteousness, propriety, wisdom and trust as the core; The outlook on life based on morality, merit and words; The life style of practicing poetry, music, chess, calligraphy and painting; the life attitude of striving constantly by self and holding world with virtue. It is not difficult to form a more objective and fair judgment by putting the specific representative figures and influential events in Jianyang's history in such a coordinate to test and examine them. In fact, in the history of more than 2,100 years of establishment, for a long time, those who promoted the progress and cultural formation of Jianyang were all successors and believers of Confucianism. Without a deep understanding of the value of Confucian culture, it is difficult to comprehensively and deeply understand the source of the Top Scholar culture, Celebrity culture and Dongguan culture.

Taoism, with Laozi (his last place of seclusion should be in or near

Chengdu) and Zhuangzi as its main labels, and which was first formed in the Chengdu Plain later, made unique contributions in discussing and practicing the relationship between man and nature. Both Confucianism and Taoism have the concept of "the unity of heaven and man". The Tao Te Ching further describes that "man follows the earth, the earth follows the heaven, the heaven follows the Tao, and the Tao follows the nature". Taoism is the first great philosophy in the world history that advocates that human beings must conform to, respect and live in harmony with nature. Taoism also regards human body as a part of nature. It believes that the most successful life is to have a healthy body and a free personality. Taoism believes that if other goals of life hinder healthy body and free personality, they can be given up; Only in the case of compatibility will we pursue. If Confucianism is the most successful collectivism in human history, then Taoism is the most gentle and kindest individualism in human history. Taoism is the special care for all living beings who have with different personalities, unpredictable life risks, unpredictable destiny. Without Taoism, there can be no distinct spiritual system formed by historical celebrities such as Yan Junping, Yang Xiong, Tao Yuanming, Li Bai, Su Dongpo, etc, It is also impossible to have the unique cultural features formed by such famous works as *Journey to the West* and *Strange Tales of a Lonely Studio*. Chengdu Plain is the stronghold of Taoism on Earth, and also a unique city that enjoys its positive energy. The Taoist philosophy that advocates nature and many legacies left by its practice are also important resources for Chengdu to build a park city demonstration area and a world famous cultural city. The history of Jianyang people's donation to build and rebuild Taoist temples is endless, which is worthy of full affirmation. It can be seen from this that in the long history, the land of Jianyang has been deeply influenced by Taoist ideas and propositions. Later, the city spirit of Jianyang, which was formed as "the main road is of simplicity, and the sun shines far away", has more or less some Taoist ideas.

How should people get along with themselves? Buddhism has made unique contributions in this regard. Buddhism originated from ancient India and today's Nepal. At the beginning of the Eastern Han Dynasty, it came to China over the Himalayas, experienced the collision and integration with Confucianism and Taoism, and later localization in the Sui and Tang Dynasties (most of the temples in Jianyang started in this period, indicating that the Buddhist transformation in Sichuan Basin, especially in the Chengdu Plain, was completely synchronized with the Central Plains). Zen and Pure Land Buddhism became the absolute mainstream (including Jianyang). If we say that the Confucian school cultivates the moral character and the Taoist school cultivates the human nature, Buddhism is the study of calming the mind. Buddhism is broad and profound, yet when concentrating on the essence, it is nothing more than the science of mind purification and mind tranquilization. Buddhism believes that the most important value of life is to always keep your heart clean and quiet. Whether you can do it or not determines whether you are happy (no worries) and the state of the afterlife. This has nothing to do with people's identity and status. The sinicized Buddhism advocates "equality of all beings" and "benevolent navigation and universal salvation" (Mahayana Buddhism), advocates doing good deeds and accumulating virtues, and advocates compatibility and adaptation with the Confucian ethics as far as possible, so as to make people good on the whole. As for the unique contribution of Buddhism to Chinese civilization in philosophy, aesthetics, linguistics, myth construction, architecture, gardens, clothing and many other fields, we can also have a deep feeling of such in Jianyang. If Confucianism is collectivism and Taoism is individualism, Buddhism is compassion and care for all living beings. The self care, self motivation and self sublimation of the pure and peaceful mind left many stories and legends. Jianyang has a large number of temples in history, and there were also many eminent monks and great virtues. Historically, there are many temples in Jianyang. There have been many acts of donating money, making efforts to build and rebuild temples by eminent monk of great virtue. There have also been a number of practitioners who have reflected the concept of Buddhism , such as the two dutiful and obedient sons in Jianzhou and many contemporary moral models who have acted bravely for a just cause and have donated money to help students. These deeds also show the mercy and care for all living beings. While placing these features of Jianyang in the perspective of historical development, we realize that the optimism, friendliness, and respect of public warfare of Tianfu culture have received sufficient response here in Jianyang.

Mr. Shu Dagang, a famous scholar of Sichuan University, summarized the positive energy that Confucianism, Buddhism and Taoism have continuously provided to the Chinese people in the following words: Confucianism makes people responsible, Taoism makes people free and easy, and Buddhism makes people open. This is undoubtedly the most incisive summary. We can also use such remarks when examining Jianyang's heritage, landscape and influence of Confucianism, Buddhism and Taoism.

In short, an accurate understanding and grasp of the core values and pursuits of the three major components of Chinese civilization is the key to understanding and even grasping of the number one scholars and celebrities in Jianyang's history, as well as the behavior of ordinary people who have produced noticeable phenomena through collective action in history, and is also the main basis for understanding the evolution of Jianyang's urban and rural cultural context since modern times.

3. The Logical Relationship between Jianyang Culture, Bashu Culture and Tianfu Culture

(1) Bashu Culture and Jianyang

Bashu culture is the regional culture of "Tianfu Sichuan". It originates in Sichuan Basin and some surrounding areas, and its center and capital are mostly located in Chengdu. It is an irreplaceable element of the pluralistic and integrated Chinese civilization with a long history and profound connotation. According to archaeologists, Bashu culture has a history of more than 5000 years. Together with the Central Plains culture, Qilu culture, Sanjin culture, etc., it has formed several major cultural systems in ancient China, playing an irreplaceable role in the creation and development of the entire Chinese civilization. Stereoscopic landscapes, rich products, diverse ethnic groups, frequent disasters and auspiciousness, and repeated migration are the five main bases for the emergence and evolution of Bashu culture. They comprehensively led to the formation of the basic values and lifestyle of calmness, self-confidence, inclusiveness, relaxation, integrity, valuing business and literature, enthusiasm and romance, which can be inherited from generation to generation.

There is no doubt that Jianyang's humanistic personality is almost consistent with the above causes of formation (except for diverse ethnic groups) and characteristics, and shows excellent charm, historical inheritance and modern expression in landscape, products, culture, education, immigration, and other aspects. Today, we study, interpret and disseminate Jianyang's culture in order to show that Jianyang and other counties and cities have both common-alities and different individual features and charms. If we take many cities and counties at the same level in Sichuan as a reference, Jianyang, which has always been known as Juyi and the gateway to the capital of Sichuan, its comprehensive achievements and influence are undoubtedly a strong pres-ence in the Bashu cultural region, and it is a representative and influential "Tianfu Xiongzhou" in many aspects. Jianyang's culture are the regional expression and vivid interpretation of Bashu culture in Jianyang. Finding the coordinate system of Jianyang's culture in the inheritance of Bashu culture is conducive to highlighting Jianyang's urban status in Bashu and improving cultural self-confidence. However, all counties (cities) in Sichuan, including the original counties (districts) in Ziyang City, as well as counties (cities) at the same level throughout the country that have economic and cultural exchanges with Jianyang, are fully aware that after Jianyang is integrated into Chengdu, it will obtain superior material and cultural resources. The expec-tations from all circles on Jianyang will also be greatly enhanced. Whether Jianyang can maintain its status as an economic and cultural "Xiongzhou" in the Bashu cultural landscape, it cannot be blindly optimistic.

(2) Tianfu Culture and Jianyang

Tianfu culture is the culture of "Tianfu Chengdu". This concept and its action are derived from the 13th Party Congress of Chengdu held in April 2017 and the 14th Party Congress of Chengdu held in April 2022, which put forward new and deepening requirements for the inheritance and promotion of this culture. Tianfu culture mainly refers to the regional culture of the administrative region of Chengdu. In some contexts, its formation and activity areas also include some areas that were once under the jurisdiction of Chengdu government (city) or had decisive influence in history, such as some areas of today's Chengdu Deyang Meishan Ziyang "Metropolitan Circle", and closely related areas of Ganzi Prefecture and Aba Prefecture. Of course, its core layer is the administrative area directly under the jurisdiction of Chengdu today. There are not only farming and animal husbandry, but also industry and commerce, including the sinicized and localized modern civilization. In addition to the mysterious romance of the predecessor of the pre-Qin Chengdu city embodied in the eight "king cities", such as Sanxingdui and Jinsha (but because no relevant words have been found so far, it is difficult to describe accurately, and their relationship can not be described), which shocked the world and became the top chapter of the city and even the Chinese civilization in the Bronze Age, Tianfu culture especially emphasizes the urban culture of Chengdu that has lasted for more than 2300 years since Zhang Yi built the city. It is the fruit and the flowers of Bashu culture, the concentration and wonderful presentation of Bashu culture, and the main representative of Bashu culture when it collides, exchanges and merges with other regional cultures in China and other civilizations in the world. The mission and function of this representative are sometimes a bridge, sometimes a guide, and sometimes both. Its goal is to inherit Bashu civilization, develop Tianfu culture and strive to build a world famous cultural city. Its core and personality as follows: innovation and creation, elegance and fashion, optimism and inclusiveness, friendship and public welfare. It was specially emphasized to shape the urban character of "innovation and creation, openness and liberality", and the humanistic characteristics of striving for happiness and being philosophical and friendly.

The proposal and practice of "Tianfu Culture" is an important measure taken by the Chengdu Municipal Party Committee to vigorously promote the Chengdu-Chongqing Double City Economic Circle, Park City Demonstration Area and Chengdu Metropolitan Circle from a new starting point. It is also the heroic recognition of historical memory, positive response to the needs of the times and outstanding pursuit of future development, which fully reflects the extraordinary aspiration of Chengdu culture in the next step of construction and development and has generated strong dissemination and mobilization power. The goal of Tianfu culture construction can be divided into two directions: internally, to form the value consensus and common spiritual home of the city's people, and to promote the healthy development of cultural undertakings and industries; externally, to make Chengdu a city, to make Chengdu a city which is attractive and respectable to general public.

The unique location and historical opportunities (including administrative system and ownership different from that of ordinary prefectures and counties) have changed Jianyang's weight and position multiple times in the Tianfu cultural landscape. Jianyang is famous for its people's hard-working, agricultural civilization and "rich culture and ingenuity". Jianyang "returned" to Chengdu in 2016, and is a full participant in the Tianfu Culture action. In the past six years, Chengdu has "empowered" Jianyang in many aspects, which has the greatest impact on Jianyang. It also enables Jianyang to enter and integrate into the "eastward" strategy of Chengdu, which meets the multiple demands for the construction of Chengdu Chongqing double city economic circle, park city demonstration area and world famous cultural city. With such urban cultural planning, cultural ideals, cultural aspirations and cultural actions as the coordinates, compared with other districts (cities) and counties in Chengdu, Jianyang today can still be called the "Xiongzhou" due to the construction of the new city area, population, general area and water area. Yet other things that can highlight the civilization of a modern, international metropolis, represented by its models, experiences and charm, which can demonstrate the material civilization achievement of Chengdu and even Sichuan, are obviously small in number. In particular, Jianyang still has room for further development regarding the protection of inheritance of cultural resources, the creative transformation and innovative development, which are widely integrated into urban development of Tianfu cultural action under the theme of "Innovative creation, elegant and fashionable, optimistic and inclusive, friendly and public welfare". However, the history of more than 2100 years of construction and the long-term interaction and integration with Chengdu have given Jianyang a deep foundation and distinctive characteristics in terms of human geography, cultural personality and other aspects. It has formed magnificent history, beautiful humanities and beautiful sceneries. No matter judging from the historical dimension or the objective reality, Jianyang should have an important position in Tianfu culture. Of course, it can become a highly recognizable regional city in Tianfu culture and make a unique contribution to the construction and development of Tianfu culture.

4. Direction of efforts

After integration into Chengdu, Jianyang culture has become an inseparable part of Tianfu culture. Therefore, Jianyang should take full advantage of the excavation, interpretation and inheritance of Jianyang's culture, quickly improve the position of cultural action, strengthen overall planning, make good use of resources, do something but not everything, and build cohesion in the creation of features and highlights, and strive to become a veritable "Tianfu Xiongzhou" in the territory of Tianfu culture. The construction of the East New Area of Chengdu with high-tech industries and high-end service industries as the main body, the construction of Tianfu International Airport with world-class facilities, and the development of its ancillary industries and undertakings, and Jianyang Municipal Party Committee and Government attaching great importance to cultural construction and making dedicated efforts, all these lay a good foundation for Jianyang to catch up in cultural construction and would allow Jianyang to glow the glory of "Tianfu Xiongzhou" city. It is a very important foundation work to scientifically, systematically and accurately understand the eight most representative cultures of Jianyang, and to wipe and build them in the coordinate system of Bashu culture and Tianfu culture, so as to make them an important support for urban development and the value pursuit of citizens' life.

Section II Theoretical Construction and Application

1. Four levels theory of measuring urban and rural cultural level

The introduction of this book has already mentioned the theory which will be explained here.

The measurement of existing cultural level of any cities and villages can be divided into four levels: being neglected, being remembered, being yearned for, and being looked up to. The so-called "being neglected" refers to the fact that cities or villages, cannot leave a positive impression on people due to its mediocrity and backwardness. Naturally, they not only cannot obtain external resources and development opportunities, but also their own people, money and things will flow away. Such places have no hope of "revitalization". The so-called "being remembered" means that people who have entered this place will have a positive impression in their hearts due to certain characteristics or personality. Such a place has certain but limited possibilities for development. The so-called "being yearning for" refers to the outstanding personality and conditions of a place which enable people who have come here to aspire to live here. This situation can be reflected by the advertisement for Chengdu made by Zhang Yimou, saying "Chengdu is a city where you do not want to leave once you come." The so-called "being looked up to" refers to a city with some unique characteristics such as loftiness, greatness, romance, kindness, warmth and elegance, all these features attracted the external audience. Just like the feeling hold by Sima Qian has when he faced Confucius, "The mountain is high, and the scenery is moving. Although one can't reach it, one still yearn for it". To be "looked up to" is the main symbol of a world famous cultural city. Because in the era of globalization, it is impossible to talk about culture without competition. Only a city that is at the level of being looked up to will not lose its outstanding descendants and other high-quality resources. All those high-quality people, money and goods from all over the world will automatically flow to this city. Therefore, it will remain invincible in the competition.

Chengdu has been one of the benchmark cities in China since ancient times. In the long history of human recognition that China is a country of civilization and etiquette, at least since the Han Dynasty, Chengdu has frequently been a world famous cultural city. Its characteristic is that it represents the high-end of Chinese culture in many ways, winning people's pride and the world's admiration. With the great rejuvenation of the Chinese nation, the goal of Chengdu is naturally to become a world famous cultural city again. The cultural construction of Jianyang urban and rural areas can refer to this theory, and according to the current resources and cultural development level, targeted planning and layout can be carried out. The bottom line is to make all communities (villages) get rid of being ignored, at least being remembered. Those who have the conditions may become yearned for and those with the best conditions may become looked up to. From the perspective of the exploration and application of historical and cultural resources, the top part of the top scholar culture, Dongguan culture and celebrity culture should strive to form a "looked up" city image, highlight its lofty, solemn and magnificent spiritual attributes, and spread and express them to form the main basis of Jianyang people's cultural pride; Longya culture, celebrity culture and commercial road culture should make efforts to form the urban and rural image of "being yearned for", highlight its attributes of being unique in China, unique in Sichuan, and attractive in Chengdu, generate strong, lasting and touching appeal, forming a deep foundation for Jianyang people's cultural self-confidence; The farming culture, mass culture and intangible cultural heritage culture should mainly start with the formation of "remembered" urban and rural images, highlight the personalized strong homesickness, "cultural prosperity and craftsmanship" and the warmth and affinity of helping each other, and help shape the image of a happy Jianyang that is suitable for work and living.

2. Four-types theories to measure the cultural accomplishment of city (village) people

The deep foundation of urban culture is the cultural accomplishment of citizens. People's cultural accomplishment can be divided into four types: lawlessness, heteronomy, self-discipline and self-motivation. The so-called lawless people refer to those who abandon themselves, lack the basic rules of conduct, and are most likely to break the law and lose morality, becoming negative social energy; The so-called heteronomy refers to the people who can only be rigidly constrained by laws and regulations, and the time and place where laws and regulations are not powerful (such as the intersection with traffic lights but no cameras), such people will run the red lights, becoming the negative energy of society; The so-called self-disciplined people, relying on self-restraint, obey and serve the collective and society, are generally the positive energy of society; The so-called self-motivated people refer to the people who have the spirit of struggle, dedication and sacrifice. They are the most powerful positive energy among the people. Our cultural construction should make the self-motivated well-known, widely respected and followed, let the self-disciplined relax physically and mentally and receive the most preferential treatment, let the heteronomous know their folly and be encouraged by progress, and let the conscience of the lawless who break the law revive, otherwise they will be severely punished or despised.

Since the reform and opening up, Jianyang, once a major agricultural county, has gradually embarked on a process of urbanization and internationalization. Especially since it was incorporated into Chengdu, this process has been accelerated unprecedentedly. It must be soberly noted that the new and old citizens have problems that cannot be ignored in the reconstruction of their spiritual home and the cohesion of their value consensus. In the face of most citizens and villagers, the goal of cultural construction should be to comprehensively eliminate people who are lawless (rule of law and culture), accommodate people who are heteronomous, expand self-disciplined population (there is much to be done in the inheritance and promotion of the healthy commercial road culture, farming culture, mass culture, and intangible cultural heritage culture), and a small number of self-motivated elites (especially among the top celebrities in history and various high-level award-winning people produced by Jianyang every year), in the construction of city and community culture, should be respected and spread to the greatest extent. This way, like every drop converging into a river, Jianyang would make contributions to Chengdu which will eventually become a world-famous cultural city. Also, Jianyang should produce more elites who can speak for Tianfu culture, Bashu civilization, and even Chinese culture (top scholar culture, Dongguan culture, and celebrity culture have great prospects in this regard).

3. Understand and apply Chengdu's lifestyle aesthetics

In recent years, the saying of "There is a kind of lifestyle aesthetics called Chengdu" has become widely known, reflecting the unique charm of Chengdu people's lifestyle rooted in tradition, responding to reality and connecting with the future. It is an important resource for Chengdu to be yearned for and looked up to. Although Jianyang has not been integrated into Chengdu for a long time, the pursuit of lifestyle aesthetics has come down in one continuous line with the connotation of Chengdu's lifestyle aesthetics. However, there is still a certain gap in the presentation of lifestyle aesthetics. By making full use of Jianyang's cultural resources, making innovative transformation and creative development, Jianyang strives to live up to the standard and keeps up with the clock. Thus, the integration into Chengdu lifestyle aesthetics in the new stage has accelerated. The so-called lifestyle aesthetics refers to the aesthetic sense of lifestyle and its connotation, which make people experience the beauty of ease, pleasure, freedom and happiness inside-out; The lifestyle aesthetics appeals to people, enabling them to obtain positive thinking about beauty. In a word, Chengdu lifestyle aesthetics is the art of life, the humanistic customs and social customs formed in the life of art. It is the "Chengdu Story" and "Chinese Story" with the most empathy, penetration and dissemination value, which are derived from

Chengdu's excellent urban personalities. Its soul is the populist humanistic concern, the artistic urban customs, and the space and landscape creation philosophy that enable everyone to quickly relax. The key words of planning and action are balance and coordination — Chengdu has always been a city where its protagonists can easily realize the multiple balance and coordination between nature and humanity, material and spirit, sensibility and rationality, individual and group, history and reality, city and countryside, and men and women. Whether it is the diversity of such balance and coordination, or the stability of such balance and coordination, Chengdu is rarely matched. Therefore, it has created a super high happiness index of people's life. For 13 consecutive years, Chengdu has ranked first in the happiness index of Chinese metropolises, largely relying on the support of its unique lifestyle aesthetics.

The pursuit of lifestyle aesthetics is in Jianyang, marked by the humanistic temperament of advocating balance and coordination embodied in the material entities, spiritual and cultural expressions, such as "eight sceneries of Jianzhou", "cultural prosperity and craftsmanship", "broad roads to simplicity, sunshine to faraway", "sincerity and commitment to all, inscriptions of Jianyang", and "The city and mountain are set against each other, and people and water coexist". It is marked by the balance between agriculture, industry and commerce, culture and education, the harmonious coexistence of Confucianism, Buddhism and Taoism here, and the equal emphasis on literature and martial arts in official and civilian life. Jianyang's civilian food, represented by mutton soup, is popular in urban and rural areas, among the refined and popular, and both young and old enjoy it. But we must see that lifestyle aesthetics, as the high-end part of typical urban civilization, has high requirements in directivity, refinement, recognition, communication and empathy. Compared with the first and second tier urban areas in Chengdu, Jianyang still has a significant gap. Jianyang urban and rural community culture should pay attention to the inheritance and promotion of Chengdu's lifestyle aesthetics, fully incorporate the connotation of lifestyle aesthetics into the construction of street and community culture, take root in local cultural resources, focus on the construction of exquisite and personalized scenes and spaces, as well as the creation of an atmosphere unique to Jianyang's folk flavour, cultural charm and artistic style, and focus on the creation of high-quality attributes of urban life and brand construction; Multi language use in window industries and shopping and consumption places; building the harmonious symbiosis of harmonious urban and rural relations, new and old citizens with goodwill, care for vulnerable groups, mutual understanding of various personalities of all strata, and adequate public space reserved for elegant and popular literary and artistic activities. The environment and program design of citizens' activity space are not only exquisite, but also human, warm, artistic, and can bring joy and happiness.

4. Perfect the "River Theory" of Fine Urban and Rural Cultural Ecology

Throughout the history of human urban civilization, the great and enduring cities are generally located at the estuary of large rivers or the geographical space where many rivers meet. In addition to the need of human for water, such geographical location is also the region with the richest biodiversity. The richness and variety provided by materials are not only the decisive basis for the richness and variety of the spiritual world and spiritual civilization, but also the conditions required to maintain biodiversity are the same as the needs of culture to maintain vitality based on diversity. We can compare the regional cultural circle to such a delta where rivers and oceans, rivers and rivers converge: the overwhelming mainstream; The tributaries with abundant water flow and distinctive features; necessary backflow; wet and dry wetlands and marshes with different depths are scattered everywhere; Various types of shoals and woods. The mainstream is equivalent to the national core values, which must be followed and implemented (among the eight major cultures, the top scholar culture, Dongguan culture and celebrity culture are its historical symbols); The tributaries are equivalent to distinctive value choices and lifestyles with positive energy in the sub region, such as the customs, festivals and intangible cultural heritage (such as the unique commercial road culture and intangible cultural heritage of Jianyang) in Chengdu or a district (city) or county with characteristics and significant influence; Backflow means that some people do not violate the public conscience and the law in their personalized choices and ways of life, such as celibacy, DINK, smoking, little rich, playing mahjong, fighting landlords(poker game), playing mobile phones, playing games, and nightclub life; Wetlands, marshes, shoals and forests are the spaces and conditions that all people may need at a certain time and in a certain state, such as homecoming, comrades in arms association, fellow villagers' associations, industry organizations, public welfare organizations and activities (the general level of the Jianyang mass culture and agricultural culture). The river theory of urban culture tells us that the foundational urban cultural construction should certainly conform to the theme of national and local cultural construction, but it must also be inclusive, considerate and highly respectful of the emotions like joys and sorrows of the aforementioned ordinary people, and seek gradual optimization on the basis of understanding, assistance and respect. It is never necessary to achieve "cultural revitalization" with the attitude and thinking of force, pressure. Because the key point of this theory is not which is more important and superior among the elements constituting this ecosystem, but that the elements should support and generate each other. So if a community culture belongs to the "mainstream", of course, it is glorious, but those belonging to the "tributary", "backflow" and "marsh" should not be discriminated against. Therefore, each community, according to its own resources and conditions, that do things conforming to the law and serving local residents well, is an irreplaceable important builder of urban culture. This theory can help us understand the connotation of cultural inclusion in Chengdu (among all cities in China, the cultural "rivers" in Chengdu provide unparalleled support for cultural diversity, but this will be discussed separately), find the basis for all communities under normal governance to make unique contributions, and think about how to achieve the creative transformation and innovative development of this excellent urban personality.

In a word, the above theories conform to the formation and operation rules of a city's fine cultural ecology, are conducive to the establishment of scientific standards for the evaluation of cultural activities and cultural undertakings, and help form a scientific plan for the development of cultural undertakings and cultural industries. On the basis of solidly carrying out the regular work that reflects the fairness and justice of the supply of cultural products and services, we should focus on high-quality resources, optimize top-level design, combine points with areas, and gradually create a distinctive personality of Jianyang with Tianfu charm, Bashu flavor and Chinese style, building a city culture card that does not lack international characteristics.

The above theories will be reflected in the following monographs on eight cultures.

Section III Culture and Urban Development

1. City is the center of cultural creation, gathering and distributing

The vast majority of Chinese cities originate from the need of political rule, military control (including resisting foreign invasion and suppressing internal rebellion) and carrying out the grandest cultural activities of religion or ancestor, gods worship. Therefore, the most energetic people, wealth and things are gathered and absorbed in cities. In ancient, modern and contemporary times, city naturally is the hub for cultural survival and development and the main stage for cultural exchange in the region. It absorbs the culture of villages and foreign regions and countries, and also exports its own culture to villages, foreign regions and countries when it has strength and channels. In this kind of absorption and output, the more "exports", the stronger the competitiveness; the more "imports", the weaker the competitiveness. According to our cultural competitiveness theory, as well as the semiotics and brand building theory, the urban competitiveness can be divided into four levels: ignored, remembered, desired and looked up. In general, no city is willing to be ignored, and no city does not want to be remembered or yearned for. It is best to be looked up to. Only a city with more moral appeal, human warmth and sense of happiness in its values and lifestyle can be looked up to and yearned for. For most of its history, Jianyang belonged to the state capital that possessed counties and was later reduced to an ordinary county. Because of its unique natural, economic, political, geographical conditions and cultural traditions, Jianyang is a "Xiong Zhou" with strong cultural creation and "exporting" ability. Jianyang, after integrated into Chengdu, becomes more advantageous in terms of time, location and people. The inheritance and promotion of the eight major cultures will not only help Jianyang to achieve greater improvement in cultural soft power and create a distinctive identity of urban characteristics, but also help Chengdu to achieve a larger scale of cultural "exports" and become an important resource and carrier of world famous cultural cities.

2. Culture is the key force for a city to survive and prosper

Throughout the ages, no ethnic group or country can always lead in all aspects, and the ups and downs are inevitable, which is the iron law of the evolution of human society. As its main survival and development stronghold, cities will also face ups and downs, or even complete destruction. All cities in the Chengdu Plain, including Jianyang, have at least experienced the great suffering of the elimination of almost all the aborigines in the late Song Dynasty and the early Yuan Dynasty, the late Ming Dynasty and the early Qing Dynasty. In human history, some countries, ethnic groups and cities will disappear forever after being destroyed. However, the Chinese nation and countless cities in China can achieve nirvana and create new glories in times of suffering. Among ancient civilizations with a history of more than 2,000 years, only China has such strength. The key lies in that the Chinese culture, with the core values of benevolence, righteousness, courtesy, wisdom and trust, loyalty, filial piety and integrity, and the lifestyle of poetry, song, music, chess, calligraphy and painting, has been passed on and carried forward from generation to generation among cadres and masses in cities like Chengdu and Jianyang. In addition, the spiritual home built also by Buddhism and Taoism, which can "absorb hundreds of rivers", breathe out the old and bring in the new, and can advance and retreat, makes Chinese cities survive and prosper. Today's socialist urban culture in China is an expression of the excellent traditional Chinese culture that keeps pace with the times. Focusing on the 14th Party Congress of Chengdu that enriched the urban character with "openness, innovation and creation" and the humanistic characteristics of "striving for happiness, being philosophical, being friendly" are the clarion call and banner for Chengdu to achieve multiple major historical missions, especially for building a world famous cultural city. Jianyang must actively gather under this banner and actively explore to transform the essence and spirit of Jianyang people represented by the history and culture into the "Jianyang Practice", "Jianyang Experience" and "Jianyang Mode" of Tianfu culture. Such Jianyang can better benefit future generations and become the beautiful scenery and decisive cultural force of Chengdu.

3. Fine cultural personality is the "only immovable property" of a city

In the wave of modernization and globalization with market economy as the lever, the most commonly used indicators to measure the development level of a city are the total GDP and GDP per capita. Although such indicators are important, they should not be addicted to. In addition to the differences in the statistical methods used by countries to generate these data and that the currency used can only reflect the currency exchange relationship, covering up part of the actual purchasing power, the differences in tax systems, the gap between the rich and the poor, and the types of goods and services that can be provided in various countries can make the total GDP and per capita GDP quite different from the real living standards of specific people. Moreover, after solving the problem of food and clothing and acquiring a basic decent life, whether the accumulation of material wealth and conspicuous consumption beyond ordinary people can increase people's happiness index, and how much happiness index can be increased, vary from person to person. However, in Chinese culture (including Confucianism, Buddhism and Taoism), such conspicuous consumption is of little value, or even despised, because people who pay attention to the balance of material and spiritual life will shift the focus of life to spiritual life after having enough food and clothing or decent material life. From such spiritual life (including doing poetry, music, chess, calligraphy and painting, academic education, collection and appreciation, benefiting hometowns, and donating to the poor) they gain the feeling of delicacy, warmth, solemnity, and loftiness of life. It is despised by people for being rich and heartless. Being benevolent and polite while being rich is the gospel of society and the sublimation of individuals. Chengdu is one of all the metropolises in China, which has maintained such a balance for more than 2000 years. The sixteen-character personality of Tianfu culture is all in causal relationship with this. All the prosperous cities in the world have excellent cultural personality with strong positive energy; In a world where the power of capital is omnipresent and almost everything can be converted into commodities and bought, only the urban culture that has become deep-rooted concepts and traditions are priceless treasures of cities. Other cities can only imitate and learn from them but cannot take them away. Therefore, Jianyang's unique fine cultural genes and personality contained in Jianyang's culture must become a strong cultural soft power and transform into a number of China's first-class and Sichuan's first-class cultural brands, which can significantly enhance the cultural self-confidence and pride of Jianyang people, even Chengdu people. When this day comes, Jianyang's outstanding talents will generally regard serving the motherland and benefiting their hometown as the highest honor. More and more superior talents, property, resources outside Jianyang will automatically flow to Jianyang. How glorious Jianyang should be at that time!

Chapter II

Formation and Development
of Jianyang City Culture

Jianyang City, located at the golden north latitude of 30 degrees, has a natural geography that is in the middle of Sichuan, of diverse mountains and waters and beautiful landscapes, with Tuojiang River running through; has an economic geography of rich agricultural resources, rich products and main commercial roads in Sichuan running through; has a political geography that is adjacent to Chengdu(most of the time in history, it was a county of Shu Prefecture and Chengdu Prefecture.),having military garrisons and wars and the most important official roads (including Tuojiang shipping) in Sichuan; has a cultural geography that values both literature and martial arts, and owns everlasting attraction and creativity of religion, literature and art for more than 2000 years. Jianyang, with its special position, is gathering and interpreting the positive energy of Confucianism, Buddhism and Taoism, and has both the common characteristics of Chinese civilization and experiences of the baptism of "the spread of Western learning to the east". There is no lack of excellent and distinctive humanistic personality of Bashu culture and Tianfu culture charm, and it has abundant resources and driving forces.

Section I Formation of Jianyang City Culture

Urban culture is the mainstream, popular, formed and stable values and lifestyle of a city. If it also has some good gifts and personality which are well inherited and promoted, they will become the "only immovable property" of the city. The Chinese love to discuss the ups and downs of important people, the rise and fall of important undertakings, and the emergence and disappearance of important phenomena from the perspective of time, location, and human conditions. Let's talk about the three factors in the formation of Jianyang's urban culture.

1. Time

We believe that the good climate for Jianyang's urban culture formation is the profound nourishment of the ancient Chinese culture, Bashu culture and Tianfu culture, and all kinds of political, economic, cultural, social and even ecological support required by successive dynasties to control the prosperity of the first city in the Southwest and for Chengdu and Sichuan to form and maintain the "Land of Abundance", as well as the immigration movement, disaster relief and tax relief activities that have helped Sichuan and Chengdu recover, develop and grow, with the government taking the leading role for many times in history. The unearthed cultural relics show that Jianyang had had exchanges with the main Chinese culture at least in the Western Zhou Dynasty, and there were military garrisons or military activities of the Shu State and the Qin and Han Dynasties, so there was a tradition of encouraging martial spirit, but also the mysterious and romantic tradition of Bashu culture and Tianfu culture continued. Li Bing's water control and Wenweng's culturing Shu are also the basis for the birth of Niubing County. Against the backdrop of the magnificent demand of the Han Dynasty to expand its territory, and the splendid cultural radiation of Chengdu's becoming a world-class great city (no doubt, during the reign of Emperor Wu of the Han Dynasty, China was a world-class power, and its "five capitals" were world-class cities), Niubing County came to the world, which also condensed and reflected the extraordinary leading power from the national and local governments. From the very beginning, in terms of administrative subordination and urban function orientation, it was subordinated to the general situation of the country, forming a fine personality of Jianyang urban culture.

2. Location

(1) Always have a large space

Jianyang has experienced the institutional changes of Niubing County, Wukang County, Yang'an County, Jianzhou County and Jianyang County in history. As a county and prefecture, Jianyang often governed 2-3 counties. Jianzhou in the Ming Dynasty also included the inspection department of Longquan Town and Ziyang Town. Only Jianzhou in the Qing Dynasty did not have any counties under its jurisdiction but included the inspection department of Longquan Town. Jianyang County has been a separate county since the Republic of China. Since the Qing Dynasty, Jianyang, without any counties under its jurisdiction, still has more than 2,500 square kilometers of space, which is a large county in the central and western Sichuan Basin. Even if Longquanyi District and Luodai District were later sectioned off, more than 2200 square kilometers still remain. Survival, reproduction, innovation and creation in a wider space, people can better move around, integrate resources, and gather strength. Of course, this is more conducive to the survival of cultural resources, the development of cultural activities, and the enrichment of cultural types. Today, most of the eight major cultures in Jianyang are related to the vastness of this space.

(2) Diversity and blending of beautiful natural and cultural sceneries

Jianyang is located at the golden north latitude of 30 degrees. The territory has plains, mountains, rivers, shallow hills and forests, especially the towering Longquan Mountain, the eastern barrier of Chengdu Plain, and the surging middle reaches of Tuojiang River. The territory is rich in animals, plants, crops, and diverse natural beauty. The eight sceneries of Jianzhou, the white pagoda of Shengde Temple, the Shi Pan Ti Ming Tower, the Hefeng word bank, numerous cliff stone carvings, the innumerable temples, halls and guilds of Confucianism, Buddhism and Taoism in history, the landscape of local gods and ancestor worship, and the inscriptions and calligraphy left by many celebrities in Jianyang are in an orderly blend with the natural landscape and urban and rural courtyards. After the completion of the East Irrigation(Dongguan) Project in the 1970s, the extensive water surface of Sancha Lake and Longquan Lake was formed, echoing Longquan Mountain from afar, forming a magnificent "two lakes and one mountain" landscape. Living in an environment with rich aesthetic feelings visually and psychologically is certainly conducive to cultivating people's love and yearning for truth, kindness and beauty, cultivating an optimistic, open-minded and positive attitude towards life, and even cultivating more intense and profound homesickness and family and country feelings. Celebrity culture, top scholar culture and mass culture are especially related to such resource endowments.

(3) Excellent geographical location

Jianyang adjoins Chengdu to the west (during the long history of Longquanyi and Luodai belonging to Jianyang, Jianyang was also directly adjacent to Chengdu on the plain) and connects with Neijiang and Chongqing in southern and eastern Sichuan through official and commercial roads (including water roads) to the east. Since the founding of New China, Chengdu Chongqing Railway, Chengdu Chongqing Expressway and Tianfu International Airport have been constructed successively. After returning to Chengdu, Jianyang has been incorporated into the transportation network of the metropolitan area. Whether it connects various high-quality resources in the Chengdu Plain, connects all parts of China, or goes global, it is a highland envied by other cities and counties. Different from the districts (cities) and counties of Chengdu to the west of Longquan Mountain, Jianyang not only can be nourished by Chengdu's economy and culture in many aspects, but also gain rich information and positive energy of people and property from the strong regions in eastern and southern Sichuan, and also radiate Jianyang's unique cultural charm to the surrounding world. Celebrity culture, commercial road culture and intangible cultural heritage are closely related to this.

3. Human conditions

In ancient and modern times Jianyang, the farming conditions are extremely superior, the people are simple and hardworking, and the handicraft industry practitioners are dexterous. From the Han Dynasty to the Song

Dynasty, the economic, cultural and social development of the Rang, Yi, Liao and other indigenous peoples who once lived on their land lagged behind the new ethnic group formed after the original Shu people and the Huaxia people mixed together. According to the literature, Rang, Yi, Liao and other indigenous peoples gradually left Jianyang later, but this process was very long, and there was no record of Han people bullying and driving these peoples away. In history, Jianyang, as long as it is a period of change of dynasties caused by peace and non-tyranny, has always been a hot land of relocation, cultivation and reading, poetry and etiquette, equal emphasis on both literature and martial arts, tolerance of culture and religious beliefs, people's watching and helping each other, and enthusiasm for public welfare. Jianyang's urban culture has been formed through the integration of local farming culture and friendly exchanges with Chengdu prefectural city and its counties and city officials and people. It keeps pace with the times and brings forth the new. In addition to the Longya culture, other cultures are closely related to the ancient and modern people in Jianyang. The Chinese language says "logical administration and harmonious people", in which "logical administration" mainly come from officials' thoughts and actions and "harmonious people" mainly come from the basic cultural qualities of ordinary people. The two are mutually causal and make each other. Since the Song Dynasty, Jianyang imperial examination had shown a good performance. One of the main reasons was that local officials paid attention to the cultivation of schools and folk education, forming a virtuous circle with the long-standing folk tradition of farming and reading in family, poetry and etiquette in family, and revitalizing family through imperial examination. Jianyang officials in the Qing Dynasty generally attached importance to school education, and many academies were helped by them and local gentry, which became the decisive basis for Jianyang to produce many successful candidates in the imperial examinations at the county, the provincial and the national level. The situation in the Song Dynasty should be better, because the author has studied the magistrates of Chengdu in the Song Dynasty, and almost without exception, they sincerely care about and support the educational activities with government schools as the main body and academies as the important support, so Jianyang had successfully produced four Number One Scholars (top scholars).

Section II Development of Jianyang City Culture

1. The Historical Veins of Jianyang Urban Culture

(1) Cultural Gene and Sources

1) The birthplace of Shu people, with its own mysterious and romantic qualities.

Jianyang area is one of the earliest places where human activities took place in Sichuan Basin. Found in Wushan County, Chongqing, there are 2.04 million years old Wushan people, belonging to the original Sichuan, but strictly speaking, this place does not belong to the Sichuan Basin. Therefore, there are only "Ziyang people" unearthed in the Tuojiang River valley of Ziyang and the Longya culture unearthed in Jianyang (about 20000 to 30000 years ago)[1]

---

[1] In view of the fact that the distance between the discovery of Ziyang people and Longya culture is only 40 kilometers, both near the Tuojiang River, some people believe that the fossils of ancient humans (female) found in Ziyang may have been impacted and moved by the flood from the upstream Longya site. Because the Longya site unearthed a wealth of late Paleolithic tools, even ornaments such as pendants, and animal fossils, including the teeth of stegodons which were hunted by humans, while the site of "Ziyang people" unearthed human skulls, but there was no animal skeleton fossil as well as trace of ancient human activity.

among the Paleolithic human remains in the Sichuan Basin, which shows that the natural geography and economic geography of Jianyang have been especially suitable for human survival and reproduction since ancient times. In the pre-Qin period, this place belonged to the ancient Shu State. At present, academic circles have different opinions on the situation of ethnic groups, political power and territory of the ancient Shu State, as well as their gathering and dispersion. However, the cultural relics unearthed at Sanxingdui and Jinsha sites show that the people of ancient Shu not only have a rich and colorful artistic pursuit and spiritual life of the integration of politics and religion, but also have common awe of gods and kingship and a rare imagination and aesthetic interest embodied in the grand sacrifices and the manufacture and production of romantic and exaggerated objects. This mysterious and romantic cultural gene has made Shu, especially Chengdu, the most active area in early Chinese mythology and fairy thinking. Later Taoism was born here, and its religious ideal of becoming an immortal after the death of its master should come from the reference to the myth and legend of the Five Ancestors of ancient Shu who became immortals after their death (even taking subjects at their side). Jianyang is also the birthplace of this romantic tradition (decorative pendants unearthed from Longya Culture are rare relics found in the Paleolithic Age). In Jianyang Museum, the bronze Lei with ox head and beast face in the Western Zhou Dynasty and the bronze Lei with multi ears and cover in the Warring States Period show that this area has had standard exchanges with the Central Plains Chinese regime from the Western Zhou Dynasty to the Warring States Period. This is a real rich and elegant life. However, the No. 3 sarcophagus of the Han Dynasty in the museum shows us the vivid and romantic spiritual world of Jianyang ancestors in the Han Dynasty—— The decorative patterns on the back and left and right sides of the sarcophagus vividly reflect the intersection of man and gods and the connection between life and death. People dance with totemic and symbolic animals (dragon, tiger, snake, turtle, lin, bird, horse). Among them, we can also see the worship of Fuxi and Nuwa (on the land surface of Jianyang, there is also the legend of Nuwa's footprints), and the myth and legend of people and animals (or their souls) floating up to heaven as immortals. They were even taken to the nether world to accompany the spirits who like such stories and beliefs. Later, the prosperity of Jianyang's literature and art became the deep foundation of the top scholar culture and celebrity culture, which had a long history of interaction with those mentioned above. Therefore, to tell the historical veins of Jianyang's urban culture, we must first start with its mysterious and romantic ancient genes.

2) Li Bing's water control and Wenweng's culturing Shu: A waterfront pavilion gets the moonlight first.

Jianyang belonged to Shu Prefecture in the Qin and Han Dynasties. Although it did not directly enjoy the benefits of irrigation brought by Li Bing's water control, it should benefit from the smoother and developed shipping after the water control, especially from the various information and resources radiated to Jianyang nearby after Chengdu Plain became a land of abundance with thousands of miles of fertile land. This is incomparable to ordinary prefectures and counties far away from Chengdu Plain. While Wenweng set up local official schools in Shu and harnessed the Jian River, Jianyang, like the waterfront pavilion, is among the first places to benefit from this. In a word, Jianyang benefited more from Li Bing's water control and Wenweng's culturing Shu than other prefectures and counties outside the big irrigation area, which was the earliest gene for Jianyang to become Tianfu Xiongzhou(strong region).

3) Military and public security sites, advocating heroes and not fearing

wars since ancient times.

No later than the Warring States Period, ethnic and political conflicts in Sichuan Basin became a common phenomenon. The Kaiming Dynasty established a large number of standing armies in the contest with the State of Ba and the State of Qin and as the "leader of barbarians living outside the northwest border" to quell internal disputes, with a special military and public security management layout. At that time, Jianyang, including Longquan Mountain, should be at least a military garrison and control stronghold. The Qin and Han Dynasties advocated military development, and this situation should continue. Among the representative cultural relics in Jianyang Museum, the weapons of various shapes in the Warring States Period and Han Dynasty are eye-catching; After Niubing County was set up, it belonged to Qianwei County, which controlled and pacified the southwest barbarians. These were direct or indirect evidences.

During the Qin and Han Dynasties, there were many wars inside and outside China. Sichuan Basin had many ethnic groups in the pre-Qin period. Chengdu, Shu Prefecture and Ba Prefecture also undertook the mission of controlling and sinicizing many ethnic groups (Sima Xiangru, Tang Meng envoyed to the southwest were typical cases). Conflicts are unavoidable. The main passes of Longquan Mountain had prominent military and public security attributes, and there were often garrisoned troops and soldiers. Therefore, the government could not ignore the governance of this area. This concern for war, military affairs and the army, and the admiration for heroes who defend the country and maintain peace have always been one of Jianyang's cultural genes. Therefore, Jianyang later worshiped both literature and martial arts. In modern times, Jianyang produced many generals and famous anti-Japanese people.

4) Once under Qianwei Prefecture, it is the base of national development

and advancement, with harmonious but different ethnic groups.

The mineral resources (except salt) in Jianyang area are quite scarce, but the conditions for men to farm and women to weave are very good, and the diverse landscapes and landforms make it extremely rich in animal, plant and crop varieties. The handicraft products that meet the general production and living needs can meet the local demand, and a little further, exchange, learn, draw lessons from and take advantage of the Chengdu industry and commerce as well as its market. Therefore, when Chengdu was almost free from large-scale wars at the turn of Qin and Han Dynasties, Li Bing and Wenweng managed the water, Wenweng promoted learning in Sichuan, the the demand for the Silk Road in the south and north and for the development of southwestern barbarian region rose rapidly, and Chengdu rose as one of the five major national cities in the Han Dynasty , Jianyang, as a city (Niubing County), was officially born in the national system (The local government office was located in ancient Niubing Town on the north bank of Jiangxi River in today's Jiancheng Town). However, the acceptance of Qianwei Prefecture (In 130 BC, the fifth year of Yuanguang, Emperor Wu of the Han Dynasty, it was set up because of the development of the southwestern barbarian region. Its government is located in the western part of Zunyi City, Guizhou Province today. At most, it has jurisdiction over 12 counties from Zizhong, south central Sichuan, north Guizhou and north Yunnan, with a total number of about 100000 households. Niubing's subordination to Qianwei Prefecture lasted until the Yonghe years, Emperor Mu in the Eastern Jin Dynasty: 345-357, spanning more than two centuries.)'s jurisdiction is an interesting but neglected clue, which can at least explain two points: First, Niubing County, which was close to Chengdu at that time, should be a military and political front stronghold of the Han Dynasty's armed forces that explored the southwest to the south and defended Chengdu to the north. Second, Niubing County should also be a place with relatively complex and diverse ethnic groups, yet historically, the ethnic groups here could always be harmonious. According to the evidence, after the destruction of Bashu by the Qin Dynasty, about 20000 people came with the Qin army and their families. It is estimated that the vast majority of them were stationed and lived in the Chengdu Plain, because the Chengdu Plain after Li Bing's water control was able to support them (except for the possible small-scale army stationed in Longquan Mountain - but no literature or cultural relics have shown this so far); Qin and Han Dynasties alternated, the world was seething, and the household registration was halved. However, there is no record of war and chaos in Chengdu Plain. Emperor Gaozu of Han was unable to help the people who were left in rags and hungry for food on the ruins of war, so he ordered them to "sell their children for a living and eat in the Shu Han". It is unknown how many of these people arrived in Shu Han, but even if they did, most of them must be in the most fertile areas where they can make a living, such as Hanzhong Plain and Chengdu Plain. It is difficult for them to reach Jianyang, west and south of Longquan Mountain; Then, many ethnic groups left over from the original Kaiming Dynasty would still be the majority of the population in Jianyang. The ethnic composition is relatively complex and diverse, which should also be an important factor for Niubing to be placed under the jurisdiction of Qianwei County. Otherwise, it would be strange not to be placed under the jurisdiction of Chengdu! It had been more than 200 years since it was subordinated to Qianwei County, which also shows that the above two factors have been playing an important role.

5) It is born of the strong Han Dynasty and the prosperity of Chengdu; For more than 2000 years, the prosperity and decline of Jianyang closely followed the fate of the country and Chengdu.

The birth of Niubing County, the earliest predecessor of Jianyang, contains most of the genes of Jianyang's cultural personality. In addition to the above four factors, it should be emphasized that it is the product of the Han Empire in the ascendant and the first great shock of Chinese civilization to the world. More prefectures and counties need to be set up to establish the period of political and military achievements. Chengdu, the center of Yizhou, became a super central city in China and even the world with the rise of the Han Dynasty, relying on such opportunities as relatively peaceful in the Qin and Han Dynasties, Li Bing's harnessing of the water, Wenweng's promoting of learning in Shu, the development of the Southwest barbarian region, and the opening of the North South Silk Roads. Chengdu had strong radiation (The unearthed cultural relics in Jianyang show the great influence of Chengdu.) and influence (Of course, this kind of communication was two-way. Niubing at that time could not have had no influence on Chengdu, but the imperial court set this influence as expanding, controlling and assimilating the southwest barbarians.) on surrounding areas. Jianyang was the result of such radiation and influence. In addition, under the system of prefectures and counties in the Qin and Han Dynasties, to create a county in a region, the imperial court could not make a decision by the emperor and the dukes and ministers suddenly opening their minds. Instead, it should listen to the opinions of the officials of the superior prefectures and counties, and even let the officials of the prefectures and counties take the lead in making a motion, reporting, discussing and making decisions level by level, so that a new county could be established. In this regard, the setting of Niubing should be based on the suggestions of the chief officials of Yizhou stationed in Chengdu and the officials of Qianwei County. The court under the leadership of Emperor Wu of the Han Dynasty had a special discussion and was decided by the emperor.

Niubing County is the product of the flourishing Han Empire, its wave of pioneering and enterprising, and the political wisdom of Shu officials.

Due to the attention of the court of the Han Dynasty, Niubing County covered a large area. During the Western Wei Dynasty (535-556), it turned into Wukang and Jinquan counties. In the last years of the Western Wei Dynasty (555), Wukang County was established, with Yang'an County and Porun County under its jurisdiction. In the Northern Zhou Dynasty, Baimou County was added to Wukang County (the county seat is now Jintang Chengxiang Town) and Jinquan County was abolished. In the third year of Renshou of Emperor Wen of the Sui Dynasty (603), Jianzhou was set up under the jurisdiction of Yizhou General Administration Office, which governed Yang'an, Pingquan and Ziyang counties. The prefecture government was still located in Yang'an. Emperor Yang of the Sui Dynasty came to power and revoked Jianzhou. Yang'an and Pingquan belonged to Shu Prefecture again, and Ziyang County belonged to Ziyang Prefecture again. In the third year of Wude (620) of Emperor Gaozu of the Tang Dynasty, Jianzhou was rebuilt and Yang'an, Pingquan and Jinshui counties were managed by it. In the first year of Tianbao(742) of Emperor Xuanzong, the national strength and household registration reached their peak, and Jianzhou was changed into Yang'an Prefecture. In the first year of Qianyuan (758) of Emperor Suzong, the Tang Dynasty, which was deeply involved in the hardships of the An Shi Rebellion, contracted politically and changed Yang'an Prefecture into Jianzhou. Jianzhou in the Tang Dynasty has always been subordinate to Jiannan Dao (Jiannan Dao was divided into East and West Chuan in 757, and Jianzhou belonged to West Chuan). During the Five Dynasties, Jianzhou was set up to manage Yang'an, Pingquan and Jinshui counties. In the Song Dynasty, Chinese cultural governance reached its peak, and Chengdu and Sichuan also reached the most brilliant period of urban civilization and regional culture. There were many registered households. The court built Jianzhou Yang'an County under the Chengdu government. However, due to the increasingly serious impact and encroachment of Liao, Jin and Mongolia, the jurisdiction area gradually changed from three counties to only Yang'an and Pingquan in the Southern Song Dynasty. The Yuan Dynasty was sparsely populated, and its political design and management were crude. In addition to the province, the local administrative agencies also had four levels of Lu, Fu, Prefecture and County. In the region which was the original Yang'an County, Jianzhou, in the Song Dynasty, Jianzhou was set up, which was subordinate to Chengdu Lu, Sichuan Province, with Lingquan Country under its jurisdiction. Yang'an County and Pingquan County under the former jurisdiction were merged into Jianzhou; Ziyang County, Zizhou, was abolished, and its territory was merged into Jianzhou. Before the eighth year of Zhengde, Emperor Wuzong of the Ming Dynasty (1513), Jian County was set up, and later, Jianzhou Prefecture was set up, all of which were under the jurisdiction of Chengdu Government. For a short time, the jurisdiction of Jianzhou Prefecture included Ziyang County, Lezhi County (1514—1522), Longquan Town Inspection Department and Ziyang Town Inspection Department. At the end of the Ming Dynasty and the beginning of the Qing Dynasty, the population of Sichuan was basically extinct, and Jianyang was no exception. Relying on Huguang to fill Sichuan, it recovered through difficulties. Jianyang's status declined further than that of the previous dynasty. In the Qing Dynasty, it was under the jurisdiction of Chengdu Prefecture, managing no counties but Longquan Town Inspection Department. In the Republic of China and the early period of New China, Jianyang region had a single Jianyang County, with many changes in administrative subordination, 1913—1935, which was subordinate to Xichuan

Dao in Sichuan Province (roughly equivalent to Chengdu Prefecture in the Qing Dynasty); From then on to 1949, it was subordinate to the Second Administrative Supervision District of Sichuan Province, of which the seat of local government was located in Zizhong County. From the founding of the People's Republic of China to 1985, Jianyang has been under the jurisdiction of Neijiang District (Neijiang District, Neijiang City) as an ordinary county. In 1994, Jianyang County was abolished and Jianyang City was established, which was directly under the provincial government and entrusted by the provincial government to Neijiang City. After 1998, it was entrusted by the Ziyang region and Ziyang City. In 1959 and 1976, Longquanyi District and Luodai District of Jianyang City were successively put under the jurisdiction of Chengdu. In May 2016, Chengdu, which has been established as a national central city, sought greater and better development. The State Council officially approved that Jianyang City would be managed by Chengdu. Integration into Chengdu would bring the best development opportunity in Jianyang's history, and the magnificent grand plan was slowly unfolding.

To sum up, three points can be summarized: First, Jianyang's rise and fall in history are completely synchronized with the fate of the nation and Chengdu. The Han Dynasty (including its brilliant reverberance - the Three Kingdoms), the Sui and Tang Dynasties, the Song Dynasty, the late Qing Dynasty and the early Republic of China, and more than 40 years after the reform and opening up, were the golden times for Chengdu to develop or show its strength. These periods are also the periods when Jianyang, because of its unique positive energy, has the highest or most valued position in the national administration. This close relationship with the country and Chengdu that they stand together through storm and stress and are bound together in a common cause has nurtured Jianyang people's deep feelings of family and country, and their cultural attachment to Chengdu. For example, Fu Chongju, the cultural giant of Sichuan in the late Qing Dynasty, was born in Jianyang and then moved to Chengdu. He lived as a Chengduese all his life. Second, Jianyang often has to make adjustments in its subordination, authority and scope of jurisdiction when the country is in trouble or in crisis. Obviously, the special location and historical context of Jianyang have been putting forward "difficulties" for Chengdu, Sichuan and even the country on how to face and settle Jianyang. The changing positioning of Jianyang's "identity" just proves that it has the potential to play the role required by a variety of countries and societies that ordinary counties and cities do not have. The foundation behind this is the diversity, plasticity and strong adaptability of Jianyang's culture. Third, since the formation of Jun, Zhou, Xian(county) system in 115 BC, Jianyang has been in a higher position than ordinary counties for most of the time, and has the status and influence of quasi prefectural city; Up till now, in the 2137-year history, it had been directly under Chengdu for about 1470 years, under Qianwei Prefecture for 465 years, and under Zizhong, Neijiang and Ziyang for 81 years in total. As Sichuan and Chengdu had experienced two mass extermination in the late Song Dynasty, the early Yuan Dynasty and the late Ming Dynasty and the early Qing Dynasty, what has the greatest impact on today's Jianyang, Chengdu and Sichuan cultures is the history created by immigrants in the late Ming Dynasty and early Qing Dynasty. Since the establishment of the Qing Dynasty in 1644, Jianyang had been under the jurisdiction of Chengdu Government for 275 years, and had been under the jurisdiction of Zizhong, Neijiang and Ziyang for only 81 years. Therefore, Jianyang's context and cultural subject belong to Chengdu, which can be expected to be the most distinctive and dynamic part of Chengdu in the future.

2. Modern Evolution of Jianyang City Culture

(1) The Culture of Jianyang in Modern Times

Since the Opium War in 1840, China has gradually fallen into the abyss of a semi colonial and semi feudal society under the impact of the strong ships and guns of the western powers who follow the law of the jungle, the commercial trade based on unequal treaties, and cultural exchanges. The Qing Dynasty itself was also plagued by age-old malpractices, and the reform was slow, which finally led to the Revolution of 1911. After the establishment of the Republic of China, the Northern Warlord regime and Chiang Kai Shek's Kuomintang regime did not represent the correct direction of China's development, as if plagued with chronic diseases and incurable diseases. Then there was the National Revolution and the great revolution led by the CPC to completely overthrow the old China oppressed by three mountains and establish an independent and free new China. All parts of China have been gradually brought into this historical process. As a part of the counties of Chengdu prefecture, which are located in the interior of China and have relatively backward transportation and information development, compared with the cities and villages of the same level along the rivers and coasts, except social unrest and that people's livelihood are not easy, western learning had spread to the east, foreign products, foreign trends of thought, and foreign customs appeared from time to time and had more and more similar impact on the middle and upper class society and the intellectual class, on the whole, for the vast majority of the people, Jianyang's economy was still dominated by agricultural life, supplemented by small-scale handicrafts, folk arts and active small and medium-sized commercial activities. The mainstream values were characterized by the worship of farming and reading, the worship of poetry and propriety, and the traditional five cardinal virtues — benevolence, justice, propriety, wisdom, and trust. In political life, the squires and the big families helped the government manage the society, and guided the folk cognition and fashion. The immigration culture, which originated from the Huguang Filling Sichuan Movement launched by Kangxi, is characterized by its diversity, guilds, mutual help, equal treatment, and Confucianism, Buddhism and Taoism mutually inclusive with various local deities and ancestor worship, forming the basic cultural ecology of Jianyang city and its countryside. Even in the period of the Republic of China, because of the late westernization, although in the early period the warlord separatist struggle pervaded (Jianyang had become the battlefield and been plundered many times) and the focus of the later period was on the War of Resistance against Japan and the Kuomintang and Communist dispute, the traditional culture of Jianyang was still relatively intact.

Under the influence of the traditional loyalty, filial piety, chastity and righteousness, family and country feelings, the tradition of advocating literature and martial arts, and the coming new trends of thought and political situations, a number of outstanding talents had emerged in Jianyang in the social transformation of modern Chengdu and Sichuan, in learning modern science and technology, in participating in the 1911 Revolution and revolutionary activities led by the Communist Party of China, in participating in the modern warlord armed disputes, in participating in the great Anti-Japanese War, as well as in cultural communication between China and foreign countries. Some have good international influence (Liu Zihua, Luo Shu). Some bravely stood at the forefront of the times and left behind merit and integrity to help the country, Sichuan and Chengdu progress in the form of revolution or improvement (Xia

Zhishi, Fu Chongju, Wu Xueqin, Dong Lang, Mao Quefei, Mao Kesheng, Peng Baoshan). Some joined the army and participated in the 1911 Revolution. They were also involved in warlord competition in the turbulent world, and even participated in the encirclement and suppression of the Red Army (all defeated by the Red Army) powerfully promoted by Chiang Kai shek, getting both praise and blame, but later, most of them were obliged to join in the War of Resistance against Japan and establish their achievements, becoming the leading figures in modern Sichuan (Liu Cunhou, Chen Dingxun, Wang Shangfang, Liao Zhen, Chen Liangji, Zeng Lie, etc.). In addition to the great achievements of the above celebrities in scientific research, literary and artistic creation and translation, social progress and the Red Revolution, and going through fire and water in the anti-Japanese battlefield, in 1944, more than 15000 Jianyang migrant workers, led by Huang Youfu, the county magistrate, and others, spent less than two months to complete the Pingquan Airport for the bombing of the Japanese by the Chinese and American air forces, relying mainly on manpower, day and night, with blood and sweat. This story is also a vivid expression of Jianyang people's patriotism and the humanistic spirit of being eager for justice and good will.

In a word, the cultural form and cultural change of Jianyang in modern times can be found in the cultural gene of Jianyang, which has lasted for nearly 2000 years. In the process of welcoming the revolution and improvement of modern Sichuan, Chengdu and their hometown, Jianyang's sons and daughters had a relatively harmonious cultural transformation and social development, and their outstanding humanistic spirit and tradition had not been lost. Therefore, at least a dozen people with great contributions to and influence on the country, Sichuan and Chengdu could emerge. Compared with its small economic strength and low political status, Jianyang can be called the cultural powerhouse of modern Sichuan and Chengdu. The core of this "power" is the values and outlook on life of family and country, attaching equal importance to literature and martial arts, and daring to be the first in the world.

(2) Modern Jianyang Culture

In modern China, the cause of revolution and construction has undergone an arduous and tortuous process of exploration. The historical mission of the Chinese nation to stand up has been completed by such undertakings as the War to Resist US Aggression and Aid Korea, the War to Resist US Aggression and Aid Vietnam, and the "Two Bombs and One Star"; The reform and opening up that started in 1978 found the right way to make the Chinese nation rich; Since the 18th National Congress of the Communist Party of China, the Republic has made extraordinary achievements on the road to becoming stronger. The cultural confidence and cultural soft power of China, Sichuan and Chengdu, which are based on the inheritance and promotion of China's excellent traditional culture, have grown unprecedentedly. In particular, through reform and opening up, Chengdu has formed its cultural ambition, cultural plan and cultural personality represented by Tianfu culture, its "post-modern temperament" with healthy economy, active culture and comfortable life as its connotation, and its widely praised "urban life aesthetics". The pursuit of Chengdu as a world famous cultural city has also been recognized by the central government and written into the planning outline of Chengdu Chongqing double city economic circle (Chongqing does not). Under such development process and era background, the main figures and events that reflect the vitality and individuality of urban culture and cultural inheritance and transformation from 1949 to 2022 are as follows:

1) Major events

(1) In 1950, at the expense of the lives of 163 teachers and students and school staff, Jianyang's army and people united bravely and quelled the armed riots caused by the remnants of the old regime, which is also an important chapter of Chengdu's revolutionary culture.

(2) The warm-blooded people enthusiastically devoted themselves to the War to Resist US Aggression and Aid Korea.

From 1950 to 1953, the War of Resistance against US Aggression and Aid Korea took place. The people of Jianyang actively responded to the call to defend their country. The warm-blooded people joined the army generously and participated in the majestic war of the Chinese nation standing "up" among the nations of the world. The number of applicants exceeded 15,000, including 120 women. After selection, 3,200 young people finally joined the Chinese People's Volunteer Army. By April 1953, there were more than 5,000 warriors in the county who went to Korea to fight, 57 of whom died honorably, and many heroes such as Xue Zhigao and Lai Wenlu emerged. In this great war, the people of Jianyang once again demonstrated their humanistic personality of advocating martial arts and heroes and made their own contributions.

(3) The East Irrigation (Dongguan) Project with a heroic spirit that conquers mountains and rivers.

In order to benefit future generations, in the early 1970s, 100,000 Jianyang cadres and masses bled and sweated for two years and five months to get through Longquan Mountain and establish supporting water storage and irrigation projects. They created a miracle of the East Irrigation(Dongguan) Project, extending the Dujiangyan irrigation area to Jianyang, leaving most of Jianyang to bid farewell to the history of water shortage. This has also formed the "East Irrigation (Dongguan) Spirit" that Jianyang people are proud of.

(See the monograph later)

(4) Since 2016, Jianyang has become a part of the jurisdiction of Chengdu again and has rapidly integrated into Chengdu in all aspects. Among them, the construction and operation of Tianfu International Airport and the establishment of the Eastern New District of Chengdu on about one-third of the land in the west of Jianyang City have brought about modernization, internationalization, globalization, and new concepts and requirements of material culture, institutional culture, and spiritual culture. Now, Jianyang is undergoing an unprecedented revolution in ideology, production, and lifestyle. "Tianfu Culture" has become the cultural attribution of Jianyang. The Municipal Party Committee and the Municipal Government keep pace with the times, fully connect the national, provincial and municipal development strategies of building a park city demonstration area, Chengdu Chongqing double city economic circle, world famous cultural city, "three cities and three capitals", metropolis circle, etc., and seek the best positioning and development path of Jianyang.

2) Key figures

(1) Zhou Keqin, winner of the first Maodun Literature Award

Zhou Keqin (1936—1990) was born in Shiqiao, Jianyang. He only went to a Chengdu Agricultural School equivalent to a technical secondary school, and had served as a teacher at a rural school and commune, as well as a storekeeper and accountant of a brigade and later part-time seed worker in Hongta District Office of Jianyang County. He was recruited as a commune cadre in 1978 and transferred to the county cultural center. He joined the Party in January of the next year. In March, he transferred to the provincial literary federation to engage in professional creation because he had published a collection of short stories, "Brothers and Sisters of the Stone Family". In August of that year, he completed a novel, *Xu Mao and His Daughters*, which describes the disaster brought by the ten years of turmoil to the farmers and their struggle and pursuit. It has a strong local color and local flavor, and the plot twists and turns and is alluring. From 1980 to 1981, his new "Not Forget Grass" and "The Mountain Moon Knows Nothing" won the National Excellent Short Story Award consecutively. n 1982, "Xu Mao and His Daughters" won the first Mao Dun Literature Award. In 1984, he moved to Chengdu and settled down. Later, he served as a leader of the Provincial Writers Association and edited "Modern Writers".

(2) National agricultural labor model Zhang Sizhou

Zhang Sizhou (1920-1980), a member of the Communist Party of China, was born in Qingfeng Town, Jianyang County. He was an expert in cotton planting. He took the initiative to set up a mutual aid group and a primary agricultural production cooperative and served as the person in charge. He once participated in the third Chinese people's condolences mission to the DPRK, visited the volunteer army in Korea, and participated in the Chinese agricultural overseas mission to visit Eastern Europe. He had won many honors and positions such as county's, special region's and Sichuan Province's model worker, representative of the National People's Congress, and commune president. He insisted on participating in production and labor for a long time and worked hard to learn to get rid of illiteracy. Later, he devoted himself to the introduction and cultivation of cotton and grain varieties and bred dozens of varieties. In 1968, he successively served as the deputy directors of the county, prefecture and provincial revolutionary committees successively, but was dismissed in 1969. He went to Beijing as a representative to attend the Ninth National Congress of the Communist Party of China and was elected as an alternate member of the Central Committee at the Ninth National Congress and the Tenth National Congress of the Communist Party of China.

(3) Two academicians: Ye Chaohui, born in March 1942, graduated from Peking University, once worked as a visiting scholar in the United States, physicist, director of Wuhan National Laboratory of Optoelectronics, and academician of the Chinese Academy of Sciences. Wei Fusheng, born in 1938, graduated from the University of Science and Technology of China. He is an environmental protection expert. He has successively served as the director of the General Office of China Environmental Monitoring Station, deputy director, chief engineer of China Environmental Monitoring Station, member of the Standing Committee of the National People's Congress, deputy director of the National Environmental Monitoring Special Committee, and an academician of the CAE Member.

In general, since the founding of the People's Republic of China, Jianyang's cultural development has shown a pattern of twists and turns, downward shift of focus, reduction of heavyweight celebrities, but an increase in events and practices embodying the group's humanistic spirit. It is related to the tortuous process of exploring socialist construction in New China, the distance and relationship between Chengdu and Jianyang, and the new development pattern Jianyang has faced in the past six years. Throughout the history of modern and contemporary Jianyang culture for more than 70 years, only Zhou Keqin and his works winning the prize, the East Irrigation(Dongguan) Project and its spirit which shocked people and attracted attention at home and abroad, and the new atmosphere and unlimited development prospects that Jianyang has gradually presented since its return to Chengdu are the heavyweight cultural phenomena that can lead to "yearning" and "looking up".The "Tianfu Xiongzhou" is coming back, but there is a long way to go. Jianyang must see its own gap (with other districts, cities and counties in Chengdu, and the gap with domestic excellent counties and cities). Especially after only six years of integration into Chengdu, many concepts and habits need to be clarified and even reshaped. The cadres and the masses need a broader and deeper consensus and empathy to make good use of resources, seize opportunities and create a new glory of Jianyang culture. The deep excavation and refinement of the eight cultures have irreplaceable and important value. Without insight into the past, how can we see the reality, and how can we look forward to and plan for the future? Isn't it the biggest waste to neglect and not to use well Jianyang's "only immovable property"?

3. Impact of population change

Throughout Jianyang's historical context and its evolution, the rise and fall of its culture, as well as the inheritance and enrichment of its personality, are largely related to population changes. The author is also the author of *Chengdu Biography* which combs the nine large-scale migration activities to the Sichuan Basin with Chengdu as the center in history. The impact of each migration on Chengdu is similar to that on Jianyang, but there are also some differences. Let me try to make a discussion:

(1) Partially assimilated by Qin

In 316 BC, Zhang Yi and Sima Cuo led a large army to destroy Shu and brought tens of thousands of Qin family members. The result was "Shu's partial assimilation by Qin", which was undoubtedly an important step for Chengdu to enter the Chinese civilization. The new Chengdu built by Zhang Yi and Zhang Ruo was constructed in a standardized way in strict accordance with the construction method of the city of Qin State. For the first time, Chengdu built the city wall (which was rammed in the past), using iron tools and brick and tile technology, which naturally made it more orderly, more solid, and more authoritative just like the Qin ruling center. In addition, the sub-regional central cities of Pi, Linqiong, Jiangzhou, Langzhong built by Zhang Ruo in the ruling areas of Shu Prefecture and Ba Prefecture also used new technologies and presented new climates. On such basis, during the Qin and Han Dynasties, "Chengdu, Guangdu and Xindu were the three capitals of Sichuan, and was named altogether as Ming city", which shows that it had become a "city cluster". The impact of this migration on Jianyang (Jianzhou) in history, a land adjacent to Chengdu, should be much the same. The State of Qin especially advocated farming and military exploits. There should be a small-scale Qin army stationed in Longquan Mountain. Such values and power allocation situation should have an important impact on the urban form of Niubing County in the Han Dynasty and the concept and lifestyle of its urban and rural people. In the Han Dynasty, Niubing County was under the jurisdiction of Qianwei Prefecture instead of Shu Prefecture, and it lasted for more than 300 years in the following dynasties, which should also be related to the influence of this immigration.

(2) Migration into Shu in Qin & Han Dynasties

Ying Zheng, the King of Qin (259—210 BC), exiled political enemy Lv Buwei (? —235 BC) and his affiliated relatives and friends into Sichuan, and Lv Buwei completed the writing of *The Spring and Autumn Annals of the Lv Family* (Sima Qian's *Bao Ren Shao'an Shu*: "Lu Buwei was exiled to Shu, so *the Spring and Autumn Annals of the Lu Family* was handed down."). Even according to the argument of some experts, this book was written before Lv Buwei entering Sichuan, which, however, brought people with top ideology and culture into

Sichuan. After the unification of the Qin Dynasty, the First Emperor of Qin had no confidence in whether the powerful people (such as nobles and merchants) among the adherents of the six countries in Shandong were loyal to the Qin Dynasty. He decided to forcibly migrate them from their original places of residence to other places, so "the roads of Bashu are dangerous, and all the people who migrated from the Qin Dynasty live in Sichuan" (*Historical Records — Xiang Yu's History*). For example, Zhuo Wang Sun and Cheng Zheng, the great iron and steel kings, were originally rich in Shandong (formerly Qi). This group brought into Sichuan advanced technology and management, as well as private capital. In the early years of Emperor Gaozu of the Han Dynasty, people were ordered to eat in the Shu Han, which at least added labor force to Sichuan and Chengdu.

The above two types of migrations promoted the great development of commodity economy in Sichuan. Chengdu became one of the five powerful capitals of the Han Dynasty, not only dominating the southwest, its commodities and fu even speaking for the Chinese civilization of the time. The trend of "giving people enough to live in, and valuing wealth "pervaded. It was a symbol of success in life by riding high chariots and horses, wearing royally beautiful robes, holding extravagant weddings and funerals, and singing, dancing, hunting, and gathering with families and friends. Sima Xiangru couldn't avoid this. His heroic words when he left Sima Bridge to Chang'an became one of the labels for Chengdu's mainstream society to express confidence, to strive to gain imperial fame through talent and enjoy a happy life (including spiritual life) in the Han Dynasty.

From the time point of view, this migration also took place before the emergence of Niubing County. Its impact on Niubing County should be similar to that of other regions in Chengdu. This migration enhanced the sense of unity of officials and people here, further integrated the local ethnic groups and the Chinese ethnic groups from the Yellow River basin, and increased the sense of community with a shared future.

(3) Badi refugees entering Sichuan

At the end of the Western Jin Dynasty, when the imperial court was divided against each other, Zhao Xin (? —301), the governor of Yizhou, lost power and was about to be transferred from Chengdu. Knowing that he had a bad future after returning to the capital, he decided to take advantage of the Badi refugees who had entered Sichuan (There was drought in Guanzhong at that time and famine in successive years, more than 100000 people of Han, Di, Qiang, Mi and other ethnic groups from six prefectures flowed into the Bashu area through Hanchuan for food. The local government did not welcome them to Sichuan.) to form his own forces to fight against the imperial court, so he recruited Li Te, the leader of refugees, in the name of the government, to send Li Xiang, Li Te's third brother, to lead a detachment of civilians into Chengdu. They set an ambush and cooperated to trap and kill Geng Teng, the representative of the imperial court. Later, Zhao Xin took over the Chengdu army of the Western Jin Dynasty and killed Li Xiang to frighten Li Te. Unexpectedly, Li Te led the refugee army to counterattack Chengdu from Mianzhu, his base area, to kill Zhao Xin and conquer Chengdu. Previously, the refugees had lived in hardships in Sichuan for two years and had accumulated grievances for a long time, so they killed officials and burned and looted Chengdu. Later, the imperial court sent Luo Shang, the general of the western expedition, to suppress Li Te. Li Te was killed because he was arrogant and belittled the enemy. However, Luo Shang was cruel to people. People in Chengdu had a song saying, "Li Te is OK, Luo Shang is killing me!", so Li Te's younger brother Li Liu and his son Li

Xiong continued to fight. One year later, Luo Shang was defeated and fled to Guanzhong, and Li Xiong was called the King of Chengdu; Two years later, in 304 AD, he established Dacheng State. Because of the extravagance and cruelty of future generations, the Dacheng State owned by Li Xiong was destroyed by the Eastern Jin Dynasty in 347 years after more than 30 years of protecting the territory and the people. This time, immigrants entered Sichuan in order to find a way to live. At first, the political situation was turbulent, refugees overwhelmed with numerical strength, and the local officials were powerless to stop them. But they entering Chengdu was the result of the local officials' ulterior motives. As for the subsequent evolution of the situation and its impact on Sichuan and Chengdu, it is difficult to say in a word, but there had been lessons learned from how to deal with the ethnic minority immigrants entering Sichuan and Chengdu.

This immigration activity is called in history the first alien regime established by the "Five Hu" who disturbed China. It is the only immigration activity with negative energy greater than positive energy in the history of many times of immigrants in Sichuan, mainly in western Sichuan, because of the great ethnic differences and estrangement, which led to large-scale wars. The impact on Niubing County should be the same. Although the population and property loss of Niubing County should be less than that of Chengdu, because the main battlefield for power and resources is not Niubing County, nor Qianwei Prefecture. The economy and culture of Niubing in this troubled time has nothing good to report.

(4) Two Emperors of the Tang Dynasty took refuge in Sichuan

Two emperors of the Tang Dynasty, Emperor Xuanzong (685—762) and Emperor Xizong (873—888) of the Tang Dynasty, fled to Chengdu successively because of the An Shi Rebellion (755—783) and Huang Chao (820-884) attacking Chang An. When the two groups of monarchs and ministers and their affiliated population entered Sichuan, there were thousands of them. As for the time of "staying in Chengdu", Xuanzong spent one year (756—757) and Xizong spent four years (881—885). A large number of imperial nobles, scholars and even eminent monks entered Sichuan. Although this was a painful note in the decline of the empire, it objectively brought about the infiltration and integration of elegant culture. Up till now, people in Chengdu and Sichuan recall that the two kings came to Sichuan for refuge, especially when talking about the related relics, such as Daci Temple, Baoguang Temple, Tianhui Town, Qingyang Palace, etc., they are still beaming with joy and feeling similar to Li Bai's feelings in "the Song of the Emperor's Visit to Nanjing in the West".

The immigrants accompanying the two emperors, especially Xizong of the Tang Dynasty, were mostly nobles, so they had a great influence on Chengdu and Sichuan. It is recorded in history that during the reign (903—918) of Wang Jian (847—918), the Former Shu emperor, "most of the nobles of the Tang Dynasty took refuge in Shu. The emperor treated them with courtesy and allowed them to participate in political affairs, so the system and cultural relics had the legacy of the Tang Dynasty". Today, when visiting the Yong Mausoleum Museum where Wang Jian "sleeps" for a long time, we can see the royal band composed of 24 beautiful women who use 21 kinds of musical instruments, and we can feel the elegant culture of the Tang Dynasty in the imperial life.

For Jianzhou, which had been under the jurisdiction of Chengdu (Yizhou, Shu Prefecture, Jiannan Dao), Tang Dynasty immigrants should also play a role in increasing population and fine cultural resources. So until the end of the Tang Dynasty and the reign of the Former Shu and Later Shu around the Five Dynasties, although the Sichuan Basin experienced several wars, including the cost of Wei Gao's brilliant military achievements, there was no change in the jurisdiction of Jianzhou over the three counties and the county seat. Wei Gao left a monument in Jianyang, which should be related to factors like Jianyang's ability to support the war and Jianyang's restoration as Niubing County in Qianwei Prefecture during his military campaign.

(5) "Huguang Filling Sichuan" in the Great Xia Regime

The Yuan Dynasty was a low point in the history of Sichuan and Chengdu, because at the time of the Song and Yuan Dynasties, Sichuan soldiers and civilians fought a very solemn and stirring war of resistance for half a century, and the population was exhausted. Although the Yuan Dynasty had 90 years, due to the brutal rule, Sichuan people were the lowest "southerners" under the four-class system, and the population growth was extremely slow. According to the research of Professor Li Shiping of Sichuan University, the total population of Sichuan was less than 800,000 at the end of the Yuan Dynasty, of which only about 200,000 people lived in Chongqing Lu and Kui Lu in Bayu region. The capital of the Daxia regime was located in Chongqing, so during the reign of Ming Yuzhen (1329—1366), in order to increase the national strength, in addition to leading the majority of Hubei soldiers and their families to Sichuan, he also recruited people from Hubei, Jiangxi and other places to Sichuan at least twice. According to statistics, in total about 400,000 people had been added to Sichuan, two thirds of whom were resettled in the Ba Yu area, where the population was particularly sparse. Among the immigrants, those from Hubei were the majority, and mainly from Huangzhou and Macheng; 112 of the 214 surnames in the statistics were from Hubei, accounting for 52.3% of the total 214, more than half. Thus, the prelude of "Huguang Filling Sichuan" was played. After the Ming Dynasty unified Sichuan, although some military immigrants were later transferred to other places, many remained. These immigrants prepared the geographical basis for the Ming and Qing Dynasties, especially the great migration in Qing Dynasty.

This time, the number of immigrants coming to western Sichuan is not very large, and the number of people coming to Jianzhou should be very small (only 30 surnames and 86 households came to Jianzhou later in Hongwu Period). At that time, there was only Lingquan County under Jianzhou. The Yuan Dynasty was mainly established on the basis of barbaric military conquest, implemented a four class system, had a crude political design, had many short-lived and incompetent emperors, and had corruption of officials early on. This led to a low point in the history of Sichuan and Chengdu, of which the economy and culture were far behind those of the Han Dynasty and the Tang and Song Dynasties. This downturn also restricted the occurrence of large-scale migration. Jianzhou experienced the same situation.

(6) "Huguang Filling Sichuan" in the Late Ming and Early Qing Dynasties

At the end of the Ming Dynasty and the beginning of the Qing Dynasty, the Chinese scholar bureaucrats and the people in war-torn areas experienced a change of ownership and psychological upheaval as though Heaven and Earth had fallen. With Zhang Xianzhong as the main force and other forces (including the Qing army, Li Zicheng, the Ming army, the bandits' "Yao Huang Zei", the forces supporting Wu Sangui's rebellion, etc.) as the auxiliary, based on the needs of political and military struggle, as well as various massacres to vent all kinds of private anger and abnormal psychology, plus plague and natural disasters, Sichuan's population was once again on the verge of extinction. The city of Chengdu was completely destroyed and its population was wiped out. Therefore, after Emperor Kangxi (1654—1722) pacified Wu

Sangui's rebellion, the court organized large-scale migration from surrounding provinces and regions of Sichuan to Sichuan, and Chengdu Plain became the core area for immigrants to fill and took the lead in recovery. For this migration, the government had promoted the officials in rank who persuaded the immigrants to enter Sichuan and properly resettled them, tried to provide management and care for the people along the way to Sichuan, let the people who had settled down occupy the land as they could, and provided temporary relief in production and life and tax relief for several years in the initial stage. In addition, in case of major natural and manmade disasters, tax relief was also available. After the gradual recovery of the economy, Sichuan became the easiest region to earn a living in all parts of China. For example, the author studied the rice prices in several major production regions of China in the Qing Dynasty (Jiangsu and Zhejiang, Hunan and Guangdong, Sichuan). For at least 100 years, the food prices in Chengdu were the lowest. This time, Huguang filling Sichuan included three consecutive periods of Kangxi, Yongzheng and Qianlong, which lasted for at least 120 years. People from more than 18 provinces across China, by the light of the moon and the stars and bringing along the old and the young, came to this new field to blaze a trail, pioneer in the mountains and build new homes. They not only inherited the cultural tradition and spiritual lifeblood of Bashu as a whole, but also brought the excellent cultures of various regions to Sichuan Basin for collision, exchange, and integration, forming a cultural value and aesthetic pursuit full of civilian feelings represented by Sichuan cuisine, Sichuan wine, Sichuan opera, Sichuan dialect, Zhuzhi Ci, and Sichuan voiceless sound. Because immigrants were all common people, and there was no cultural and identity discrimination in their earliest cultural genes of getting along with each other. Later, it was difficult for gradually rich families to have the kind of cultural and identity arrogance based on blood relationship. Even if some people showed signs of such arrogance, it was also difficult to get widespread recognition and respect. Popularization and the peaceful coexistence of Confucianism, Buddhism and Taoism in Chengdu and Sichuan had further strengthened the openness and inclusiveness of Bashu culture. As for why beautiful women and handsome men were in large numbers in Chengdu and Sichuan, biological and genetic evidence could also be found in the marriage of immigrants from 18 provinces.

Jianyang's situation was almost the same as above, and the immigrant culture had far-reaching influence. Because the livelihood of Jianyang was more difficult than that of Chengdu Plain, but better than that of most other prefectures and counties in Sichuan, and it was directly adjacent to Huayang County, Chengdu, Jianyang culture had a more prominent civilian character, and its people were more diligent and active in farming and reading. It can be seen from the folk customs of Jianyang in the Qing Dynasty, the grassroots and simple nature of intangible cultural heritage, the extensive establishment of private schools and academies, the loud and clear voice of book-reading, and the advocacy of imperial examinations. Luodai, a Hakka cultural stronghold (guild hall), was also a part of Jianyang at that time. Jianyang's Yingdi Lotus Pond and Naming Pagoda, together with the rare in Sichuan and magnificent and diverse character library tower, also tell us that Jianyang is similar to Chengdu in endowment and common destiny, but it also has its own good personality in some aspects (such as martial arts worship, being particularly industrious and simple, valuing reading and imperial examination, Hakka culture concentration, and women taking more responsibilities inside and outside the family).

(7) A Gathering Place of Elites During the War of Resistance Against Japan

In 1937, the "July 7th Incident" broke out, and the Chinese nation started the comprehensive national defense war against the arrogant and cruel Japanese fascists. The National Government moved its capital to Chongqing. China's most important industrial and mining enterprises, academic and cultural institutions, and national elites represented by university teachers and students, scientists, engineers and technicians, and various literary and artistic masters came to Sichuan and gathered in Chengdu and Chongqing. Most of them had spent years of hard time in Chengdu, Chongqing, and Sichuan, and had been supported and treated kindly by Sichuan's army and people who had lived and died together and shared weal and woe. This period was the warmest and most seamless connection and integration of Bashu culture and national axial culture. After the victory of the War of Resistance Against Japan, both the Kuomintang and the Communist Party have made high profile announcements to thank Sichuan and the people of Sichuan for their great contributions. Many modern celebrities were filled with unforgettable warm memories of their time in Sichuan, and Chengdu and Sichuan people are also proud of this history. Today, the Anti-Japanese War Relics Museum in Chongqing, the Jianchuan Museum in Dayi, Chengdu, and the Yibin Lizhuang on the Yangtze River have recorded the anti-Japanese war life in the minds of Sichuan people, as well as the martyrs and heroes they revere, which have become the spiritual landmarks of these cities. In addition, the international friendship established by Sichuan people during the War of Resistance against Japanese Aggression with soldiers, politicians, diplomats, journalists, academics, cultural and educational exchange personnel from anti-fascist countries has also become the common wealth and heritage of human urban civilization. This has helped Sichuan, especially Chongqing and Chengdu, greatly improve the level of internationalization.

During the Anti-Japanese War, with the arrival of a large number of immigrants, Chengdu's industry and commerce also took a leap. According to the statistics in the mid-1940s, there were 28480 stores in the urban area of Chengdu, a net increase of 15167 compared with that before the War of Resistance Against Japan. A prosperous commercial downtown has been formed with Chunxi Road as the center, Zongfu Street and Tidu Street in the north, and East Street in the south. Finance and real estate also were unprecedentedly active. Take Chunxi Road as an example. In the middle of the War of Resistance against Japan, land prices soared to a very high point. For a single room shop, the rent was as high as tens to one hundred taels of gold.

Migration to Sichuan during the Anti Japanese War certainly added resources to Jianyang. However, Jianyang, which was not easily accessible at that time, had limited attraction and far less impact than the Chengdu Plain, because high-quality people and property were more concentrated in the plains dominated by Huaxi Ba and in Lizhuang, Yibin, which was safer from Japanese bombing. However, because of the unprecedented business of commercial roads (including waterways) and post roads, the construction of Pingquan Airport, and the latest international and domestic information sent back by relatives and friends in Chengdu, including the repeated bombing of Chengdu by Japanese aggressors, the ups and downs of the fate of the Chinese Air Force, and the story between Song Meiling and Jianyang Big Ear Sheep, the people of Jianyang also got rich positive energy generated by this immigration. The vision, knowledge and ideas of Jianyang officials and civilians had been comprehensively impacted and improved.

(8) Third-line Construction Ushers in Industrialization and Population

The third line construction refers to a large-scale construction of national defense, science and technology, industry and transportation infrastructure

197

in 13 provinces and autonomous regions in central and western China from 1964 to 1980 with the guiding ideology of war preparedness. These regions are located in the strategic rear area of the war with the United States and the Soviet Union, so they are called "the third line". The background is the Sino Soviet hostility, the Soviet Union stationing millions of troops on the Sino Soviet border, and the war clamors and threats from the United States from time to time (including repeated nuclear blackmail from the United States and the Soviet Union against China).

The central government invested a huge amount of 205.268 billion yuan, accounting for 40% of the country's total investment in capital construction in the same period; Four million workers, cadres, intellectuals, soldiers of the People's Liberation Army and tens of millions of migrant workers, under the call of Chairman Mao to "prepare for war, prepare for famine, and serve the people" and "well men and well horses head to the third line for construction", crossed mountains and rivers, entered the deep mountains and valleys, desert and wilderness in the great southwest and northwest, slept in the open air, shouldered heavy objects, and built more than 1100 large and medium-sized industrial and mining enterprises, scientific research institutions, and colleges and universities with hard work, sweat and life. During 1964-1980, the state approved more than 1100 medium and large construction projects. There were many new and large-scale projects in Guizhou, the mountainous area in the east of Sichuan, the plain area in the middle of Sichuan, Hanzhong, the northern foot of the Qinling Mountains and other regions. A large number of industrial people had moved in. Among them, Sichuan Chengdu mainly received light industry and electronics industry, Mianyang and Guangyuan received nuclear industry and electronics industry, and Chongqing was a conventional weaponry manufacturing base. After the third line construction, a large number of ancient cities and towns, such as Chengdu, Chongqing, Xi'an, Lanzhou, Guiyang, Anshun, Zunyi, had been industrialized for the first time, bringing them closer to the eastern cities. Millions of builders had sacrificed their youth, sweat and even precious lives in these places, making China one of the few countries in the world with a complete national economic system and an independent national defense production system, despite its low per capita income, when the reform and opening up began in 1978.

In this historical period, hundreds of thousands of scientific and technological workers, engineering technicians and excellent industrial workers from developed cities in the east had been accepted, and their integrity, rigorous scientific spirit, selfless struggle consciousness, management culture of modern large enterprises, and supreme craftsmanship of great countries had been accepted. Therefore, the humanistic personality of Chengdu and Sichuan people had undoubtedly added an extremely important new connotation that was in line with the development of the times.

Although Jianyang had not become a key area and city in the third line construction (perhaps because it did not belong to Chengdu), it had also received solid benefits. According to the population records in *Jianyang County Annals*, after the founding of the People's Republic of China, from 1953 to 1985, there were 669,262 people moved in (664,733 people moved out in the same period, basically the same), with an average annual population of 20,883. From 1958 to 1960, a total of 100,856 people moved in, with an annual average of 33,619 people, which is a peak of migration, especially in 1958, which reached 50,967 people. A total of 75,290 people moved in from 1975 to 1977, with an annual average of 25,096 people, which was another peak period. The immigrants in the 1950s were mainly military and southward cadres, provincial cadres transferred to Jianyang, and those who came to Jianyang because of marriage or coming to live with relatives. In the middle and late 1960s, the country strengthened the construction of the third line in southwest China, and a number of industrial, mining and enterprise populations successively moved into Jianyang. As for the reasons for the outflow of population, they are mainly marriage, employment, border support, college entrance, military participation, etc. According to the industrial records in *Jianyang County Annals*, from 1965 to the mid-1970s, there was a great increase in state-owned industries domestically, and factories belonging to the "third line" were moved into Jianyang, and a total of eight were built and put into operation. By 1985, they had 10,268 cadres and workers, and their product sales revenue was 109,652,000 yuan, accounting for 56.2% of the independent accounting state-owned industrial enterprises in the county; The tax revenue provided was 9.109 million, accounting for 55.44% of the independent accounting state-owned industrial enterprises in the county. They not only strongly supported the local economy and drove the enthusiasm of Jianyang County to host state-owned enterprises, but more importantly, they showed the flavor, concept and style of modern industrial civilization of new China to the people of Jianyang. In addition, without the technology, knowledge and skills intensive population (including their families and children) provided by these third line construction factories, and the improved economic and spiritual life of Jianyang, many indicators of population flow in and out of Jianyang would be much worse, and the city and regional image of Jianyang would also be far behind.

(9) The City of Happiness Attracted a Large Number of New Immigrants during Reform and Opening-up

In 1978, China's reform and opening up opened the curtain with Deng Xiaoping (1904—1997) from Guang'an, Sichuan Province, as the chief designer. So far, China has achieved great take-off and peaceful rise. Chengdu and Sichuan have also achieved historic leaps. In 1993, Chongqing became a municipality directly under the Central Government. Half of the space belonging to the Ba cultural circle and most of the economic and cultural resources in the former east Sichuan Province were allocated to Chongqing. The historical narrative of the new Sichuan began from then on.

In any case, Chengdu's status as the first city of old Sichuan and new Sichuan has not changed, but its administrative status and respective missions with Chongqing, the twin star of Bashu culture, have presented a new pattern. In general, Chengdu is the main destination for immigrants from other provinces and even international friends to enter Sichuan during this period, and the destination for immigrants between regions in the province is mostly Chengdu (especially after Chongqing is directly under the jurisdiction of the Central Government). The main charms of Chengdu to attract immigrants are: it has a unique natural and cultural environment, its own unique "life aesthetics" and natural post-modern temperament; It has the highest happiness index in China for 12 consecutive years; Its urban and rural planning and infrastructure construction are good; Extremely convenient transportation and communication, synchronous growth of hard power and soft power; Build a world famous cultural city with the construction of "three cities and three capitals"; Various policies and measures to attract talents. These are core competitiveness that cannot be ignored. The solid action of "inheriting the Bashu civilization and developing the Tianfu culture" is continuously injecting new momentum for it to take root in history, care for reality and lead the future. Chengdu, Sichuan, will surely become one of the leading cities on the road of competing for national and global outstanding immigrants.

It is a pity that Jianyang did not belong to Chengdu in the first 38 years of the 44 years of reform and opening up, so it received less demographic dividend than other districts (cities) and counties in Chengdu. The economic and cultural vitality increased by the continuous inflow of high-end and high-quality population naturally lags behind. For example, the modern and international vision required to compete with domestic and international first-class cities, the high-end and sophisticated communication awareness required for constructing landscape, scene and brand, the concept of regarding talents and efficiency as the soul of development, the awareness of rule of law and citizen behavior norms, the optimization of business environment, the urban and rural planning and integration of high-quality preservation of urban context and charm, and the discovery and optimization of the unique life aesthetics of the city under the guidance of "Tianfu Culture", all have deficiencies in one way or another. It has become the consensus and action of Jianyang Municipal Party Committee, the municipal government and the people of the city to belong to Chengdu administratively, to integrate its development into Chengdu, to fully integrate into Chengdu spiritually, but also to build up the cultural personality of "Tianfu Xiongzhou" and to establish full cultural confidence and cultural pride. Accurate urban positioning, broad development prospects, clear development paths, and urban ecology suitable for work and living are also the confidence and guarantee for Jianyang to re-realize the positive interaction between population migration and its own development.

Finally, summarize my theoretical thinking. Generally speaking, the trend of population change conducive to cultural development is: it is better to increase the total population than to decrease it, because it means that its material civilization, institutional civilization, spiritual civilization and even ecological civilization form a strong bearing capacity for human happy life; The more tolerant of more ethnic groups, the better, because it means that the culture here is open and inclusive, and respects individuality; The longer the average years of education and the higher the level, the better, because this means that the number of people who can engage in cultural activities is large, and the market potential for consuming cultural products and services is large; The younger the average age is, the better, because culture should be innovative, and culture is not only a career, but also an industry, the latter needs young people's vitality and courage; The more freely flowing in and out, the better, because this means that it is possible to hybridize multiple cultural genes, the offspring must be stronger, and the new fruit must be sweeter; The less discrimination between old and new residents and residents of different classes, the better, because the entrenched class estrangement, as well as the self-righteous or arrogant as support for discrimination, have always been the enemies of "people with virtue and culture"; The closer the ratio of men and women is, the better. In such cities, because people's basic desires are met, there are the least people who are perverse, violent or even abnormal. Only religious philosophy and literary and artistic activities based on the balance of yin and yang, which have the broadest human sympathy and usually have a sense of happiness over bitterness, can naturally flourish, and thus people can generally find out and taste from the various spiritual lives, literature and arts presented by the official, civil, individual organizations the beauty and happiness. In addition, attracting important external cultural and artistic figures to visit, stay and stop, or even leave literary and artistic works and praise because they like, appreciate and love the place, is an indicator reflecting whether the city's culture has charm or not, and how much charm. From the last indicator, Jianyang has many top scholars and celebrities (including celebrities produced here; celebrities who use this place as an activity stage; and celebrities who left poems, songs, calligraphy, painting, and even films and TV works praising this city because of its beautiful and diverse landscapes. Its relics should be protected, restored or rebuilt as much as possible), and there are many cultural landscapes of the three religions and immigrants, the unique charm of featured food (such as Jianyang's "Nine Wonders of Food and Beverage") and custom festivals (such as Jianyang's intangible cultural heritage activities, several festivals being created with great efforts integrating commerce, tourism, entertainment and local scenery display), together with the official and commercial roads connecting western and eastern Sichuan, all are quite outstanding. The so-called "the first prefecture to come to Sichuan from the east", "the most suitable place to visit in Sichuan is Jian prefecture" and "the east gate of Chengdu" are not empty reputations, but the collective memory of many scholars in history. Among them, Xue Tao's "Rewarding Guo to Send Oranges from Jianzhou" and "Jiangyue Tower" are the most famous. The pleasure felt by the beautiful poetess when she received the delicious oranges sent by the officer surnamed Guo of Jianyang, and the beautiful scenery she saw when she visited Jianzhou and boarded the Jiangyue Tower, a famous scenic spot in Jianyang, and the admiration that can be compared with seeing the beauty of regions south of the Yangtze River, are all vivid records of the charm and happiness of Jianyang in the Tang Dynasty.

CHAPTER III

Cultural Connotation of Jianyang City

Section I Longya Culture

1. Excavation of Longya Site

At the end of April 2010, when building houses in Longya Village, Jiancheng Town, Jianyang City, villagers found two ivory incisors, the long one about 3.15 meters long. In the subsequent field survey, it was found that the site was accompanied by hand-made stone products, which was initially presumed to be a Paleolithic site. From July to September 2010, Sichuan Institute of Cultural Relics and Archaeology, together with Jianyang Cultural Relics Administrative Office, carried out rescue excavation of the site, with the actual excavation area of 87 square meters. The site is located on the gentle slope terrace of Kangjia River, the second tributary of Tuojiang River, with a height of about 398m. The current surface is fruit forest and seasonal crops. The excavation process was in strict accordance with the field archaeology regulations. The excavation was carried out from the north to the top and then to the bottom, from late to early. To the cultural layer where animal fossils and stone products are buried, the site was divided into squares of 1×1 square meter, and 10 cm was taken as a layer. The excavation was carried out horizontally downward, and the excavation coordinates of the specimens were accurately recorded. Archaeologists surveyed and mapped the burial status of some specimens, used the water sieve method to collect small specimens, and collected some early soil samples. The stratum accumulation of Longya Site is divided into five layers from top to bottom, of which the fourth layer is the Paleolithic cultural accumulation layer. Mainly animal skeleton fossils, stone products and decorations were unearthed at the Longya Site. More than 180 mammalian bones, teeth and horns, as well as thousands of animal bone fragments, were unearthed in the excavation area. These fossils are no less than 6 genera and 15 species, mainly including oriental stegodon, Chinese rhinoceros, deer, cattle, sheep, pigs, badgers and bamboo rats. According to the preliminary arrangement of bone fossils (according to the mandible), it is known that there were at least 3 oriental stegodons. There are dents of different sizes on the surface of some bones, which may be hit or scraped. More than 3,000 pieces of gravels were unearthed at the Longya Site, including more than 700 pieces of stone products, most of which were made of fairly good quartz sandstone gravels, reflecting the traditional characteristics of the gravel industry in the south. The unearthed stone products mainly include stone cores, stone chips, chopping tools, adze tools, scrapers, pointed tools and stone balls.

There are also three ornaments unearthed at the Longya Site, one of which is made of animal bone, and the other two are made of mammalian molars. The perforation technology is a two-way drilling method. The hole diameter at both ends is slightly larger than the middle part, and the hole diameter is about

1.5-2 mm. The drill hole for hanging of animal skeleton is located in the thin position in the middle of the skeleton, and the drill hole for hanging of tooth is located in the root of the tooth. The teeth would be trimmed and thinned before drilling to facilitate drilling. The cultural layers of human activities in the Paleolithic Age of the Longya Site cannot be layered, and the horizontal bedding of rivers and lakes cannot be seen in the buried deposits. A large number of stone products are slightly weathered and abraded. Animal skeleton fossils are scattered in the excavation area, and there is no sign of fixed direction arrangement. It is speculated that the stone products and animal skeleton fossils of the site may not have been exposed for a long time or transported from a long distance before burial.

The stone products of Longya Site are mainly large gravel stone tools, accompanied by many kinds of animal fossils such as oriental stegodons and giant panda fauna. At the same time, drilling technology which may be in the late Paleolithic age, was discovered. The Longya Site is located in the Tuojiang River basin. The famous "Ziyang people" were found in the eel creek more than 30 kilometers downstream of the site. The cultural features and nature of the two are relatively consistent. The excavation has added new data for exploring the early human culture in the Tuojiang River basin. At the same time, the scientific excavation of ancient geology and topographic feature is also helpful to summarize the investigation methods of early culture in hilly areas. At the later stage of the excavation, Sichuan Provincial Academy of Arts and Culture invited relevant scholars from the Institute of Vertebrate Paleontology and Paleoanthropology of the Chinese Academy of Sciences, Sichuan University, Chengdu Institute of Cultural Relics and Archaeology and other institutions to hold an expert demonstration meeting and visit the site of the excavation. The experts at the meeting agreed that "Longya Site is an important late Paleolithic site newly discovered in southwest China. The site has a clear stratum and rich unearthed relics, which is of great scientific research value for studying the history of the survival and evolution of ancient humans in the region and discussing the environmental changes of Sichuan Basin".

2. The Historical Value of Longya Culture and Its Significance to Jianyang

1. It provides abundant information about the production tools, daily necessities, associated animals and plants of ancient people in Sichuan Basin in the late Paleolithic Age, and the climate of Sichuan Basin at that time was warmer than today. So far, this has been a unique precious resource. Since the "Ziyang people" discovered before it had only one skull, and there was no other evidence, and the locations of their discoveries were only 40 kilometers apart, the possibility that "Ziyang people" were Longya people who were washed to Ziyang after their death by the flood cannot be ruled out. At least both of them prove that Sichuan Basin is one of the earliest regions in China where human beings lived and multiplied.

2. It provides evidence that the constructors of ancient Shu civilization — the most prominent archaeological excavations, of course, are the evidences of human bronze age activities shown by Sanxingdui and Jinsha sites — are from the Western Sichuan Plateau, or the indigenous people in the basin, or the ethnic groups formed by the integration and combination of the two.

3. Where is the origin of the mysterious romance of Bashu culture and its strong aesthetic taste and ability? The decorations of Longya culture provide the earliest physical evidence.

3. Summary of Humanistic spirit

Longya Culture, the most important Paleolithic site in the past 30 years, is a unique "cultural immovable property" in many aspects. It proves that this place was most suitable for human survival and reproduction in ancient times. At that time, people had already had artistic aesthetic pursuit, even primitive religious belief. It also proves that Jianyang area is one of the earliest origination and activity areas of ancestors in Sichuan Basin. The Chinese culture attaches great importance to "being cautious with endings and pursuing the future", and the consciousness of the Chinese national community that President Xi Jinping emphasized is also related to this. In addition, the Longya Culture is only 40 kilometers away from the excavation site of "Ziyang People" (in the upper reaches of the river) which is a bit earlier. Therefore, we can at least conclude the cultural connotation of Longya Culture as follows: **the hometown of Shu ancestors, the hometown of art, the harmony between God and man, and the coexistence and growth of all things.**

Such summary and expression can establish Jianyang's unique image of the ancestor of the Land of Abundance ethnic group and culture and art in the historical context of the diverse Chinese culture as an organic whole and the origin of Bashu ethnic groups. The inheritance and promotion of this mysterious and romantic cultural resource will effectively strengthen Jianyang's fine cultural attribute of "being remembered" and "being yearned for".

Section II Farming Culture

1. Origin and endowment of farming culture in Chengdu and Jianyang

The author and Dr. Ma Yingjie jointly wrote the book *Approaching Tianfu Farming Civilization* (Sichuan University Press, 2021.07), which systematically combs and demonstrates the farming civilization under the vision of Tianfu culture. The so-called farming culture is explained in Baidu Encyclopedia and 360 entries: "farming culture is a custom culture formed by people in long-term agricultural production. It is one of the earliest cultures in the world and one of the cultures that have the greatest impact on human beings. Farming civilization integrates various folk cultures, forming unique cultural content and characteristics. Its main body includes the concept of national management, the concept of interpersonal communication, language, drama, folk songs, customs and various sacrificial activities. It is the most extensive cultural integration in the world. Farming civilization determines the characteristics of Han culture. In fact, this is a rather vague and general definition that is difficult to understand, grasp and discuss. In my opinion, farming culture is a stable and continuous values and way of life based on the economic life of men farming and women weaving, and its associated and coupled religious beliefs and customs.

Archaeological excavations and a large number of documents can prove that the Chengdu Plain and its surrounding areas are one of the birthplaces of China's agricultural civilization. Her unique natural and geographical conditions and the stable and continuous humanistic character created by the ancestors through "morality, meritorious service and speech" ensured the prosperity of its farming civilization. Even if she encounters severe natural and man-made disasters, she can quickly repair and continue new creations and development. Jianyang is also one of the participants and constructors of this process and tradition because of its close relationship with Chengdu in history in terms of geography and administrative subordination.

The vast soil and deep foundation on which the four excellent gifts of Tianfu culture can continue for a long time is its remarkable farming civilization. In particular, its most prominent personality—optimism and inclusiveness, and its "superior and beautiful" farming life, which blends with each other and complements each other, continue to be inherited in the impact of modern industrial civilization, modernization and globalization. The integration of family and country in the excellent traditional Chinese culture; The core value system represented by loyalty, filial piety, integrity, benevolence, righteousness, courtesy, wisdom and trust; The spiritual home of the trinity of Confucianism, Buddhism and Taoism; The sense of a community of shared destiny through thick and thin, sharing weal and woe, and helping each other in times of adversity; The customs and habits of fearing heaven, gods, nature, elders and sages mainly lay the foundation and are rooted in the most mature, stable and continuous farming culture of mankind. Tianfu farming civilization is an important and unique part of it. Mr. Tan Jihe believes that the "Duguang Zhiye (Chengdu Plain is its center)" is a place of origin of China's agriculture. It is characterized by water control, and symbolized by the civilization of Jiangyuan. It breeds and develops a "superior and beautiful" Tianfu agricultural civilization. This is the first and most important feature of the Western Shu culture. Mr. Tan Jihe pointed out that the origin of ancient Shu's agricultural civilization started from the Minshan River valley, including the Chengdu Plain, Linqiong (today's Qionglai), Jiangyuan (today's Chongzhou), and Nan'an (today's Leshan) triangle. Meng Wentong, a master of Chinese culture, has specially demonstrated in the article "Problems in the History of Bashu". He believed that "in ancient times, Chinese agriculture developed independently from three regions, one is Guanzhong, the other is the lower reaches of the Yellow River, and in the Yangtze River basin, it started from Shu". He advocated that "agriculture enters the Chengdu Plain from Jiangyuan. Jiangyuan and Linqiong are the valleys of Minshan Mountain. The culture of Shu may begin here". The valley of Minshan Mountain is "Duguang Zhiye", and the Chengdu Plain is its center. It is the origin of the Shu culture, that is, the Jiangyuan agricultural civilization. Its origin started from Dujiangyan water control, then developed to Linqiong and Jiangyuan, and then to Wenjiang and Shuangliu (Ancient Guangdu, in history, Niubing, Jianzhou and Jianyang have been directly adjacent to them). Wenjiang gets its name "because the snow water has been warm since then", which indicates that the earliest high-quality agriculture appeared in Wenjiang, and it is more suitable for irrigation because the snow water from Minshan Mountain reaches Wenjiang and other central areas of Chengdu Plain. It is precisely because this is the origin of agriculture that the legend of Hou Ji, the farmer ancestor of Zhou Dynasty, who was buried in the Duguang Zhiye recorded in *the Book of Mountains and Seas*, and the legend of Du Yu, the farmer ancestor of Shu, meeting with Zhu Li in Jiangyuan (today's Chongzhou) and becoming a couple emerged. The origin of agriculture in Western Shu was linked to the culture of Dayu, Bieling and Li Bing who successively controlled floods. On this basis, the Tianfu agricultural civilization with distinctive characteristics and superior beauty was developed. Therefore, Western Shu has a particularly long farming era and distinctive farming culture, which has become a decisive factor in the basic nature of Western Shu culture and its presentation. Till modern times, after entering the industrial society, the decisive factor of agricultural civilization also played a deep-rooted role in the urban and rural civilization and ecology and culture of Western Shu, as well as the psychological state, lifestyle, mode of thinking and social customs of Western Shu people. The author believes that Jianyang has always participated in or shared the outstanding endowment and personality of Tianfu farming civilization. In addition to the wisdom and great achievements in water control (in history, Jianyang has enjoyed the huge benefits brought by Li Bing's harnessing of the Minjiang River and Wen Weng's harnessing of the upper reaches of the Tuojiang River; the East Irrigation (Dongguan) Project completed by Jianyang people with a heroic spirit that conquers mountains and rivers in the 20th century directly included Jianyang in the Dujiangyan Irrigation Area, a paradise for farming on earth), the connotations should also include: farming and reading in family became a common practice, laying a solid foundation for the ancient Wenzong (person whose writing is followed by all) to emerge from Western Shu (Jianyang's number one scholars and literary giants can prove that Jianyang is one of the leaders in such field of Tianfu culture); It nurtured the irreplaceable important position of Chengdu in the history of human silk civilization and the Silk Road (Niubing County served the development and integration of southwestern barbarians, which was the fundamental guarantee for the formation and maintenance of the Southern Silk Road); The forest plates in western Sichuan and the vibrant market-towns are the excellent resources to maintain the high happiness index that ordinary people in Chengdu often have in peacetime and to realize the strategy of revitalizing the countryside in the future (the forest plates in Jianyang have unique features of shallow hills, and have a distinct beauty of differentiation from those in cities and counties of Chengdu to the west of Longquan Mountain); It has bred famous families with the main merits of education, learning, literature and art, and a local culture characterized by attaching importance to and devoting to various public welfare undertakings in the hometown and being willing to solve problems for the elders, connecting the urban and rural areas of officials and people, leading, nurturing and benefiting Tianfu (represented by the "Liu's Three Streams" in Jianzhou in the Song Dynasty and the families and local sages and folk heroes of the Qing Dynasty who attached great importance to farming and reading, poetry and etiquette, imperial examinations and philanthropy, Jianyang can also keep pace with other cities and counties in Chengdu in this regard); It is the deep soil for the birth and development of Taoism in Chengdu, greatly reducing the ancient and modern discrimination against "agriculture, rural areas and farmers" (there are many Taoist strongholds in Jianyang, and there are many records of people donating money to build and rebuild Taoist temples in local literature); The local concept of "men are superior to women" is weak, and women are quite respected. A large number of talented women with world-famous poetry and prose skills and heroines who dare to act bravely emerged (Jianyang has the tradition of Nuwa worshipping; Luo Shu left famous works standing at the forefront of the times and was respected and publicized by Ba Jin; 120 women signed up for the war to resist U.S. aggression and aid Korea; Jianyang women actively participated in the East Irrigation (Dongguan) Project with the spirit of holding up half the sky, and young women in the flower season also undertook and completed the most difficult tasks; Jianyang women supported by Hakka culture are industrious and dexterous, which is a very prominent scene in Sichuan and Chengdu); Its people having a strong sense of family and country and unity, Jianyang has become a reliable strategic rear area that has experienced many major disasters in China's history and a "back garden of China" in peacetime (especially in the late Song Dynasty, when Li Daquan, the governor of Jianzhou, fought bravely against the Yuan army and died for his country, leaving behind "loyalty to Qishan Mountain" and "Huabi Temple" and other historical sites; A large number of anti-Japanese generals emerged in the bloody battlefield; 15000 people bled and sweated to complete the Pingquan Airport needed for the War of Resistance in advance; actively joined the army in the War to Resist US Aggression and Aid Korea; actively adapted to the new China's construction layout with administrative subordination and zoning having changed many times; Actively committed to the construction of parks and cities where cities and mountains are in harmony and people and water coexist); Respectively abide by their own distinctive local gods and sages worship (especially the worship of Erlang God and Li Bing and the harmonious coexistence of various spiritual beliefs and customs represented by the immigration guild halls); It has created a comfortable and romantic atmosphere of the city that integrates the garden city, the flower city, the silk city, the music city, the poetry city, the book city, the food city, and the leisure city (as for these eight cities, Jianyang mostly have relative historical background, which is worth setting a good position for itself. Do something and do nothing, participate actively, and highlight personality and characteristics).

Today's Chengdu and Jianyang inherit the attributes and charm of these eight cities. The industries and the attributes of the eight cities they created cannot do without the healthy development and innovation of the countryside, farmers and agriculture. A lot of opportunities lie in revitalizing the countryside.

In a word, for more than 2000 years, all the positive energy contained in and carried by the above connotations of Chengdu and Jianyang's Tianfu farming civilization, which can be referred to as "superior and beautiful", is a strong support for Chengdu's optimistic and inclusive humanistic character.

Although in modern times, especially since the reform and opening up and the return to Chengdu, the main economic support of Jianyang, measured by its share in the total GDP, is no longer agriculture but various modern industrial civilizations that stand at the forefront of the tide and strive to catch up. However, Jianyang still has a distinctive development feature of "small city leading large rural areas". All kinds of modern industrial civilizations cannot change the unique personality of Tianfu culture formed by the accumulation of agricultural civilization for more than 2,000 years. Moreover, with the creative transformation and innovative development of Tianfu's agricultural civilization that keeps pace with the times, and its benign connection with the secondary and tertiary industries, it will strongly weaken the individualism, pragmatism, opportunism, tool rationality, consumerism carried by modern industrial civilization with Western systems and concepts as the basic coordinates, as well as their impact on and destruction of the city's existing spiritual homeland and humanistic tradition. In particular, it prevents the increase of material desires, the dominance of commodities, currency and fetishism, the indifference of interpersonal relationships, and the widening gap between rich and poor, so as to preserve and increase the natural post-modern temperament of Chengdu since the reform and opening up — that is, the city has a healthy economy, an active culture, and a comfortable life at the same time, so that it has always been a city with outstanding sense of happiness for ordinary citizens in China and even the world. Keep a clear understanding, do a good job in top-level design, and take strong actions. Jianyang, rich in natural and cultural resources, with the goal of urban development that is suitable for work and living, will surely fly together with the cause of new rural construction and urban-rural integration.

2. A summary of Jianyang's farming culture

The natural environment, economy and cultural geography of Sichuan Basin, especially the Chengdu Plain, determine that it has a "superior and beautiful" farming civilization. Located on both sides of the Tuojiang River, the Jianyang people are hardworking and intelligent. Jianyang is adjacent to the central urban area of Chengdu in the west and connects Chongqing in the east. Its farming activities marked by men's farming and women's weaving have superior conditions. After thousands of years of accumulation, Jianyang has bred the cultural tradition of **diligence and honesty, farming and reading, hometown love and patriotism**, produced numerous material and spiritual wealth, and supported strong homesickness and family and country feelings. Jianyang is an important representative of Tianfu farming civilization. Its historical accumulation and contemporary expression are at least the deep soil for it to be "remembered" and "yearned for".

Section III Top Scholar Culture

1. Top Scholar Culture and Its Value

Since the Sui and Tang dynasties had the imperial examination system to select officials, the top scholar was the honorary title of the first person who stood out in the metropolitan examination hosted by the imperial court (usually the Ministry of Rites) and the final imperial examination ordered by the emperor in person. For thousands of years, it had been the highest peak that countless students hoped to reach; It was the best and most shining way to enter the official career and realize fame, the glory of family, the glory of hometown, and the loyalty to the monarch and the country; It is the ultimate happiness among the four types of happiness generally recognized by traditional Chinese people (a good rain after a long drought, meeting an old friend in a distant land, wedding, and succeeding in the government examination). Although the imperial examination system has some drawbacks, the statistics tell us that the ancient imperial examination system not only has obvious advantages over disadvantages, but also is highly coupled and mutually promoted with the concept of "unification", ethics, education system, scholarship, literature and art. Compared with the relevant fields of other countries in the world at the same time, it is undoubtedly the most fair and equitable, and also the most guaranteed talent selection system. Therefore, it is called the fifth great invention of China by western scholars who have a deep understanding of the Chinese culture. The western civil service selection system since modern times, to a large extent, has learned from the ancient Chinese imperial examination system. China's current civil servants "must take exams every time they enter", and the examination procedures should be as fair and just as possible, which is also the contemporary inheritance of this historical and cultural heritage. Therefore, **the so-called Top Scholar Culture is the values and the lifestyle needed by the generation and use of top scholars with the core connotation of respecting teachers and valuing education, advocating scholarship, respecting poetry and prose, fair competition, and pursuing excellence.**

The imperial examination system is a complete negation of the "aristocratic clan system", which relies on lineage to inherit senior officials' positions and titles or monopolizes high origins in social concepts. It also has the significant effect of preventing class solidification, making it possible for all classes to achieve rise and fall mobility, and greatly enhancing social vitality and national cohesion. Since the Song Dynasty, China had formed four classes of "scholars, farmers, workers and businessmen". Although they could move up and down, "scholars" (especially those who have obtained the titles of Xiucai, Juren and Jinshi) had become the most respected and influential group and class. This had made it a common phenomenon in the grass-roots society of valuing farming and reading in families, valuing poetry and etiquette in families, prospering through imperial examinations, and achieving fame. In fact, this was the most humane and warm humanistic scene in traditional China that best reflects the temperament of a civilized and ceremonial nation. Almost all parts of China, without exception, regard the top scholars who had emerged in history and their number, as well as the reason why they are such a group that makes the elders and descendants of their hometown proud, as the best resources for cultural construction. The number of top scholars had also become one of the main indicators of the academic, literary and artistic prosperity of the region.

2. The Cause and Embodiment of Jianyang Top Scholar Culture

(1) The Causes and Manifestations of Commonality

Jianyang has a history of 2,137 years of urban and rural development since the birth of Niubing County in the second year of Yuanding (115 B.C.) of Emperor Wu of the Han Dynasty, including about 1,470 years, during which it directly belonged to the Chengdu government, or the office was located in Chengdu. If measured mainly by the achievements of the imperial examination, it ushered in its own peak of development in the Five Dynasties, especially in the Song Dynasty. This is consistent with the ups and downs of

Sichuan and Chengdu in history. The author is the author of the book *Cultural Mechanism of the Emergence of Many Talents in Sichuan in the Song Dynasty*, in which a basic conclusion is that the most important reason why Sichuan in the Song Dynasty had so many talented people (Chengdu Fuxue alone had cultivated thousands of Jinshi, known as the best in Tianxia), and thus shone in China and the Confucian cultural circle in East Asia is the temperament of Bashu culture which has achieved the best coupling in history with the national temperament that Zhao and Song created. That is, they insisted on advocating civil administration (including the unprecedented improvement of the imperial examination system, which reflected fairness and justice, and the fact that the children of Zai Fu and officials were not allowed to become the top scholars), never punishing with words and never killing scholar officials. This has formed the best environment for talents in Bashu region to stand out through the imperial examination system and the severe test and selection of the state to deal with internal and external problems (It is very obvious from the three Jinshi from the Song Dynasty) and make contributions. In addition, when the kings of the Song Dynasty ruled Chengdu, because of the painful lessons of many uprisings and mutinies, including Wang Xiaobo's and Li Shun's uprisings, which were triggered by the early treatment of being frivolous and arrogant to Shu people, the emperor and prime minister carefully chose Sichuan and Chengdu's chief executives. Therefore, for the officials who came to Chengdu, few of them were corrupt, immoral and incompetent, and most of them were very concerned about and supported local education and had a broad mind to be a Bole. They actively found, encouraged and recommended young and middle-aged talents and scholars in Sichuan.

Chengdu had been one of the cities with the strongest atmosphere of respecting teachers, valuing education, advocating scholarship, and advocating poetry, prose and art since Wenweng promoted education in Sichuan. During the Five Dynasties and the Later Shu, Chengdu was a relatively pure land and a highland of culture, education and art in China's troubled times for more than half a century. The famous "Stone Classics of Meng and Shu" and the *Revealing Treasures* after the founding of the Song Dynasty and other collection of great classics were engraved in Chengdu, which proved the profound cultural foundation and strength of the Later Shu (this was the basis for Jianyang to produce the top scholar Wang Guipu in the period of Later Shu); In the Song Dynasty, the economy and material technology of the Land of Abundance (including papermaking, printing, and book publishing) could provide strong support for these value pursuits. It was also inevitable that Jianyang had three top scholars. ①

(2) The Causes and Manifestations of Personality

1) There were fewer uprisings, mutinies and disasters in the early Song Dynasty.

When the Northern Song Dynasty unified Sichuan, Meng Chang of Later Shu quickly chose to surrender. Madame Huarui later signed about this, "The flag of surrender was lowered on top of the king's city wall. The king's concubine living in the deep palace had no way to be informed of so. 140,000 soldiers took off the armour, none of whom showed manhood!" In the early

---

① During the Southern Song Dynasty, the land was more cramped, and the capital moved eastward to Lin'an (now Hangzhou). Chengdu and Sichuan were more important to the country. Sympathizing with the difficulties of Sichuan students going to Lin'an to participate in the metropolitan examination, the court set up provincial examinations for Sichuan and Shaanxi. The first place was equal to the third place in the capital's metropolitan examination and could further go to the capital to participate in the final imperial examination. The rest would be given the title of Jinshi.

period of the Northern Song Dynasty, the Northern Song court was culturally and psychologically arrogant to Sichuan and transported the plundered wealth of Meng Shu to Kaifeng for a long time. Plus the misdeeds of the Northern Song officers and soldiers and the widening gap between the rich and the poor in society, there were large-scale mutinies, such as Quan Shixiong mutiny, Wang Xiaobo and Li Shun Uprising, and Wang Jun mutiny that the court had to send soldiers to suppress. Wherever the fire of war came, it naturally caused a lot of destruction. However, these wars and disasters hardly caused serious damage to the region where Jianzhou is located. During this period, Jianzhou's economy and culture had been well developed.

2) Affiliated to Chengdu and connected to the south and east of Sichuan.

Jianzhou in the Northern Song Dynasty had three counties under its jurisdiction (shrunk in the Southern Song Dynasty), which directly connected the Chengdu Plain and Zizhou in the central and southern Sichuan. It could also be directly connected to eastern Sichuan by water. Such a geographical location makes Jianyang more successful than ordinary counties in obtaining the civilized resources of Chengdu, including government schools, Jiaozi, Printing, Shi Er Yue Shi, and several academic and educational families, and receiving the influence of Chengud's high respect for literature. However, the economic and cultural conditions in Jianzhou must be more difficult than those in the Chengdu Plain, so the scholars in Jianzhou were naturally more diligent and hardworking, which is also clearly reflected in the personal styles of the three top scholars.

This character analysis also helps today's Jianyang to think about how to inherit and carry forward its own cultural and educational characters in the greater Chengdu; Jianyang should not only inherit Chengdu's advanced urban civilization, international vision in life aesthetics, efficiency concept, refined consciousness, urban and rural planning and community governance experience, but also continue to maintain the simplicity, diligence, tenacity, both civil and military traditions, and personality of the people of Jianyang, so that it would have its own unique competitiveness and vitality compared with Neijiang, Ziyang and other brother counties, as well as the districts, cities and counties in the first and second circles of Chengdu. This will be an important topic for Jianyang (even the East New Area of Chengdu)'s future cultural inheritance and development and cultural soft power building, which should be considered and planned. The analysis of the reasons for the formation and embodiment of the Top Scholar Culture can present a mirror of history.

3) The Cultural Highlights Formed by the Four Top Scholars in Jianzhou.

In Jianyang's history, there were four top scholars, namely Wang Guipu, Xu Jiang, Zhang Xiaoxiang and Xu Yi. Viewing from the county level within the country, this number of top scholars is commendable. It can be seen that the appearance of the four top scholars in Jianzhou one after another had brought a highlight moment for the formation and accumulation of the Top Scholar Culture. The study of Jianyang's Top Scholar Culture should focus on this and analyze its core and extension.

Wang Guipu was the first top scholar in Jianzhou's history. According to the *Ten Kingdoms Chunqiu · Later Shu · Ben Zhuan*, "He was from Jianzhou. When he was young, he was intelligent and good at writing. Between 938 and 965 AD, he won the top scholar, and had never been heard of since." Qianlong's *Jianzhou Annals* and Jiaqing's *Sichuan General Annals — Election Chapter* recorded that "Guipu was a Jinshi in the Tang Dynasty, and the year was not examined."

Xu Jiang was the second top scholar in Jianzhou's history. According to *Jianyang County Annals* from the Republic of China, "In the eighth year of

Jiayou reign (1063 AD), Emperor Renzong of the Song Dynasty, he won the first place in the imperial examination of Guimao Branch. He was a Xueshi official." He had successively served as the prefect of Chengdu, the prefect of Dingzhou, the minister of the Ministry of Rites, the prefect of Henan, etc.

Zhang Xiaoxiang was the third top scholar in Jianzhou's history. According to *Jianyang County Annals* from the Republic of China, "In the 24th year of Shaoxing (1154 A.D.), Emperor Gaozong of the Song Dynasty, he won the first place in the imperial examination, and he was later a Xueshi official." He was a famous patriotic poet in the Southern Song Dynasty. His style was bold and generous, and he occupied a place in the history of Chinese literature. He wrote *Yu Hu Ji* and *Yu Hu Ci*.

Xu Yi was the fourth top scholar in Jianzhou's history. According to *Jianyang County Annals* from the Republic of China, "In the fifth year of Qing Yuan (1199 AD), Emperor Ningzong of the Song Dynasty, he won the first place in the imperial examination." He once was the prefect of Suining and Tongchuan, among many posts he served.

3. The Spiritual Core and Manifestation of Jianyang's Top Scholar Culture

(1) Spiritual Core

Selecting talents and officials through imperial examinations is a great institutional civilization in which the Chinese civilization breaks the consanguinity and identity monopoly and selects talents and officials in a fair and just way. The number of top scholars produced throughout regions of China has always been one of the most important indicators to measure the cultural and educational level in the history of the region. In Chinese history, there were no more than 674 top scholars with names. Today, there are more than 2000 counties in China, that is, an average of 3-4 counties can possibly produce a top scholar. In the history of Jianyang, four top scholars emerged, which is very rare in Sichuan and other counties in western China except Shaanxi. This is a very precious and unique cultural resource in western Sichuan. Moreover, the activities of the four top scholars were all positive energy of the country and society in history. Jianyang's Top Scholar Culture is a spirit of **fair competition and pursuit of excellence**. It is also an elegant style of **poetry and wisdom serving the country**. In particular, it can stimulate the cultural confidence and pride of Jianyang people. Jianyang should strive to inherit and carry forward this most precious historical and cultural heritage, making it Jianyang's urban endowment of "being remembered" and "being looked up to".

(2) How to express

Mr. Chen Yinke has a famous saying: "The culture of the Chinese nation has evolved for thousands of years and has been extremely developed in the Song dynasties." The same is true of Sichuan's history and culture. In the Song Dynasty, Chengdu was prosperous in economy, culture and education, and only experienced the devastation of the war against Mongolia in the final years. Thus, the quality of its government schools was No.1 in China, and for a long time, Chengdu performed the best in the imperial examinations nationwide. Jianyang, as the subordinate county of Chengdu Fu Lu, had created the miracle of delivering three top scholars for the Song Dynasty, namely Xu Jiang (the eighth year of Emperor Renzong Jiayou, the top scholar in 1063), Zhang Xiaoxiang (the 24th year of Emperor Gaozong Shaoxing, the top scholar in 1154), and Xu Yi (1170—1219, the fifth year of Emperor Ningzong Qingyuan, the top scholar in 1199). As far as the author can see, in the history of Sichuan

Province and even the whole Southwest China, there is no other county that can beat Jianyang in this regard. Therefore, the evaluation of Jianyang's Top Scholar Culture can be expressed and highlighted in terms of "the pearl on the crown of Bashu culture in the peak period of Chinese civilization", "the crown of Sichuan culture and education in the Song Dynasty", and "the brilliant representative of Chengdu in the Song Dynasty".

Section IV Celebrity Culture

1. Sorting out the cultural resources of Jianyang celebrities

Due to the superiority of natural geography, cultural geography, economic geography and political geography, and the fact that most of the time in history Jianyang was the heartland of the Sichuan Basin directly under the Government of Chengdu, plus some coincidences in the historical evolution, Jianyang's celebrity cultural resources[1], compared with the same level of counties and cities, are top in Sichuan and at the middle and upper levels of Chengdu. In a comprehensive review, Jianyang's celebrity cultural resources have the following main types and characteristics:

(1) Main types

1. An influential family: In Jianzhou of the Song Dynasty, the big academic

---

[1] Generally, the criteria for identifying regional and urban historical celebrities (such as two groups of Sichuan's top ten historical celebrities) are: born here; have lived and been active in here for a period of time, and have made great achievements in virtue, writing or meritorious service; native place is here, and father's generation was born here (this is controversial, but it has been generally accepted).

family represented by "Three Xi of the Liu Family" ("Qianxi" Liujing; "Dongxi" Liu Boxiong; "Houxi" Liu Guangzu) was active in the top palace of politics, academia, literature and art of the Song Dynasty with significant positive energy. Apart from the three top scholars, Jianyang (set up as Yang'an County of Jianzhou at that time), in the Song Dynasty, maintained a continuous educational and academic prosperity, with a large number of talents. At that time, Jianyang was one of the most brilliant regions in culture, education, and imperial examinations among the counties of the same level under the jurisdiction of Chengdu Fu lu. Moreover, on the map of Chinese culture, education, and imperial examination, Jianyang was also brilliant and could not be ignored. Many leading figures in the Song Dynasty were friends with the three Liu, including Wang Anshi (Liu Jing's Bo Le and recommender), Su Shi, Su Zhe brothers (friends who had close contacts with Liu Jing and they sung poems and lyrics together), Huang Tingjian (Liu Jing's close friend), Zhao Ruyu (a virtuous minister who highly appraised Liu Boxiong's morality and learning), Zhu Xi (who respected Liu Boxiong's moral and ethical articles and respected Liu Boxiong as the "elder" in his letters), Wei Liaoweng, Zhen Dexiu (Liu Guangzu's lifelong colleagues and best friends, whose epitaph was also written by Zhen Dexiu). It can be seen that their moral articles had an important influence and strong positive energy in the Song Dynasty. Liu Guangzu's virtuous wife, Li Shi, not only helped him cultivate three of his four sons as Jinshi, but also treated people very kindly. How can such a kind-hearted family not be harmonious, peaceful and prosperous! In fact, in history, Jianyang became an attractive (yearned for or even looked up to) "Xiongzhou", largely because of the family and its activity relics, plus the memorial landscape built by the officials and people who admired them in their hometown in the

Ming and Qing Dynasties (the most important was the Three Xi Temple^① built by Yan Shouyi, the governor of Jianzhou in the late Qing Dynasty). Wang Xiangzhi (1163—1230), a geographer in the Song Dynasty who had the status of Jinshi, learned a lot and was indifferent to fame and wealth. He left a poem in his elaborate *Yu Di Ji Sheng · Jianzhou*, which said, "It is best to visit Jianjun when entering Sichuan, and it is necessary to visit Liu's family when looking for mountains", which became the most objective, sincere and influential "public-interest advertisement" in history praising and recommending Jianyang's humanistic charm.

2. Three heroes: In the history of Jianyang, for the sake of the just cause of the country and the nation, there were many heroes who dared to take justice for their own sake. However, in terms of their weight, three of them are particularly memorable. Li Daquan, the governor of Jianzhou, led the army and people of Jianzhou at the end of the Song Dynasty and the beginning of the Yuan Dynasty to resist the Yuan troops and died bravely in battle. Not only the official history recorded him as a martyr, but also in order to commemorate him, people had built many historical sites in Jianyang, such as "loyalty to the Qi Mountain" and "Huabi Temple". Xue Zhigao (1930—1952, born in Wuli Village, Jiajiachang, Jianyang) bravely killed the enemy in the Shangganling Campaign of the War of Resistance against American Aggression and Aid Korea. He still participated in the attack even though he was seriously injured and died bravely. He was awarded the special-class merit once and won the title of second level combat hero of the volunteer army; Lai Wenlu (1931—1952, born in Pingquan Town, Jianyang), his squad was responsible for holding the 194 highland of position 82. On September 23, 1952, the atrocious "united nations army" delivered tens of thousands of artillery shells to their positions.

---

① It would be great if this temple could be restored as it is.

In addition, seven tanks and a battalion attacked them. They were only a squad, but they beat back more than ten enemy charges. Finally, he fought back the enemy five times alone, and his cap had seven holes (it was collected by the Central Military Museum). Later, together with the two soldiers who came to reinforce after breaking through the artillery fire, he held out until the next day and was replaced. He was awarded an international medal by the Korean government, a first-class merit by the headquarter of the Volunteer Army, and a second level hero by the Central Military Commission.

3. Four top scholars: Wang Guipu in the Five Dynasties, Xu Jiang, Zhang Xiaoxiang and Xu Yi in the Song Dynasty. Even if only the three top scholars of the orthodox Chinese dynasty (Song Dynasty) were counted, this was rare in southwest China, and all three of them were scholar bureaucrats who were honest, loyal, talented and loved people in history. For example, Xu Jiang, with his extraordinary temperament and talent (including archery), went to Liao to resolve the disputes initiated by Liao, which not only won the respect of Liao's monarchs and officials, but also caused the event that Liao's capital became empty, as all the people went to "see the top scholar of Song Dynasty". This was the most memorable scene in the diplomatic activities of the Song dynasty, which were often humiliated and compromised. The author has read through such masterpieces as *History of the Song Dynasty*, *History of the Liao Dynasty*, *History of the Jin Dynasty*, *Long Editions of the Continuation of History as a Mirror*, and *Records of the Year Since Jianyan*. I am well aware that the history of China in the Song Dynasty cannot be judged completely from the standpoint of the Han people. At that time, the Song Dynasty often did not have the upper hand in war, but in culture, it was always an example for the courts and the commonalty of Liao, Jin, Xia and Mongolia to learn and imitate secretly, and was their teacher. This kind of cultural soft power is the most profound decisive force in the difficult integration of the nation and is also the most valuable type of celebrity culture in the Song Dynasty. Without doubt, Xu Jiang not only maintained the dignity of the Northern Song Dynasty, but also radiated the cultural power of the Northern Song Dynasty. His effect reached the peak in the diplomacy with no military advantage. In the past, the attention and evaluation of this point was seriously insufficient. With regard to the life stories of the four top scholars, the two books *Jianzhou Celebrities* (December 2006, China Culture and History Press) elaborately prepared by Jiang Xiangdong, Chen Xueming and Chen Shuizhang and *Tianfu Xiongzhou, Happy Jianyang* (October 2013, Sichuan University Press) prepared by Comrade Wang Hongbin as the director of the editorial board have well introduced and summarized them. This research report will not repeat that. However, when two of them are considered literary giants, their relevant lives will be introduced here.

4. Eight literary giants:

(1) Yong Tao (805—?), a native of Chengdu, was a Jinshi in the 8th year of Dahe (834), Emperor Wenzong of the Tang Dynasty. He served as the Imperial Censor and then worked at the Imperial College. Later, he served as the governor of Jianzhou in 854, and after that lived in seclusion in Lushan until death. He liked to travel, and his footprints covered most of China. He had a distinctive personality and was used to singing poems and drinking wine to amuse himself. According to historical records, his lvshi (a poem of eight lines, each containing five or seven characters, with a strict tonal pattern and rhyme scheme) and jueju (a poem of four lines, each containing of five or seven characters, with a strict tonal pattern and rhyme scheme) were the best and he was also good at Fu (descriptive prose interspersed with verse). He was an important landscape poet in the late Tang Dynasty. His life and deeds were recorded in *the Yun Xi You Yi* Volume (I), the *Tang Poetry Chronicle* Volume 56, and the *Tang Scholars' Biography* Volume 7. Although his ten-volume poetry collection was lost, and only one volume can be seen from Volume 518 of *All Tang Poems* today, there is no problem that he was in the first-class position among landscape poets in the late Tang Dynasty. What is important is that he renamed Jianyang's "Love End Bridge" across Dongda Road as "Zheliu Bridge" and wrote poems about his feelings, leaving Jianyang with a romantic story about the interaction between writers and traffic, which moved many later generations. Even modern architect Mao Yisheng had paid attention to this bridge, especially Yong Tao's poems. It can be seen that the story of Yong Tao and this famous bridge is a point in history where people could yearn for and look up to Jianyang. It is a pity that the bridge was destroyed due to the construction of Chengdu Chongqing Highway.

(2) Xu Jiang (1037—1111), a native of Jianzhou, immigrated to Hebei, and was smart since childhood. He was called a little prodigy. There is a folk story about little Xu Jiang and an elder man in his hometown playing couplets games. In the eighth year of Emperor Renzong Jiayou (1063), He became a top scholar at the age of 26. He had served many different posts successively, such as a local magistrate and general judge. In the seventh year of Xining, he was on a diplomatic mission to Liao. Relying on his erudition, he talked calmly and rejected Qidan's unreasonable demands. He also won respect by hitting the target with one shot in the bow and arrow competition. After returning to China, he was widely praised. He then served posts such as a scholar in the Imperial Academy, the prefect of Kaifeng, an examiner in the metropolitan examinations, a minister of the Ministry of War, the prefect of Chengdu, etc. During this period, he was also involved in the struggle between the old and new parties and was fiercely retaliated and persecuted for opposing the "new" faction. Xu Jiang was not only an outstanding politician and diplomat, but also a top literary giant. According to historical records, he worked in poetry, especially in fu. After he succeeded in the imperial examinations and became the top scholar, Ouyang Xiu read his fu and said: "Your fu's style is like Duke Yi's, you will have a bright future and way to go!" Duke Yi was the honorable title of Wang Zeng. Wang Zeng (978—1038), a native of Yidu, Qingzhou (today's Qingzhou City, Shandong Province), was a famous minister and poet in the Northern Song Dynasty. Wang Zeng was a lonely boy when he was a teenager and good at writing. During the era of Xianping, Wang Zeng ranked first all the way from county examination to provincial examination and to palace examination and was later granted the title of Duke Yi. He had a high reputation among the scholar bureaucrats and literati in the Song Dynasty. Xu Jiang became the governor of Chengdu in the 8th year of Yuanfeng (1085), and he worked for three years. During this time, he wrote back and forth especially poems to his famous friends in the West Garden (then Chengdu's famous garden). Today, people can see 10 pieces of their works. Xu Jiang also wrote the poem "Guan Lan Pavilion" for his hometown of Jianzhou, which is lofty, powerful and heroic. It is the important cultural deposits of "Four Cliffs and the Moon", one of the eight scenic spots in Jianzhou. Only two of Xu Jiang's poems can be seen today, "Cherish the Yellow Flower, The Voice of Wild Goose Breaks at Night" and "Immortal at Linjiang", which are masterpieces with vigorous writing and feeling and setting happily blended.

(3) Zhang Xiaoxiang (1132—1170), a native of Jianzhou in the Southern Song Dynasty, was the top scholar at the age of 22 in the 24th year (1154) of Shaoxing. He had successively held the posts of prefects of many places. In his life, he abhorred evils as deadly foes, was loyal to the monarch, was patriotic, opposed Qin Hui, supported Yue Fei and advocated the Northern Expedition, so he was suppressed many times and experienced several ups and downs. He was talented and excellent in poetry, ci, prose and calligraphy. Qin Hui almost made him lose his top scholar title, but during the palace examination, he not only wrote with ease tens of thousands of words as magnificent prose, but also wrote beautiful Chinese characters. According to the history, Emperor Gao Zong, who liked calligraphy, saw his calligraphy and painting that were powerful and outstanding. Thus, "Zhang Xiaoxiang was suspected of being a banished immortal, and was the first choice for personal promotion." In the history of literature, Zhang Xiaoxiang was recognized as one of the most representative and influential patriotic poets in the Southern Song Dynasty.

(4) Liu Jing (1043—1100), a native of Yang'an, Jianzhou, was a Jinshi in the 6th year of Xining (1073), Emperor Shenzong. He was awarded the Doctor of Imperial College between the year 1078 and 1085. In the first year of Yuanyou (1086), he was impeached by the imperial censor Wang Yansou (who was also the top scholar, brilliant, but belonged to the old school that opposed the reform and was a fierce figure of Sima Guang's faction), and served as the magistrate of Xianyang County, and later as the general judge of Chengdu, the magistrate of Fangzhou, and so on. [1] Between 1098—1100, he served as a fifth-grade official, and then passed away. In the chaotic political situation in the late Northern Song Dynasty, Liu Jing had no significant influence as a politician, but as a literary giant, he was deserving. According to historical records, he "boarded the door of Su Zizhan early", and had close contacts with Su Shi and Su Zhe. He "devoted himself to learning", and was a scholar "famous for literature", which was compiled into the *200 Famous Officials of the National Dynasty* and *History of the Song Dynasty · Biography of Literary Gardens*. In the

---

[1] In the field of history, it is extremely difficult to judge the right and wrong of Wang Anshi's political reform itself and the contest and dispute it initiated between the literati and officials in the Song Dynasty. So far, there is no widely accepted conclusion.

extant *Complete Works of Dongpo*, there are three pieces of changhe (changhe: write and reply in poems, using the same rhyme sequence) works between Su Shi and Liu Jing, and one piece of prose about Su Shi's response to Liu Jing; In Su Zhe's poetry collection *Luancheng Collection*, there are four works of changhe between him and Liu Jing. Liu Jing's painting and calligraphy skills were also extraordinary. In addition to collecting a large number of ancient paintings and calligraphy, he was good at painting woods, pine, bamboo and stone. He, together with the then famous Mi Fu and Chang'an native Xue Shaopeng, called Mi Xue Liu: "The three figures have uninhibited and carefree demeanor, and they are first-rate people." Liu Jing had a friendly relationship with Mi Fu. Mi Fu mentioned him many times in his works *History of Books*, *History of Painting* and *Collection of Baojin Yingguang*. In addition, Liu Jing had also written books of historiography and philology such as *The Western Han Dynasty Brought into Play* and *Chengdu Stone Carving Catalogue*.

(5) **Liu Guangzu (1142—1222)**, a native of Yang'an, Jianzhou, was a Jinshi in the fifth year of Qiandao (1169), Emperor Xiaozong. He once served many posts such as the governor of Suining, an imperial censor in the palace, and resigned after ascending to the third- grade official for some years. When he was the Imperial Censor, he "critiqued factions, destroyed the evil and attacked the strong, and seldom avoided these people". Thus, he was known as the "Iron faced Imperial Censor". Of course, he was also oppressed by political opponents. He made significant contributions to the gradual reduction and cessation of suppression of Neo-Confucianism represented by Zhu Xi in the late Southern Song Dynasty, so he was highly praised by Zhao Ruyu (Zhu Xi's supporter) and Zhu Xi himself. His academic and literary attainments were very high, and his works were rich, including classics, prose, poetry and ci. Eight of his poems were recorded in Volume 2,611 of *The Complete Song Poetry*, 21 pieces of his Ci were

recorded in Volume 3 of *The Complete Song Ci*, and 6 pieces of his writings were collected in Volume 6,313 of *The Complete Song Literature*. Literary historians commented on his solemn and beautiful poems; Its style is of little decoration but strong in simplicity and honesty, and its straightforwardness is the most valuable; Zhen Dexiu commented on his ci "particularly clear and sweet". Its cemetery was located in Hehua Village, Yangmahe River, Jianyang. It was a grand one. The local people called it "Official Grave Valley", but unfortunately it was destroyed in the "Cultural Revolution".

(6) Luo Shu (1903—1938) was mentioned before. Although she died young, her "Born a Wife" and articles on the theme of patriotism and the War of Resistance against Japan have made her rank among the best female writers of her time. The attention and love she received from Ba Jin and other great writers shows that Luo Shu should have a glorious place in the history of Chinese literature, especially women's literature.

(7) Zhou Keqin (1936—1990), a native of Shiqiao, Jianyang, was born in poverty and had only received education from Chengdu Agricultural School, but he loved his hometown and was obsessed with literary creation. He won the National Excellent Short Story Award twice, and his local novel *Xu Mao and His Daughters* won the first Maodun Literature Award. He inherited and carried forward the spirit of local-flavored literature of Ai Wu, Sha Ting and other famous writers, leaving a vivid and moving picture of production and life of the people in his hometown. He has the status of a first-class writer in modern China. He served as the deputy secretary of the Party Leadership Group and executive vice chairman of Sichuan Writers Association, which is the pride of Jianyang, Chengdu and Sichuan.

(8) Li Mingsheng (1956—2022), born in Jianyang, is a famous contemporary writer, the winner of the three "Lu Xun Literature Awards" (1996;

2000; 2010), the vice president of the Chinese Reportage Society, and the chief documentary writer of "Chinese Writers". He is praised by the literary world as "the first person in China's aerospace literature", "the second leader in China's science and technology topics after Xu Chi", and "the most conscientious writer" by netizens. His work "Seven Series of Aerospace" has influence both at home and abroad. The three award-winning works are "Out of the Global Village", "China 863" and "The epicenter is in the heart".

5. Ten Unusual Talents:

(1) Li Chunfeng (602—670), a great astronomer in the Tang Dynasty, was a native of Jianzhou and was buried in his hometown after his death. In his life, he was proficient in astronomical calendar and the science of yin and yang, which were considered the most mysterious and abstruse by both the court and the commonalty at that time. He also had many amazing inventions. For example, when he was in his twenties, he attracted Emperor Taizong's attention by participating in the guidance and revision of the "Wuyinyuan Calendar", and then proceeded to work in the grand astrology administration; He made the most advanced Huntian ecliptic armillary sphere in the world at that time; He wrote 7 volumes of Faxiang Zhi, which systematically summarized the gains and losses of all generations of the armillary sphere; He was promoted to Doctor Taichang and then Taishi Cheng Hou (an official who holds astronomy and calendar), and wrote the most difficult parts — astronomy, legal calendar, travel and chronicles in the *Jin Shu* and *the History of the Five Dynasties*. According to the evaluation of later generations, *Jin Shu · Astronomical Annals* is the best of all official astronomical records, so he was made a Baron; Li Chunfeng also surpassed the *Wu Yin Yuan Calendar* and developed a more advanced *Lin De Calendar*; Among the many magical stories about him, the most famous one is that he bet with Taizong and successfully predicted the exact time of the solar eclipse. He was also a great mathematician who annotated ancient mathematical classics and enriched ancient Chinese mathematical literature. In the second year of Longshuo, Emperor Gaozong of the Tang Dynasty (662), he was granted the post of a Mige Langzhong (namely, the imperial astronomer), and remained in the post until death. Li Chunfeng also used his prestige as an astrologer to prevent Taizong from believing the prophecy that "the Tang Dynasty becomes weak, there will be a female king of Wu", and wanting to kill all the suspects. Li Chunfeng was also a top figure in the field of "geomantic omen", as evidenced by his *Yi Si Zhan, Tui Bei Tu, Bai Jue Tu* and *History of Chinese Science and Technology*. Maybe people today will remember what metaphysics is when they face Li Chunfeng. Li Chunfeng was also the first person in human history to rate the wind. He divided the wind rating into 8 levels from small to large. More than 400 years later, British navigator Beaufort expanded the wind rating to 13 levels on Li Chunfeng's basis. Dr. Joseph Needham (1900—1995), a great British master of history of science and technology, had the highest evaluation of Li Chunfeng in the history of science; for example, he believed that the *Jinshu · Astronomical Annals* was a treasure house of astronomical knowledge; He praised Li Chunfeng as "the greatest annotator of mathematical works in the whole Chinese history" in Volume 3 of his brilliant masterpiece "History of Science and Technology of China". Li Chunfeng is a superstar who can make his hometown and motherland looked up to.

(2) Deshan Xuanjian (782—865), the top eminent monk of the Tang Dynasty, had an impact on both ancient and modern times, both at home and abroad. He was a Buddhist reformer in the history of Han Buddhism, who shocked both the monks and the secular people at that time. He was the first who dared to "denounce Buddha and scold ancestors", breaking the shackles of individual consciousness brought by idolatry; He invented the "Deshan stick", "head slapping" the beginners and stupid disciples to alert them (In history, many people were stimulated and rebounded by such doubts and challenges to authority and idols, including Emperor Yongzheng of the Qing Dynasty, who once ordered Deshan Xuanjian to be removed from the list of eminent monks!). Deshan Xuanjian was the founder of Zen Yunmen Sect and Fayan Sect and the earliest proponent of "humanistic spirit" in Buddhism. His life had left many classic stories. For example, when he was in Chengdu, he was the "first to speak about the vajracchedika-sutra and became famous in Chengdu", but then he travelled thousands of miles out of Sichuan to challenge the Southern Zen School, which advocated satori, and finally they competed in Liyang, Hunan. In the end, he was enlightened by the Chongxin arch mage who lit and blew the lights at night to see him off. He got the koan of Chongxin, and then was sincerely convinced. He burned the once complacent *Qinglong Scripture* he brought from Jianzhou (now there is a sutra burning altar in Qianming Temple in Changde, Hunan Province to commemorate this event), and became a firm member of the satori sect. He then said goodbye to Chongxin and went to compete with Master Nanyue Weishan Lingyou (the martial uncle of Xuanjian by seniority), and finally gained the upper hand. Weishan predicted that Xuanjian would end up denouncing Buddha and scolding ancestors. Although Xuanjian in history had a distinctive personality, his virtue was pure, and people admired that. His followers were numerous. Therefore, his third-generation disciples were able to establish the famous Yunmen and Fayan sects in the Southern Zen, which have been passed down to this day, with believers all over the world (especially in Japan, South Korea, and Vietnam). Based on various factors, after Deshan Xuanjian left Sichuan, his main activity stronghold was Changde, Hunan (today's Changde has already spread and created Xuanjian as their Buddhist cultural card), and never returned to Sichuan. However, he was a native of Jianyang, and had formed and demonstrated the foundation and belief of Buddhism in Jianyang and Chengdu and was endowed with the distinctive characteristics of Bashu culture and Tianfu culture (see the previous discussion). He had gone out of Sichuan and become a landmark monk of innovation and change in Chinese Buddhism and Buddhist history. The ancient Wolong Temple where he became a monk is in Jianyang. He is a cultural resource that has not been fully developed for Jianyang.

(3) Chan Master Chushan Shaoqi, Shijing Temple. Shijing Temple is located 18.64 miles northwest of Jianzhou (now Jianyang, Chengdu, Sichuan Province). It originally belonged to Jiulongchang Township, Jianyang, and now belongs to Chadian Town, Longquanyi District, Chengdu. It is 23.92 miles southeast of Chengdu and a major Buddhist scenic spot in the southern suburbs of Chengdu. It is said that the Shijing Temple was built in the late Eastern Han Dynasty (220). In the Shu Han Dynasty, it was the home temple of General Zhao Yun. According to the records in *Jianyang County Annals* from the Republic of China, Shijing Temple, formerly known as Tiancheng Temple, is located at the south foot of Tiancheng Mountain in the middle of the Longquan mountain range. During the Zhengtong period of the Ming Dynasty (1436—1449), Chan Master Chushan from Zhejiang stayed here for nearly 30 years. Chushan was a famous monk at that time. After coming to Sichuan, he kept in touch with King Shu Ding and Chengdu dignitaries from time to time, singing poetry and drinking alcohol with them, and was highly appreciated and treated with courtesy. King Shu Ding also paid money to make additions to Tiancheng Temple. In the ninth year of Chenghua (1473), Chushan died in Qihuan Nunnery behind Tiancheng Temple. The monks then moved his corpse to the Gongshan Cave and put him into a Bodhisattva sculpture who was named Chushan Zushi, for devout men and women to worship. The human body of Chushan was destroyed during the Cultural Revolution. The Chushan Monk wrote *Chushan Quotations,* and his poems were handed down from generation to generation. Tiancheng Temple leans on the southern foot of Tiancheng Mountain in the Longquan mountain chain, and a seven-story hall is built along the mountain. Entering the mountain gate is the Heavenly King Hall, the left is the Buddha Hall, and the right is the Five View Hall. Going up along the wide straight stone ladder, one sees the Mahavira Hall, which was built by the construction workers dispatched by king of Shu in the Ming Dynasty. The structure is very magnificent. The murals and painted Buddha statues in the hall are vivid and lifelike. The left side is the Hall of Hell. From the right side of the Mahavira Hall, climb more than 300 broad stone steps, one reaches the rear hall. Then climb up again, one reaches the Guanyin Hall, the Ancestor Hall and the Lantern Hall. On the right side of the Ancestor Hall are the general affairs room, the clothing shack, the abbot's room, the garden, the guest hall and the dormitory. Before liberation in 1949, there were more than 300 rooms in the whole temple. The whole temple, built according to the mountains, is magnificent and tall, surrounded by mountains, with lush trees and beautiful scenery. It is really an excellent Buddhist summer resort in western Sichuan. At the end of the Ming Dynasty, when Zhang Xianzhong entered Sichuan, the insurrectionary army were strictly disciplined and protected temples wherever they passed. Seeing the tall and rugged Tiancheng Temple, they paid more attention to protecting it. Later however, the monks fabricated the myth that Zhang Xianzhong wanted to light a fire to burn the temple, and that "when he lit fire three times which was put out three times, he was frightened and left". As a result, there were more people who believed in Chushan, and people from nearby prefectures and counties came one after another to the temple to pray and worship him.

In the 32nd year of Qianlong's reign in the Qing Dynasty (1767), Song Siren, the governor of Jianzhou Prefecture, visited the Tiancheng Temple. He loved the beautiful scenery and admired the moral knowledge of Chushan, so he sent a copy of *Vajra* Sutra to be carved on 32 huge stone tablets which were erected in the temple. Thereafter, Tiancheng Temple was renamed Shijing Temple. The monks in the temple spread a myth again that the old lady of the Mu family in Songzhou suffered from eye disease and made a wish to Chushan. Then her eye disease was cured, and she presented this stone carved *Vajra Sutra* to the temple for gratitude and to show off the "efficaciousness" of Chushan, which attracted the masses to the temple. This stone carved scripture, after the war, had only one stone tablet left by the time of liberation in 1949, and was regarded as the "the treasure of the mountain" in the temple.

(4) Wu Ang, "Crazy Painter" (1801—?), was born in Yuzhou (today's Chongqing). He was well informed and knowledgeable. He worked in calligraphy and painting. He was also good at feng shui. He was unyielding and did not seek fame and wealth. About the tenth year of Daoguang (1830), he left home alone and traveled to Jianzhou, where he was welcomed and treated by the magistrate. He had a good relationship with Fang Zhaochun from Shipanpu, so he moved to the Wan Shou Gong from the county bureau. Although he was economically poor, he regarded it with equanimity. He often drank and sang poems with the literati and scholars from the countryside. He could chat with the people and even beggars all day long but could speak nothing with the dignitaries. He lived alone every day, or did not eat for days, or slept for days, or played with others, so he was regarded as "crazy", and he did not care. Once he painted, he worked for days without stopping, and when he finished, he clapped his hands and cheered. Although he created many paintings, it was not easy for ordinary people to get them. Only some close friends could get them. He also accepted the help of his intimate friends but did not hand over his works to dignitaries. Judging from the existing works (most of which are inscribed with poems), Wu Ang was a painter with distinctive personality, broad-minded ambition, advocating farming and reading, with a unique and lofty style, mainly focusing on landscape painting and flower painting. In Jianyang, there are also legends about his background that he was a staff member of Hong Xiuquan of the Taiping Heavenly Kingdom, might have come to Jianyang to hide from disaster and pretended to be crazy, and that he proposed to build local famous landscapes—Ti Ming Tower and Iron Light Pole, so as to bring benefits such as wealth, culture and beauty of nature. Wu Ang is not included in the celebrity dictionaries of important figures in Sichuan and Chengdu (including the latest *Chengdu Historical and Cultural Dictionary*, of which the author is the deputy editor in chief), which is related to his personality, lifestyle and level, narrow dissemination of works and other factors. But at least, he was a "person of unusual ability" in the local urban culture who had a clear manifestation of the characteristics of Bashu culture and Tianfu culture.

(5) Yu Fazhai (1854—1946), the local "fist king", was born in Shipanpu. His ancestor, Yu Fei (nicknamed "Sai Yanfei"), immigrated from Huguang to Jianyang during the Shunzhi period. Yu Fei liked martial arts and had a bold and forthright personality. He once met an eminent monk and took in a master from Henan Province who escaped bullying from the powerful. Yu Fei learned their unique skills in martial arts. He combined Seng, Song, Yu and Northern and Southern fist styles, and created "Yu Men Fist". It was passed on to Yu Fazhai who was already the 14th generation. In 1918, Li Guochao, the bodyguard of Xiong Kewu, Commander in Chief of the Jingguo Army in Sichuan, set up a challenge arena in Qingyang Palace and was defeated by Yu

Fazhai who had overcome all the difficulties on the way. In 1928, Yu Dingshan, Yu Fazhai's eldest son, defeated Chen Niu, a man of unusual strength, and was hired to teach at the Chongqing National Martial Arts Gym. Yu Dingshan had many disciples. In 1930, Yu Dingshan participated in the "Examinations and Meetings of Martial Arts Warriors" hosted by Pan Wenhua, Mayor of Chongqing. There were 15 people who won the title of hero, and 12 of them were Yu clan disciples. After the founding of the People's Republic of China, Yu Shaohua, the descendant of Yu Men Fist (Yu Fazhai's grandnephew), was employed as the martial arts coach at Chengdu College of Physical Education, participated in national competitions twice, and entered the Chinese martial arts celebrity dictionary. Later, as the descendants moved to other places, the propagation centers of Yumen Fist moved out of Jianyang (mostly in eastern Sichuan). In 2010, Jianyang Martial Arts School established the Yumen Fist Research Association. In 2016, Yu Menquan was selected as an intangible cultural heritage project in Chengdu. With the support of the government and society, the descendants are gradually restoring in Jianyang this fist technique with the gene of Hua Tuo's "Five-Animal Exercise". Yumen Fist was formed in the middle of the Ming Dynasty and developed in Jianyang in the Qing Dynasty. It is a kind of boxing with varied techniques and a martial arts culture integrating "martial arts ethics", "benevolence" and "nourishing qi".

(6) Fu Chongju (1875—1917), the pioneer of modern civilization in Chengdu, was from Shipan, Jianyang. He was born in a Juren family and had liked learning and collecting since a child. He moved to Chengdu with his father and loved the city very much, so he always called himself a Chengduese. He once studied in Zunjing Academy and was deeply influenced by the ideas of constitutional reform and modernization. He was determined to help the people, especially devoted to the spread of science and technology to enlighten people and the establishment of newspapers to open the public's vision. He also had many "Sichuan First" practices, such as establishing a jinrikisha company and issuing lottery tickets. He was kind-hearted and could not help making hypocritical officials and bad friends, which finally made his undertakings wither and himself dejected. In his later years, he mainly focused on writing for his hometown. In more than 10 years, he collected and published the large-scale *Fu Series*, which provided a lot of valuable information needed for the progress of Sichuan and Chengdu. Among them, the 310000-word *Chengdu Survey* is the most contributive, with more than 400 columns, which introduces in detail all aspects of Chengdu at the end of the Qing Dynasty and the beginning of the Republic of China, and was known as the "encyclopedia" of Chengdu society at that time. Fu Chongju therefore became one of the greatest cultural giants and local sages in Chengdu at that time. Today, Jianyang has been restored to be a part of Chengdu, so it is an inevitable obligation of cultural construction to make efforts to carry out cultural creation and various forms of communication with his deeds and ideas, and to build the cultural confidence, consciousness and pride of the city.

(7) **Zheng Ziren (1878—1973), a legendary doctor**, was born in Wumiao town of Jianyang. Because he was often ill in his childhood, he once worshipped the living Buddha and became a Buddhist. Later, he learned medicine from the famous doctor Zheng Xiangchen. He also studied Tibetan medicine and received the monastic precepts in the Sakya Temple of Gongga Mountain in Tibet. In 1915, he went to Beijing to take the civil service examination. After passing the examination, he had a short experience as a judge and military law officer in Shenyang and Chengdu. He spent most of his time working as a military doctor. In 1935, he served as a professor in Chengdu National Hospital. He was a person with extraordinary willpower and aspiration.

He had entered Tibet eight times and gone to India twice in order to learn Buddhism and medicine, and his footprints covered all provinces of China. He was very intelligent, familiar with Sanskrit and Tibetan, and had great attainments in philology. He gave full play to the "fight poison with poison" therapy of traditional Chinese medicine and Tibetan medicine. His tiger wolf like formula was often terrifying, but it could cure difficult or chronic diseases. The famous general Liu Xiang had been successfully treated with his tiger wolf formula. He was also able to make a variety of pills. The process and method were very mysterious, and he successfully cured the bone disease of the famous Sichuan female athlete Wang Xiaojun who won the national sprint and relay championship at that time. Even in today's medical community, this disease is a difficult problem.

(8) Yang Yongxian (1838—1956), a famous Chinese cursive pen saint, was nicknamed "Yang Caoxian" and was born in Yangjiahe, Jiang Yuan, Jianyang. He worked as a village teacher, then worked as a private adviser in Anhui, and finally moved to Shenyang, Japan, Shanghai, Southeast Asia and other places. He died in Singapore at the age of 118. His longevity alone is amazing. In terms of family and career choice, he was headstrong and stubborn, and took the path of selling calligraphy for a living. When he arrived in Southeast Asia, his wife broke off contact with him. After his calligraphy went popular in the market, he made a lot of money. When he was in Japan, he encountered a volcanic eruption and there were heavy civilian casualties. He donated 200,000 yuan to help. So that when he returned to Shanghai, his family sometimes needed financial help from friends. His cursive art had a strange and peculiar style, but it was highly praised by the media because of its extraordinary character. Some media even praised him as "the first sage of cursive writing in 3,000 years", which shows that his admirers were enthusiastic. His thoughts, speech, personality, articles and art all have their strong points. "Possessing the sovereignty of civilization and progress, he can be called the quintessence of China". It can be seen that his reputation is high. Every time before he started writing, he also had a leap movement, "like a Chinese martial artist chopping a broadsword, dancing with a long sword, and wielding a copper hammer and iron rod, which are extremely portable"; He could "use both hands, one hand at a time, sometimes from left to right, and sometimes from right to left, or do the writing with both hands and finish in one smooth motion." The audience invariably enjoyed themselves to the full, all shouting and applauding. As a result, his characters were valued as high as 10,000 to 20,000 yuan per character. At the age of 91, he performed and exhibited his own works in Taiwan, which won great popularity. His cursive plum blossom style was rated as "the first Chinese sage of rapid cursive writing" by Japanese celebrities at that time. In addition, Yang Yongxian was also an excellent poet who had attainments in both ancient style poetry and modern poetry, and had made unique contributions to the expansion of the influence of Chinese culture both inside and outside the Confucian cultural circle.

(9) Liu Zihua (1899—1992), an astronomer who speculated about new stars in the solar system using the studies of the *Book of Changes*, as born in Luodai①, Jianyang. He was an apprentice when he was young, studied in an old-style private school, and learned English from his uncle (an English teacher in Jianyang Middle School). In 1918, he was admitted to the preparatory work study program for studying in France. One year later, he

---

① Longquanyi District (including Luodai) had long belonged to Jianyang in history. Today's Jianyang can rightfully regard the celebrities before the separation as its own historical and cultural resources. However, when it comes to the development and utilization of these resources, Jianyang City and Longquanyi District should strengthen communication and coordination, strive to achieve a win-win and a better layout, and prevent falling into an either this or that dispute.

won the travel allowance to France with the third-place academic result and arrived in Paris. He participated in the revolutionary activities of the CPC who studied in France in the early days. In 1923, he was admitted to the University of Paris (preparatory course), and in 1926, he studied in medical school. In 1932, his thesis won the "Special Honorary Award" in the essay contest held by the International Union of University Students on the issue of the League of Nations. Later, someone asked him to explain the *Book of Changes*, which Westerners thought was very mysterious. Liu Zihua turned his research to astrophysics. From 1937 to 1939, living in the cheapest apartment, he was often tortured by coldness because he could not afford heating. With great efforts, he completed his doctoral thesis "The Eight Diagrams Cosmology and Modern Astronomy — Prediction of a New Star", submitted it and participated in the thesis oral defense. The thesis spans ancient and modern times, China and the West, and is too recondite. Several professors read it separately which amazed them. In June 1940, the fire of fascist war had reached France. In order to dodge air raids, Liu Zihua studied in the cemetery. He received his doctorate in November. When it came to solving the problem of publishing funds, this paper won support from the scientific research institution led by the famous scientist Jolio Curie (Madame Curie's husband) and the French Ministry of Foreign Affairs. According to convention, there should be a picture of the author on the book, but Liu Zihua insisted on attaching a picture of his mother. As a result, with the special permission of the University of Paris, a picture of Chinese rural women was printed on the scientific work formed by his doctoral thesis. In 1943, the thesis earned him the title of National Doctor, the highest degree in France. This was the first time that a Chinese work study student going to France had won this honor. The University of Paris invited Liu Zihua to teach in the university after the war. However, in

1945, the National Government called on overseas Chinese to return, and Liu Zihua returned to his motherland. After returning to China, the Kuomintang party asked him to participate in politics to strengthen the ruling power. He did not cooperate because he did not like politics. In addition, his theory was regarded as a heresy in the domestic academic circle that was full of stories of worshipping foreign things. Liu Zihua fell into the predicament of being jobless, and he led a difficult life. Although he served as a counselor of Sichuan Provincial Government after the founding of the People's Republic of China, he also experienced hardships. After the reform and opening up, his doctoral thesis and contributions were finally fairly evaluated.

(10) Fu Yuantian (1925—1997), a Taoist leader who cleverly protected the heritage of Qingcheng Mountain, was born in Jiulong, Jianyang, from a poor family and was constantly ill. He only went to an old-style private school for a short time. In 1946, he became a monk in Huanglong Temple, Wenchuan County, following his mother's orders, and learned from Zhang Yongping, the leader of the Longmen Sect of Quanzhen Dao. From then on, he dedicated his life to Taoism. He went to Qingcheng Mountain Taoist Temple in 1955 and was successively elected as the leader of Shangqing Palace, the president of Qingcheng Mountain Taoist Association, and the president of Chengdu Taoist Association. In 1986, he was elected Vice President of the Chinese Taoist Association. In July 1988, Fu Yuantian founded the Qingcheng Mountain Taoist School. In March 1992, at the fifth national representative meeting of the Chinese Taoist Association, Master Fu Yuantian was elected as the president and concurrently served as the president of the Chinese Taoist Academy. At the same time, he also served as a member of the Standing Committee of the CPPCC National Committee. Fu Yuantian has been industrious and plain all his life, never using his position to pursue perquisites and prestiges. He was sincere, approachable and amiable. His demeanor can be regarded as one of the best interpretations of "broad roads to simplicity, sunshine to faraway".

Fu Yuantian's most legendary wisdom was prominently reflected in the "Cultural Revolution". When the Red Guards went up the mountain in a threatening manner and was about to "destroy the four olds" in the Taoist temple, he and Master Yi Xinying led the Taoists to cover all the cultural relics inside and outside the Taoist temple with pasted papers, which were filled with "the highest instruction" (Chairman Mao's speech) and the most "revolutionary" slogan at that time: Long live Marxism Leninism! Long live the CPC! Long live Chairman Mao! Thus, the Red Guards had to leave angrily. Later, he and Master Yi Xinying led the Taoists to move the cultural relics to the Shangqing Palace, hide them, and take care of them every day. At ordinary times, in order to prevent other thieves from thinking about cultural relics, he led Taoists to work in the ground during the day and arranged patrols at night. He dared not be careless. During the "Cultural Revolution", the cultural relics of Qingcheng Mountain survived very well, thanks to the courage and wisdom of him and Master Yi Xinying. In addition, in order to solve the livelihood of Taoists in the chaotic state and stabilize the team, he spared no effort to organize Taoists to plant tea and exchange tea for food. He made "Taoist Dongtian Dairy Wine" through hundreds of blending experiments using the Taoist ancestral secret recipe of kiwi plain wine, and built a factory to produce it. The winery was later brought down by the intervention of political forces. After the reform and opening up, the "Dongtian Dairy Wine Factory" was rebuilt, and its product became one of the tourism commodities of Qingcheng Mountain. These stories are legendary.

In addition, Fu Yuantian also had a lofty demeanor in taking the lead in public charity and donation. For example, in 1993, he donated 1 million yuan to the Hope Project on behalf of Qingcheng Mountain.

6. 12 Generals. According to *Jianzhou Celebrity* compiled by Jiang Xiang-dong, Chen Xueming and Chen Shuizhang and *Tianfu Xiongzhou Happy Jian-yang* collectively compiled by Jianyang, there are at least 12 generals who have had an important impact on the country and Sichuan in history, with varying degrees of historical positive energy and commemorative value:

Jian Yong, General Zhaode of Shuhan who was deeply respected by Liu Bei during the Three Kingdoms Period.

Wei Gao (741—805), a native of Jingzhao (now Xi'an, Shaanxi), was an outstanding figure in the middle of the Tang Dynasty. He was awarded the title of Grand General after he established a remarkable feat in the process of pacifying An Shi Rebellion and the rebellion of the warlord Zhu Ci who proclaimed himself emperor. In the first year of Zhenyuan (785), he was appointed as the governor of Chengdu and the governor of Xichuan in Jiannan. He lived in Sichuan for 21 years and became an outstanding strategist and politician in the southwest of China.

Wei Gao, as a famous person in Jianyang, may cause controversy, but he basically meets the criteria of the regional historical celebrity that were explained earlier. He was a governor of Xichuan in Jiannan of the Tang Dynasty for a long time. His main historical contribution was to win over and contact the Nanzhao regime and the Dongman regime, deal with the Tubo regime, ensure the peace of the southwest of the Tang Dynasty, and make great military achievements. Wei Gao sent troops to fight against the Tubo regime for many times, restraining its main force and ensuring the northwest frontier defense to a certain extent. He dispatched troops to fight several times and recovered lost territories many times. It is said about him in the history that "480,000 Tubo soldiers were defeated, 500 to 1,000 governors, city lords and officials were killed, more than 50,000 peopele were beheaded, 250,000 cattle and sheep were gained, and 6,300,000 weapons were collected, which was the highest contribution in the southwest." In addition to military achievements, Wei Gao, as the military and political leader of the Southwest, also used both grace and authority in politics, which made him quite popular. Emperor Dezong of the Tang Dynasty named him the King of Nankang, so later generations addressed him[1] respectfully as Wei Nankang. And Jianyang, as an important base and support for his military achievements, officials and people here had also made important contributions. So, in the year of Wei Gao's death, Emperor Dezong of the Tang Dynasty decided to "engrave stones to show loyalty", and personally gave an oral edict. The crown prince (later Emperor Shunzong of the Tang Dynasty) personally wrote the content of the Jigong Monument (more than 1,200 words), and then sent the trusted eunuch Li Xianshou, who served as the overseer, to read the order, and the local officials of Meizhou and Jianzhou organized the engraving.[2] Because of the special interaction between Wei Gao and Jianyang embodied in this monument, and the backward attention and application by Chengdu and Sichuan of Wei Gao as a historical and cultural celebrity resource, Jianyang can certainly regard him as its own historical celebrity. According to the comprehensive historical

---

[1] Although it is true that Wei Gao was an overly powerful minister in his later years. Yet this is not comparable to his meritorious service. In addition, he went from being close to opposing the Wang Shuwen and Liu Zongyuan Group, and even participated in forcing Tang Shunzong to abdicate in favor of Tang Xianzong. Such gratitude and resentment, merits and demerits are difficult for later generations to simply praise and criticize.

[2] In addition, Wei Gao's memorial monuments for meritorious deeds were located in Zizhou (now Zizhong) and Xuzhou (now Yibin). The former was established by Wei Ding, the great grandson of Wei Gao, when he was the governor of Zizhou, while the latter was established by Zhang Jiuzong, the governor of Xuzhou, in the fifth year of Yuanhe (810). These two monuments are less important than those of Meizhou and Jianzhou. Today, the other three monuments have disappeared. Only Jianyang has retained this monument and the historical evidence that Jianyang is a hot land closely related to this hero.

data of *Jianzhou Celebrity* written by Jianyang experts Jiang Xiangdong, Chen Xueming and Chen Shuizhang, Wei Gao once led troops to garrison and train in Jianzhou for a long time when he was fighting against Tubo. Therefore, Jianzhou was an important location for him to make achievements, which should be no problem. According to historical records, Wei Gao wrote the *History of the Restoration of the Southwestern Barbarians* (which has been lost). He should think of Jianyang as the Niubing County when the Han Dynasty explored the Southwestern Barbarians.

Xia Zhishi (1887—1950), a native of Hejiang, Sichuan, once traveled to Japan to study military affairs, participated in the Chinese Revolutionary League, and served in the Chengdu New Army after returning home, and engaged in revolutionary activities. After the Railway Project Crisis in 1911, on November 5, as an ordinary officer, he was publicly recommended as the Commander in Chief of the Revolutionary Army, leading the Longquanyi garrison and firing the first shot of the 1911 Revolution in Sichuan. After the uprising, he led the army to Chongqing and served as the deputy governor of Chongqing Shu Military Government. Afterwards, he also served as the commander in chief for the grand admiral Sun Yat sen. After he retired from office, he also founded Jinjiang Public School in Chengdu. He was killed by mistake in his hometown Hejiang County in 1950, and was rehabilitated in 1987.

Liu Cunhou (1885—1960) was born in Xinglongchang, Sancha Town, Jianyang. He studied in the Imperial Japanese Army Academy, participated in the Chinese Revolutionary League, participated in the war for the protection of the nation, participated in the warlord competition, and sheltered Wu Peifu. In 1933, on the order of Chiang Kai shek, he served as the commander in chief of the sixth lu of the "Communist suppression" army in Sichuan, fought with the Red Army, was defeated utterly, and was dismissed by Chiang Kai shek. He lived in Chengdu for the next 16 years. In 1949, with the help of Yan Xishan, an old classmate, he fled to Taiwan and stayed there until death.

Tian Songyao (1888—1975), a native of Longquanyi, Jianyang County, graduated from Baoding Military Academy of Land Force. He once served as brigade commander and division commander of the 21st Sichuan Army Division, land force general of the Beiyang Government, and commander of the 29th National Revolutionary Army. He participated in warlord wars and was defeated by the Red Army. He took part in the 1949 uprising of Liu, Deng and Pan, had performed meritorious service, and thus later served as the counselor of the provincial government. In his later years, he was enthusiastic about the cause of education in his hometown and made positive contributions.

Chen Liangji (1890—1952), from Pingxi, Jianyang. During the Anti-Japanese War, he was a general and division commander of the national army who had made great contributions to the defense of Changsha. He was the winner of the "Commemorative Medal for the 60th Anniversary of the Victory of the Chinese People's War of Resistance against Japanese Aggression".

Huang Yin (1890—1969), born in Longquanyi, Jianyang County, graduated from the Baoding Military Academy and was a Confucian general in the Sichuan Army. He used to be the lieutenant general in the Kuomintang, the commander of defense works along the Changjiang River in Sichuan, and the first mayor of Chengdu since the founding of the city in modern times. He rose in Chengdu in 1949 and served as the deputy commander of Chengdu Military Region after 1950.

Liao Zhen (1890—1949) was born in Sancha Town, Jianyang. He studied in the speed-up military educational program in Sichuan, served in Sichuan Army, and gradually showed up prominently. His anti-Communist and anti-Japanese actions were outstanding, and his highest military position was the commander of the 44th Kuomintang Army. He was the winner of the "Commemorative Medal for the 60th Anniversary of the Victory of the Chinese People's War of Resistance against Japanese Aggression".

Chen Dingxun (1893—1973) was born in Sanchaba, Yihe Township, Jianyang. He once participated in the warlord competition in Sichuan, but later he made outstanding contributions to the war against Japan and returned to Sichuan in his later years to bring benefit to his native place. He was the winner of the "Commemorative Medal for the 60th Anniversary of the Victory of the Chinese People's War of Resistance against Japanese Aggression".

Dong Lang (1894—1932) was a native of Ping'an Township, Jianyang County. He was a student of Huangpu Military Academy and was one of the important military commanders of Nanchang Uprising, and one of the founders of Hailufeng Revolutionary Base. He was once the chief of staff of the Fourth Red Army (of which the Commander was He Long). He was a famous general of the Red Army who unfortunately died of Wang Ming's left deviation purges. In 1954, he was recognized as a revolutionary martyr.

Wang Xiafeng (1899—1953) was born in Baishiba, Jianyang. He was the nephew of Liu Cunhou and gradually promoted under Liu's command. He became brigade commander in 1932. He attacked the Red Army with Liu Cunhou, and his troops were completely defeated. He escaped alone at night. He sneaked into Nanjing and studied at the Central Army University. He served as a division commander in the Anti-Japanese War, fought bloody battles with the Japanese aggressors for many times, and later won the "Medal of Blue Sky and Bright Sun". He was promoted to lieutenant general commanding the 47th corps, and was captured in the War of Liberation. He was the winner of the "Commemorative Medal for the 60th Anniversary of the Victory of the

Chinese People's War of Resistance against Japanese Aggression".

Zeng Lie (1901—1945) was born in Shizhongtan, Jianyang. He graduated from Chengdu Martial Arts School and joined the Sichuan Army soon after. In 1937, as the Chief of Staff (Major General) of a brigade of the 20th Army (Commander Wang Zanxu), he went out of Sichuan to fight against Japan (his hometown, Pingwo Township, Jianyang, sang a grand play for him for three days "seeing off Chief of Staff Zeng from Sichuan to fight against Japan"), and participated in the battles of Anqing and Suizao. In particular, he participated in and commanded the "Changde Battle" (one of the most powerful battles in the frontline battlefield), which gave a heavy blow to the Japanese army at the end of 1943, wiped out more than 29,000 enemies and successfully recovered the city. He was the winner of the "Commemorative Medal for the 60th Anniversary of the Victory of the Chinese People's War of Resistance against Japanese Aggression".

In an ordinary county, there are so many generals that cannot be ignored in the history of the country and Sichuan, which is very rare in Sichuan.

The above six types of celebrities are the main representatives of Jianyang's humanistic personality, urban spirit and excellent traditional culture. Of course, "celebrities" mainly refer to their great reputation both in life and after death, which does not mean that they are all perfect. Especially for the twelve generals, some of them, like almost all senior officers under the old regime at that time, had historical regrets of participating in warlord scuffles, anti-communism, and people raiding in the modern history of constant change. However, the Chinese culture is tolerant of those being aware that they have strayed from the right path, admiring those abandoning the dark and turning to the bright, and welcoming those who return to their roots, especially regarding the establishment of meritorious deeds in the war to defend their country as very important and glorious, so the author summarizes such a list.

Of course, Jianyang, as a truly influential region in history, is a hotbed of humanities and talents. There are also county sages represented by Xu Hexuan (1882—1957), Li Shuangru (1873—1959) and Wu Xueqin (1872—1952) who devoted their lives to serving their hometown, benefiting their people, and making contributions and setting an example; Mao Quefei, a revolutionary martyr who had participated in the War of Resistance against Japan and shot down Japanese planes, decided to cast aside the dark and turn to the bright in the War of Liberation. As the captain of a landing ship, he led the officers and soldiers to revolt, but unfortunately was caught by the Kuomintang secret service agency and died; In the early days of the founding of the People's Republic of China, those who were outstanding among the martyrs who died bravely in the food collection and the suppression of violent banditry; Ye Chaohui, Wei Fusheng, etc., from Jianyang, academicians of the Chinese Academy of Sciences, who have made important contributions to the scientific and technological cause of new China, they all deserve the attention of today's people and deserve to be remembered by future generations.

2. Value induction of celebrity culture

The mainstream culture of Confucianism in China advocates that "people should remain famous, and wild geese should keep their voices". The ultimate standard is morality, meritorious service, and speeches and writings to determine whether people can remain famous in the history. Historical celebrities play an important role in the process of social and historical development. Their influence is not only the great achievements they have created, but also the material and spiritual heritage they have left behind, which has become a huge wealth that affects future generations. They embody the excellent traditional Chinese culture, the pursuit of the lofty values of benevolence, righteousness, wisdom and trust, loyalty, filial piety and integrity, the solemnity of killing one's life to preserve benevolence and sacrifice one's life for justice, the great spirit and integrity, and the warm feelings of loving one's hometown and benefiting it. These are valuable resources for Jianyang to form a high-end cultural image. It can be summed up as: **to be determined to make meritorious contributions, to be benevolent and righteous, and to be famous by blessing**. Most of them can become the eternal historical resources and spiritual power by which Jianyang is remembered, yearned for and looked up to.

Section V Dongguan Culture

1. The great project with a heroic spirit that conquers mountains and rivers

In the modern history of Jianyang, there is a great feat that must be kept in mind and is worthy of praise. This is the "East Irrigation" (Dongguan) project. The "East Irrigation" (Dongguan) project was started in the spring of 1970 and completed in 1980. More than 102,000 cadres and migrant workers of Jianyang County participated in the construction. By 1985, the total irrigation area had reached 1,151.56 square kilometers, with 830,700 mu of arable land, accounting for 53.58% of Jianyang's arable land, benefiting 175,100 households and 689,800 people. The water diversion project is divided into four stages: the first stage is the Longquanshan Water Diversion Project, including the main diversion canal, Longquanshan Tunnel, Zhangjiayan Reservoir, and the south and north main canals. It had been prepared since August 1969, started in February 1970, and completed in August 1973; The second stage is the auxiliary project, including the excavation of the three main canals of Jiangyuan, Jianzi and Yangma, which began in November 1972 and was completed in the spring of 1977; The third stage is the Sancha Reservoir Project, including the reconstruction and expansion of the South Main Canal and the excavation of the Low South Main Canal. It had been prepared since September 1973, started in March 1975, and completed in February 1978; The fourth stage is Shipan Reservoir Project, which had been prepared since October 1976, started construction in August 1977 and completed in October 1980.

Since Li Bing and Wen Weng succeeded in harnessing the water and Chengdu thus benefited from flood control, irrigation and shipping, Chengdu Plain has rapidly replaced the Guanzhong Plain and become the world recognized "Land of Abundance". Ancestors of past dynasties have continuously increased auxiliary projects, which has expanded the area of benefit, and a part of Jianyang's villages and towns in the west of Longquan Mountain has also been included. However, the main body of Jianyang can only look at the water and heave a sign because of the barrier of Longquan Mountain, which stretches 200 kilometers from north to south. Especially after Longquanyi was incorporated into Chengdu and set up as a separate district in 1959, Jianyang basically has no connection with the Dujiangyan irrigation district. After the founding of the People's Republic of China, Jianyang left Chengdu and went under the jurisdiction of Neijiang District, which is of course subject to the overall situation of national construction, but after all, its "geographical advantage" has shrunk. Especially under the impact of the

"Cultural Revolution", the population of Jianyang naturally grew rapidly, but the production development was slow. The harm of natural disasters, especially drought (Jianyang is located in the transitional zone between the summer drought in western Sichuan and the summer drought in eastern Sichuan, and is plagued by the double drought, known as "one severe drought in ten years, two droughts in three years, and dry winter and dry spring every year"), became increasingly prominent, prompting the cadres and masses of Jianyang to produce and quickly demonstrate, declare, mobilize, organize, and start construction, get through Longquan Mountain, and immediately build supporting projects, so that the water in Dujiangyan can benefit Jianyang forever. In the early 1970s, 100,000 Jianyang people, against the background of poor political situation, weak scientific and technological support, and tight capital and equipment, successfully drilled through Longquan Mountain, drawing the torrent of the Daguan District, with the spirit of sacrifice and human resources as the main force, bleeding and sweating for more than two years. Through supporting projects, 700,000 mu of land are turned into fertile land and beautiful soil free from flood and drought, and the magnificent mountains and rivers of Jianyang are laid. *Tianfu Xiongzhou Happy Jianyang* wrote that in February 1970, the first battle of the project, "Longquan Mountain Diversion Tunnel", began. In order to complete such a huge project, more than 30,000 people's commune members, with their own dry food, hoes, carrying poles and other tools, marched into the barren mountains. They did not know the technology, so they went around to find the masters and learned it while working; In the absence of machinery, they relied on manual handling. There was strength in numbers. At the same time, the people of the county responded positively, workers, peasants, soldiers, students and businessmen mobilized together, the little old lady carried river sand with her handbag, the elderly in the nursing home took out the saved meat coupons, the teachers and students of primary and secondary schools picked up stones and made mandarin bags, the doctors sent medical treatment, the hairdressers went to barber, the theater and film teams went to perform, and the shops, post offices and bookstores moved to the construction site ... The farmers in Hedong who could not benefit temporarily also put forth their strength without hesitation. After two years and five months of hard work, they finally overcame many difficulties and finished the mountain diversion tunnel, which is 6,432 meters long, 3.4 meters high and 4.3 meters wide ... People call it Happy Water. Then, the people of Jianyang made unremitting efforts to build Zhangjiayan Reservoir, Sancha Lake Reservoir, and Shipan Reservoir (Longquan Lake) one after another ... A large-scale water conservancy project integrating water diversion, saving, and irrigation has emerged on the land of Jianyang... More than 1 million mu of farmland has been irrigated, rice yield per mu has increased from 275 kg to 514 kg, and cotton yield per mu has increased from 44 kg to 71 kg ... The history of water shortage is gone forever.

No matter in China or other countries, there is no second similar water conservancy project completed at a similar cost under the condition of similar materials and technologies. If the supporting projects are included, millions of people in Jianyang have worked together with the strength of the whole county. Over the past ten years, a total of 100,000 people (including thousands of women militia) have been invested, 87 million working days, 119 people have died, and 1,739 people have been disabled. The power behind these figures is the integration of will and belief, wisdom and sweat. During this period, many touching stories of cadres and the masses, workers and peasants, technicians and migrant workers working with one heart, sharing weal and woe, and working overtime emerged. From the central, provincial and municipal leaders to the ordinary people, they have formed numerous touching pictures that are the most impressive and reflect collectivism and selflessness. After the project is gradually completed and improved, it becomes a monument of China's water conservancy industry. There is an endless stream of domestic and foreign visiting, investigation, learning and exchange teams, bringing unique pride and glory to Sichuan, Chengdu and Neijiang.

Dongguan Culture is for achieving better development of hometown. Facing huge difficulties and dangers, people took the initiative. Provincial, prefectural and county leaders and professional departments worked together. Chengdu provided technical and transportation support. Jianyang workers, peasants and soldiers worked together and built a culture of fighting and heroes, which is Dongguan Culture. There is also a beautiful scenery, that is, the women of Jianyang. Jianyang women actively participated in the Dongguan Project with the spirit of holding up half the sky. Women accounted for more than 15% of the water conservancy project team throughout the year. They fought in exploration, design, construction, testing, drilling, mechanical and electrical engineering, tunneling, and driving, leaving many impressive and heroic stories:

There were more than 20 women in the "Women's Climbing and Driving Platoon" of the Lingxian Engineering Team in the Horse Raising Work Area. They learned to turn on certain machines for the first time. Their whole bodies were numb as the machine vibrated. The backs of their hands were red and swollen, and some were burned by electric leakage. They were exhausted after work. They also raised stones to practice their arms and carried out revolutionary competitions with male migrant workers.

In 1975, at the construction site of Sancha Reservoir, the "Iron Girl Class" of the Red Flag Engineering Team in the Slate Work Area set up the banner of the first female lathe erector and female artillery worker for the project.

Some of the cadres and the masses who participated in the project in those years have died, and the vast majority of them are aged people now. Reading their memoirs, or talking with them about their common memories, they become emotional and proud. For young and middle-aged Jianyang people and their descendants, we must not let them forget the hardships and excellence of the great project of "Dongguan". Jianyang's cultural and creative activities, cultural tourism, local education, urban and rural landscapes, and commemorative projects must create new highlights in the territory of Tianfu culture and the field of party and national history education. Jianyang thus has great potential.

2. Summary of spiritual and cultural values

We believe that the "Dongguan" project reflects the tenacity of the people of Jianyang to face the difficulties under relatively difficult conditions (cultural revolution turbulence, frequent droughts, not belonging to Chengdu), to realize a better life **without fear of danger, with self-reliance, unity of purpose, and fortitude.** It is the highest realm of Jianyang's mass culture, and the best illustration of Jianyang's fine cultural personality and cultural potential that can be passed on through ages.

President Xi Jinping stressed at the conference celebrating the 40th anniversary of reform and opening up: "As a large country, we should have ambitions." The Dongguan Project is designed to benefit future generations. With scientific methods, careful planning and organization, it brings together the spirit of hard work and bravery of officials and people. It is a great practice. As a collective value with dedication and sacrifice as the core, it is difficult for other projects in peacetime to be as impressive and touching as the Jianyang

Dongguan Project. With an eye to the present, Jianyang has ushered in new opportunities and development. It must be clearly seen that compared with other districts (cities) and counties in Chengdu, there are many weaknesses in the construction and development conditions of New Jianyang. In order to keep up with the development pace of Chengdu, and make unique contributions by developing strengths and avoiding weaknesses, Jianyang not only needs strategic vision and scientific planning, but also needs to continue to carry forward the spirit of Jianyang people's self-reliance, unity of purpose and fortitude. This makes Jianyang shine in the aspect of "being remembered" and "being looked up to".

Section VI Intangible Cultural Heritage

1. Reasons for the Formation of Jianyang Intangible Cultural Heritage

The so-called intangible cultural heritage refers to the forms of expression of various traditional cultures passed down from generation to generation by people of all ethnic groups and regarded as part of the cultural heritage, as well as the objects and places related to the forms of expression of traditional cultures. Generally speaking, those who have been formally recognized by the government and required to protect their heritage after declaration or rescue are important components of excellent traditional culture. Since the reform and opening up, its protection, inheritance and even development with the times have become an important task of urban or rural cultural construction from the national level to the local level. Compared with "material cultural heritage", it is usually a kind of skill, method or spatial form with specific connotation, implication and value, which can not only express the spirit and artistic pursuit, but also express a way of life and life purport that people like or hope for. The Chinese culture is broad and profound, open and inclusive, with a vast territory and a large number of ethnic groups. All regions have intangible cultural heritages that have both the common characteristics of Chinese culture and personality. Since ancient times, the people have been industrious and intelligent, the local culture has been active, and various talents have come forth in large numbers, especially Jianyang, which is "rich in culture and skillful in workmanship". However, due to the widespread destruction of Sichuan's cities and villages in the late Ming and early Qing Dynasties, the aborigines almost disappeared. The intangible cultural heritage culture that can be seen and has value today is almost all the destiny and space that immigrants from more than ten provinces have reshaped in production, life, trade and various exchanges since the Kangxi Emperor of the Qing Dynasty, and then has been preserved in the urban and rural evolution of more than 100 years of modernization and globalization.

(1) The factors belonging to the similarity of Bashu culture and Tianfu culture

1) Civilian

Today, most of the ancestors of Jianyang people came from the migration movement of "Huguang Filling Sichuan", which started in the 33rd year of Kangxi (1694) and was supported by the government for more than 100 years. Ordinary civilians in more than a dozen provinces across the country had experienced thousands of miles of travel and ethnic conflicts. In the decades' period of time, they had overcome the attacks of tigers, wolves and bandits by relying on their indomitable will. With the government's sympathy and assistance, as well as the mutual assistance of immigrants, a civilian culture had been formed, which is the main soil for intangible cultural heritage. There are few noble families and powerful "upper class society" people that discriminated against intangible cultural heritage practitioners and their skills, and Jianyang is no exception.

2) Grassroots

Sichuan and Chengdu in the Qing Dynasty had a difficult recovery process accompanied by a century old migration movement. Migrants are generally very hard-working people. After the war stopped, the tiger and wolf problem gradually disappeared, plus the government's preferential exemption and care in taxes and corvee, the people gradually got rid of hunger and cold. There was a prosperous scene. For 100 years, the grain price was the lowest in the major grain producing areas in China. Urban and rural areas were generally rebuilt and revitalized, and families that valued farming, reading, poetry and etiquette began to emerge, laying the foundation for academic, cultural and educational recovery. However, the population growth rate of the Land of Abundance was unparalleled in China. In the late Qianlong period, it was already overcrowded, and the economic development reached its limit. More and more vagrants emerged due to overpopulation. Gradually accumulated malpractices in the administration of officials and social contradictions intertwined resulted in serious problems of White Lotus Sect and Paoge. Therefore, in Sichuan and Chengdu in the Qing Dynasty, the common people and the grassroots society, from their ideas to their lifestyles, always maintained a clear grassroots nature—in intangible cultural heritage activities. They were characterized by simplicity, accompanying villages, spontaneity and diversity, and relatively casual inheritance and dissemination. In terms of technology and style, they mainly adapted to the cheapest consumption capability and expressed the hobbies and interests of the bottom people. This also determines that the intangible cultural heritage of Jianyang mainly belongs to mass culture, rather than celebrity culture, commercial road culture, etc.

(2) The personality factor of Jianyang's own evolution

1) The influence of Hakka culture

The Chengdu Comprehensive Survey, written by Jianyang's modern out-standing talent and great sage Fu Chongju at the end of the Qing Dynasty and the beginning of the Republic of China, records that: "Today's Chengdu people are all from other provinces." He also gave a detailed introduction to the proportion of immigrants from various provinces. According to statistics, Hakka immigrants are a major ethnic group second only to Hu Guang immigrants, accounting for 33% of the total population of Sichuan at that time. [1] Jianyang in the Qing Dynasty and since the end of the Ming Dynasty and the beginning of the Qing Dynasty had been the main stronghold of Hakka culture in western China, especially in the area centered around Luodai. Hakka culture has many outstanding advantages, such as respecting ancestors, respecting etiquette, emphasizing cultivation and study, being good at cooperation, and daring to work hard. In particular, women are very hardworking and responsible. They are more responsible than women of other ethnic groups in terms of family rearing and making money.

2) Continuous martial spirit

Jianyang's modern military, war and banditry activities were relatively numerous, which prompted the continuation of the tradition of emphasizing both literature and military.

---

[1]　Hakka's Entering Sichuan — 2020 *Tianfu Guangji*, Issue 12, Chengdu CPPCC

3) Transportation progress

The geographical location of Jianyang determines that with the connection of various modern transportation tools between Chengdu and Chongqing, Jianyang is the first beneficiary. The internal and external exchanges of intangible cultural heritage talents, skills, resources and culture are more convenient, and the link between Chengdu and Chongqing economic circles is obvious, which brings more and more obvious benefits to the inheritance and development of intangible cultural heritage that keeps pace with the times.

2. Jianyang's major intangible cultural heritage

In the past ten years, with the joint efforts of relevant government departments and inheritors, 10 intangible cultural heritage items in Jianyang have entered the list of intangible cultural heritage items in Chengdu (including 8 items in the fifth batch and 2 items in the sixth batch), including Heishui Temple stories, Zhang's guqin making skills, Shiqiao hanging noodles making skills, Tuojiang boatman's horn, Jiulian lantern, Yumen Fist, Zhang's earthenware making skills, traditional lamb soup making skills, Six God tune, Li's Hua'an Hall plaster. These reflect Jianyang people's unremitting pursuit of a colorful and happy life, the industriousness and intelligence of craftsmen, and the benevolence and justice spirit of benefiting their hometown. From the perspective of the Jianyang characteristics and contributions to the humanistic integration of park city and the fostering and enhancement of Chengdu's life aesthetics, these are precious resources for cultural innovation and activities, even for industrial development.

According to the author's understanding, these 10 intangible cultural heritage items, according to their own attributes and development prospects, and the size of the population that may be integrated or affected, the traditional mutton soup making techniques, Zhang's guqin making techniques, Yumen Fist, and Jiulian Lantern are the most worthy of inheritance and promotion, so I will give a special discussion here.

(1) Mutton soup and its food series

Chengdu is the first "World Food Capital" in Asia awarded by UNESCO, and Sichuan cuisine is its sufficient strength. There is a Sichuan dish that can be served both in a mansion and a humble house. And it is mainly a delicacy that reflects the needs of civilians. It is the mutton soup.

Jianyang people have a long history of being close to sheep, and a large number of sheep fossils have been unearthed in Longya Culture. Shushan, an ancestor of ancient Shu, belonged to the ancient Qiang people. The Qiang people worshiped sheep. Most of the totems and ornaments representing their beliefs are in the sheep form. Jianyang has both mountains and rivers, plains and river valleys, which are suitable for the growth of sheep. There is a local "fire pimple sheep" of strong vitality. During the Anti-Japanese War, because Ms. Song Meiling liked to drink milk from cows and sheep, Chiang Kai shek took advantage of the wartime alliance and introduced dozens of the famous goat breed, Nubian, from the United States into China. Song Meiling left Sichuan after the war. During the process of transfer, these sheep dispersed to the mountains and hybridized with "fire pimple sheep", resulting in a new breed—big ear sheep of strong adaptability, tall physique, short growth cycle, tender meat and small smell, which became a favorite food of Jianyang people. The folk mutton soup has been developed into a highly civilian Sichuan cuisine variety that has both commonality and individuality and has kept pace with the times to the 21st century. On the basis of the unchanged diet style of the common people (It mainly adapts to the consumption level and habits of ordinary people. It is delicious, cheap, and fresh, while the dining environment, service, and grade are not important), it has derived into a series of delicious foods to adapt to various consumption levels and types. This highlights the love of Jianyang people for life, their new enthusiasm for delicious food, and their nostalgia for the countryside and homesickness. Mutton soup and its series are a collection of the cooking wisdom of many immigrants from 18 provinces, giving consideration to the profound health preserving cultural demands of Confucianism and Taoism that focus on life experience, quality of life and physical and mental health, and integrating the life philosophy of treating diseases in traditional Chinese medicine diet. In particular, on the basis of being folk, being local, being delicious, being affordable, having excellent ingredients and other traditional characteristics, it seeks to keep pace with the times and achieve the coordinated development of food culture and food industrialization and branding which complement one another. The positive energy for economy and people's livelihood is stable and growing. For example, in 2013, Jianyang produced about 1.5 million goats, including 200000 to 500000 big ear commercial goats, and they were sold to Chengdu, Chongqing, Guizhou, Yunnan, Hunan and other places.

In general, the core skills of intangible cultural heritage are mainly passed down from generation to generation through the father, son and grandson within the family, or through a specific relationship between teachers and apprentices. In addition, the number of people involved in the general intangible cultural heritage activities is quite limited. However, the delicious mutton soup created by Jianyang people from their ordinary diet, which has become "popular" since the 1980s, and is suitable for the rich and the poor, old and young, has the following five characteristics: First, in order to better spread the mutton soup, all famous stores have published "recipes" of "bussiness secrets" such as raw materials, production procedures and methods used for some dishes, which reflect the simplicity and kindness of the people of Jianyang and their self-confidence. Secondly, Jianyang is deeply influenced by Hakka culture. Hakka culture is characterized by women being particularly industrious and intelligent and daring to undertake various responsibilities, including increasing family income. Therefore, the hosts of famous mutton soup stores in Jianyang are mostly women, or couples working together and starting businesses. Moreover, in some famous stores, when families teach key skills, they pass them on to both males and females. This especially reflects a good character of Tianfu culture: respecting women and women daring to do everything, both promote each other and complement each other. Third, the perfect combination of "local" and "foreign" reflects the importance of the international exchange of food culture. Fire pimple sheep and Nubian sheep are the most successful combination of native and foreign genes (Jianyang was later introduced with high-quality British sheep breeds); The sheep introduced by Song Meiling turned into food, and finally became the favorite of Jianyang and Chengdu grassroots civilians (up to now, Jianyang's status as the "first soup in the west" has basically taken shape, and at least the Chengdu and Sichuan people I know basically recognized that). These are all vivid and interesting, but also enlightening food culture stories. Fourth, as for Jianyang mutton soup intangible cultural heritage skills and food culture inheritance, there have been two lines: family intergenerational inheritance; the inheritance by apprentices based on their moral character and reliable nature. The latter is not limited to where the apprentices come from, and whether they will return to their hometown to start their own businesses. For example, Hu Guiguang of a

Jianyang mutton soup family and Li Hanjiang, an apprentice who opened up his own shops, all face the inheritance of skills with such an open mind. Li Hanjiang, well-known in Jianyang (who has passed away), led 28 apprentices, including 8 from Zhejiang, Fujian and other places. These people's return to their hometown is of great significance to the spread of Jianyang and its food. Fifth, Jianyang mutton soup, with its cultural style of benevolence, affinity, openness and keeping pace with the times, has changed from a snack "soup" to a rapidly growing exotic flower in Sichuan cuisine, originating from homesickness and is higher than homesickness, connecting urban and rural areas and benefiting more and more people—For example, through the continuous efforts of the mutton soup masters, the number of Jianyang mutton based dishes has already exceeded 150; The way of making mutton has developed to ten processes, such as stewing, frying, steaming, boiling, roasting. High quality sheep breeding has become an important industry of distinguishing feature in Jianyang. The festival, which started with mutton soup, has become the Jianyang scenery of the park city construction. The folk cuisine with mutton soup as its soul has become an independent cuisine. The price ranges from 30 to 50 yuan for a pot of soup to 1,000 yuan for a table of whole lamb dishes, inheriting the core essence and competitiveness of Sichuan cuisine (and Sichuan food culture):The industrious and intelligent ordinary people from all over China, against the background of sparsely populated Sichuan and sufficient land supply in the early Qing Dynasty, in the process of having to actively work together to deal with cannibals, bandits, and poverty, on the one hand, helped each other develop the economy, married each other, and built a society, on the other hand, made use of the extremely rich and inexpensive ingredients in the Land of Abundance, and integrated the cooking skills of ordinary Chinese people, having produced and sold thousands of delicious food with the main characteristics of good taste and low price. The cultural ecology in which Tianfu culture, Bashu culture, Confucianism, Buddhism and Taoism coexist harmoniously and complement each other, The heart refusing to format people and embracing heterodoxy and individuality, the values that value physical and mental health, life and the true quality of life, and the life aesthetics in which food, clothing, housing and transportation can improve life happiness index by adding interest (artistry) in details, all of them have been vividly interpreted in the rise of mutton soup, a wonderful work of Sichuan cuisine and Jianyang intangible cultural heritage. Jianyang has also been working hard for its further growth into a towering tree and a city card.

(2) Zhang's guqin making technique

Chengdu has been the music capital of China since ancient times. Its predecessors, Sanxingdui and Jinsha, embody the fine and exquisite bronze culture, jade culture, and gold ware making. All cultural relics and the silk unearthed prove its extremely mysterious and romantic cultural and artistic temperament. Without music, those grand sacrificial activities or activities giving orders are unimaginable. Large musical instrument stone chimes (the larger one is in Jinsha) were unearthed at Sanxingdui and Jinsha sites. As the capital of music, Chengdu has a history of at least 2,500-3,000 years. In ancient music activities, the seven stringed guqin was undoubtedly the king of musical instruments. The most valuable ancient qin that has survived in history is the Lei qin "Jiuxiao Huanpei" made by the Lei family, which produced a large number of qin masters for more than a century in Chengdu in the Tang Dynasty. This is undoubtedly the peak production and remains of Chinese classical musical instruments.

Coincidentally, Jianyang, a city that shared joys and sorrows with Chengdu in most of its history, also has a 35-year-old inheritor, Zhang Yong, who began to learn how to make guqin at the age of 15 and three generations from his family have inherited the skill (his father's generation was engaged in making and repairing musical instruments in Beijing National Instrument Factory). His guqin making technique is highly skilled, and the spirit of the craftsman of a great country has never been lost. Therefore, his products are not cheap, and can be used in major cultural venues in Chengdu (located in Jiangyuan Town, Jianyang City. His guqin is used in qin halls of Dufu Thatched Cottage, Emei Mountain, Dujiangyan, etc.). It has been widely reported by many media and recognized and praised by professional institutions. In September 2015, his work "Traditional Handicraft Guqin" participated in the "Look at Sichuan — Excellent Works Exhibition of Folk Literature and Art Creation Projects", entered the top ten among thousands of works, and won the "Excellent Works Award".

According to relevant introduction, Zhang's guqin making skill (called "Zhuo qin" in the industry) has the following characteristics:

Strict craftsmanship spirit of the great country — in terms of procedures and techniques, he insisted on standards and kept improving. It takes 3-4 months and 90 processes to complete each qin.

Strong brand awareness — in the face of the market in short supply, he would put quality before quantity, and firmly maintain the reputation of the brand.

An open-minded and broad-minded sense of inheritance — According to the special page of "Jianyang Culture" on the Internet, the first-generation person inherited Zhang's guqin is Zhang Yongsi, who taught himself the technique to make guqin. During the Cultural Revolution, he was stopped making it and became a stonemason because of his landlord background. Later, he passed on the guqin making skills to his four sons. Among them, Zhang Yiquan (Zhang Yong's father) was the most talented. He had studied from famous teachers in Beijing, Luoyang, Xi'an and other places. Therefore, the range and quality of his guqin can be rated as unique and excellent. Zhang Yong had learned to make guqin with his father since he was 15 years old. Later, he returned to Chengdu, where he was cultivated by Zeng Chengwei, a master of Sichuan guqin making. At the age of 18, he became famous and gradually had his own style. Later, he was praised by Nanjing's Chenggong Liang, Taiwan's Ge Shucong, Li Kongyuan and other famous scholars, which obviously was an encouragement to him. The inheritors of the intangible cultural heritage skills should not only perpetuate well their unique skills (for example, Zhang Yong's skills must first come from the edification or guidance of his ancestors, and he always insisted on completing most of the processes by hand), but also learn from and draw on the strengths of many parties, so as to avoid being conservative and lagging behind the needs of the times. Exactly because of this, Zhang Yong studied and learned from Cao Long of Guangling School successively and returned to Jianyang in 2005 to found "Zhang's Guqin". Now, it has become an intangible cultural heritage card of Jianyang City and has a promising future in the construction of Chengdu as a music capital.

(3) Yumen Fist

Jianyang is a place that worships both literature and martial arts, so there have been so many generals and heroes from Jianyang since modern times. Among its intangible cultural heritage, there is a folk martial arts school — Yu Family Fist, which has distinctive immigrant cultural characteristics in Sichuan, integrates the essence of many Chinese schools, and has been passed down for more than ten generations. In the aforementioned celebrity culture part, the entry of Yu Fazhai, the local "fist king", has already introduced Yu Family Fist, so I will not repeat it here.

There is both worry and delight, as for the inheritance and promotion of this intangible cultural heritage in Jianyang. The worry refers to that for more than half a century, Yu Family Fist has been spread mainly in Zigong and Neijiang in southern Sichuan, Chongqing, Fuling, Wanxian and Daxian in eastern Sichuan, with tens of thousands of disciples. In Chongqing alone, more than 8000 people learned Yu Family Fist, participated in martial arts competitions at all levels, and won more than 100 awards. In Jianyang, however, there are relatively no qualified successors. The survey at the beginning of this century showed that only around ten people in the city learned Yu Family Fist, which is a pity. The delight means that over the past ten years, Jianyang's people of insight have discovered such problem of Yu Family Fist, and the government has begun to pay attention to it. Through efforts, Yu Family Fist has been included in the list of intangible cultural heritage in Ziyang City and Chengdu City. The government also took other measures, such as conducting research to find a solution; Established relevant research associations; Held Yu Family Fist fellowship and exchange activities inside and outside the province; The media paid attention, reported, and provided various assistances. The situation is improving. If Yu Family Fist were to be carried forward in Jianyang, in addition to the above efforts, we should encourage its inheritance not only confined to the descendants of Yu Family. The development, transformation and dissemination of Yu Family Fist should try to adapt to the urbanization process of Chengdu. In particular, we should seize the good opportunity of the relocation of Chengdu Institute of Physical Education, which features martial arts teaching and research, to Jianyang (later under the jurisdiction of the East New Area of Chengdu), to further strengthen the cooperation between universities and local areas and attract talents back. At the same time, we should learn from the experience and practice of Yu Family Fist in southern and eastern Sichuan, attract more teenagers to practice Yu Family Fist, and carry forward this important intangible cultural heritage in Jianyang.

(4) Jiulian lantern

In Sichuan in the Qing Dynasty, local officials and schools advocated and disseminated the mainstream culture with Neo Confucianism as the core, which affected various social strata, scholars, farmers, artisans and merchants. Exactly because of this, Bashu culture and Tianfu culture maintained their similarity to the Chinese axial culture. However, at the level of practical application, the main groups affected by Neo Confucianism were literati and intellectuals (and the first goal is usually to pass the imperial examination). For the masses of the people who occupy the absolute majority of the population, they are more influenced by the family customs and instructions and the local customs, human feelings, and folk customs, that is, to seek and reflect the meaning of life, "scholars" are mainly following "etiquette", and "people" are mainly following "custom". The former is more ritualistic, procedural and decorative, while the latter is undoubtedly more concise, simple and authentic. From this broader and true mass perspective, the Bashu culture and Tianfu culture, which are created mainly by immigrants from 18 provinces of "Huguang filling Sichuan" and have strong inclusiveness and prominent civilian characteristics, are reflected in the folk beliefs and customs that all gods have their own believers, and all kinds of folk customs have their own inheritance regions and populations. When these people gradually merge into "fellow villagers" of "Sichuan people", "Chengdu people" and "Jianyang people" due to intermarriage, production, trade and festivals, their original gods and customs will inevitably be grafted, assembled and integrated. The Tianfu cultural factors supporting such grafting, assembly and integration include: the harmonious coexistence and mutual benefiting of Confucianism, Buddhism and Taoism; Folk literature and art (including myths and legends) are colorful; Being far away from the capital and the democratized social fashion make the folk expressions here best reflect the "harmony but difference" of Confucianism. Under the above background, the Tianfu cultural region has rich minority, small regional tangible or intangible cultural heritage inherited to this day. The jiulian lantern of Jianyang Stone Bridge is such a small flower of folk custom.

The Jiulian Lantern is a kind of performing art that combines the cultural connotations of gods, witches, Buddhas, and Taoists, expels evil spirits and prays for blessings, and expresses the people's yearning for a safe and happy life. It is difficult and has strong visual and auditory impacts. At first, it was a supporting activity for butchers to make wishes and fulfill their wishes in order to drive away disasters and take refuge. Later, it gradually evolved into a performing art with both fitness and entertainment effects. As a folk custom activity, it is usually held on the day when a city's patron saint, the town god, makes a tour. Nine men wear silk scarves on their heads, their upper bodies are naked, their lower bodies wear shorts, and their feet wear straw sandals. Several oil lamps are hung on their forehead, two breasts, the left and right sides of their front abdomen, and the left and right sides of their back, and two oil lamps are hung on their arms; Nine people form a single column, and the first eight people each use two wooden poles to support a dragon head with colorful lanterns hanging on it; The last man holds up a long bamboo pole with his hands and there are several bamboo blocks fixed on it. Nine colored lanterns are hung on the top of the pole and the bamboo blocks, and they are called "Zuo Du lantern". Performers sing as they walk along the road, the content of which is to eliminate disasters and turn bad luck into good luck. Coupled with the percussion of gongs and drums, there are many onlookers and the scene is quite spectacular. In October 2012, the shooting team of CCTV's "Far Home, 30 degrees North Latitude" filmed it in the Stone Bridge Middle School.

The Jiulian Lantern Performance is mysterious, plain, coarse and unconstrained, and has the flavor of primitive sacrifice and prayer, showing the diversified and integrated immigrant culture, religious culture, folk culture and local culture. For the descendants of Jianyang and nonlocal tourists, it has the function of helping them understand the ancestors of Bashu culture and Tianfu culture: the life and struggle process of hard work, the strong will of not fearing hardship, moving the gods and pursuing a safe and happy life, and the humanistic character of being able to harvest happiness under difficult and poor circumstances.

In the process of building a park city in Chengdu, culture must be embedded. Jiulian Lantern, a unique intangible cultural heritage of Jianyang, must be protected and inherited. As far as performance is concerned, we can moderately keep pace with the times. On the premise of retaining its basic form, connotation and style, we can do something to add a comprehensive aesthetic feeling. In addition, Jiulian Lantern is more suitable for appearing as a highlight in a series of folk custom exhibitions, which is better than appearing alone. At least, it can be the reason why Jianyang is "remembered". In the cultural river ecology, it is at least a unique small tributary.

(5) Tongue painting and finger ink painting

The so-called tongue painting and finger ink painting, that is, using the tongue and fingers to paint, have special and unique effects. The recognized ancestor of tongue painting is Huang Ernan, whose ancestral home is Daxing

County, Hebei Province, in the late Qing Dynasty, while the history of finger ink painting can be traced back to Zhang Zao, the established ancestor in the art circle of the Tang Dynasty. Min Ke'er, a teacher in Jianyang, studied with tongue painters Huang Ernan in regions south of the Yangtze River and Liu Laiyun in the northwest. Min Ke'er and his disciple Wang Yide had always insisted on research and creation and created a large number of artistic works. Now their works are displayed in Jianyang Planning Museum.

Tongue painting and finger ink painting are a kind of painting style that combines elegance and vulgarity. Their pioneering and creativity in the art field reflects Jianyang people's creativity and innovation in refining beauty from daily life. Although tongue painting and finger ink painting do not belong to the mainstream painting school, their distinctive local character has become Jianyang's "being remembered" character and trait. Therefore, in the process of inheritance and development of tongue painting and finger ink painting, we can try to balance the relationship between elegance and popularity, so that this intangible cultural heritage can be put on the stage of elegance, so that the common spiritual value pursuit of citizens can be demonstrated in an orderly inheritance, and thus it becomes an important part of the city's bright cultural attribute. In Jianyang's literary and artistic activities, the frequency of the appearance of tongue painting and finger ink painting can also be appropriately increased, so that this non-mainstream art category can become a unique existence and be widely recognized and remembered.

(6) Technique of making Shiqiao fine dried noodles

Shiqiao fine dried noodles, also known as elevated fine dried noodles, originated in the Song Dynasty, prevailed in the Yuan Dynasty, and has a history of more than 900 years. Shiqiao fine dried noodles are made of fine and exquisite materials. They are as thin as silk, round, and hollow, white and delicious. They are still fresh when boiled overnight. Shiqiao fine dried noodles are handmade, and the production process is exquisite. It needs to go through more than 20 processes, such as kneading, rubbing, oiling, flour supplement, fermentation in the tank, drawing, rolling, shelving, and lifting. Therefore, about its production process, there is also a doggerel, which roughly means: "Since 'leaving my husband', I have been 'dressing up and wiping oil' in the morning, making friends with 'two bachelors', 'playing around with romantic', and only saying 'forever', but who knows 'cutting off two ends'."

Shiqiao fine dried noodles have a long history, which embody the hard-working and intelligent spirit of Jianyang people for thousands of years and demonstrate the craftsmanship spirit of Jianyang people to keep improving and focus on innovation. The ornamental and participatory nature of shiqiao fine dried noodles production techniques, and the closeness and relevance of shiqiao fine dried noodles and daily life are conducive to re-awakening the glory of this intangible cultural heritage in the development of cultural tourism industry and catering industry. The intangible cultural heritage, which is integrated into daily life, can most arouse people's emotional resonance, make people consciously participate in the process of inheritance and development, and become a memory point of Jianyang culture. Vertically viewing, Shiqiao fine dried nooldes have a long history and are worth remembering; Horizontally viewing, among the numerous traditional techniques of making fine dried noodles in China, Shiqiao fine dried noodles also have outstanding personality and distinctive characteristics, which is worth inheriting. Therefore, we can learn from the experience of inheriting and carrying forward other traditional hanging noodles in China, integrate this intangible cultural heritage into the daily life of Jianyang people, and shape it into a cultural characteristic with memory points.

3. The Summary of the Connotation of Jianyang Intangible Cultural Heritage

It is recorded in the literature that Jianyang is rich in natural resources and the people are industrious and intelligent, so Jianyang's literature and craftsmanship are prosperous and it has rich intangible cultural heritages. The most representative local creations, such as mutton soup, Yumen Fist, Jiulian Lantern, tongue painting and finger ink painting, reflect Jianyang people's food aspiration to adapt to local conditions and improve; The ideal of martial arts that pays equal attention to both civil and martial arts and cultivates both merits and virtues; The desire to live a safe life by eliminating disasters and bad lucks; And the simple artistic purport of simplifying and beautifying life. On the whole, it can be further condensed as **"local nature, Sichuan flavor and Tianfu memory"**. Inheriting the above intangible cultural heritages, people can feel the unique local customs of Jianyang. A unique picture of a city "remembered" or even "yearned for" is formed.

Section VII Commercial Road Culture

1. The emergence of commercial road culture

Before the arrival of modern transportation tools, Sichuan Basin was a geographical unit with internal circulation mainly and external circulation as the auxiliary in economic life. Although compared with most countries in the world, this unit is large enough, but on the economic territory of China, the huge inconvenience and cost of getting in and out of the basin in ancient times represented by "the way to Sichuan is difficult, more difficult than getting into the sky" has always maintained the state that most people and their belongings cannot go out to participate in the direct economic and cultural exchanges with the outside world. Therefore, the ancient ancestors who did not want to be constrained had long ago cut through thorns, crossed mountains and rivers, conquered the miasma and beasts, and created the Southern Silk Road. There are real objects (Sanxingdui, Jinsha cultural relics; Han Dynasty Shu brocade armguard unearthed in Nya, Xinjiang "Five Stars Out of the East to Benefit China") and documents (according to the *Historical Records*, Zhang Qian went to the Western Regions and saw the Chinese goods Shu cloth and Qiongzhang from Sichuan in Da Xia, that is, in today's Afghan market) as reliable basis. The ancestors of Sichuan Basin were the earliest representatives of the communication between Chinese civilization and South Asia and West Asia; Chengdu is the starting city of the Southern Silk Road, and Sichuan is the earliest chapter in the human economic and cultural history of important and high-end participants of the Northern and Maritime Silk Road. In the Sichuan Basin, Chengdu and Chongqing, the capitals of Ba and Shu since the Qin and Han Dynasties, are undoubtedly the decisive economic hubs, the main gathering and distributing places of people and property, the source of various economic and cultural innovation and vitality, the production, gathering and distributing places of the best quality and bulk commodities, and the main residence, visit and travel places for foreign and ethnic giants, scholars and calligraphers. By comparison, in most periods, especially after the birth of the provincial system in the Yuan, Ming and Qing Dynasties, Chengdu was the only political, economic and cultural center in Sichuan (except for the period when Yuzhen took over Sichuan in the Ming Dynasty, the period of the War of Resistance against Japan, and the period after the construction of the third front). Located at the eastern gateway of Chengdu, Jianyang was directly under the jurisdiction of Chengdu for most of the time in history. The major land and waterway transportation lines of Chengdu and Chongqing converge here. Jianyang, which has many garrisons and special security agencies (such as the specially set patrol inspection department) to maintain safety in history, has become a powerful region with excellent commercial and trade positions besides Chengdu and Chongqing. Its land and waterway channels are active and prosperous in the commercial trade in peaceful times, which has always provided a constant source of vitality for the formation and enrichment of Jianyang's humanistic personality. In addition to its excellent farming civilization, Jianyang also has a continuous power to stimulate and promote the development of local commercialized agriculture and handicraft industry. Jianyang also has more people who are directly engaged in or benefited from commercial trade than other counties, and its wharf culture of waterway is also more active than other counties. Jianyang attaches great importance to agriculture, but does not discriminate against industry and commerce, avoiding the traditional "favoring agriculture and disfavoring commerce" that many urban and rural areas in China do. The social ethos of respecting scholars and valuing agriculture over commerce have provided Jianyang with the economic and cultural soil for rapid connection with modern and contemporary industries since Jianyang's modernization.

In particular, the ancient Shiqiao Town, which has a history of more than 2,000 years, was once a land and water transportation hub and material distribution center connecting western, central, eastern and southern Sichuan. From the late Qing Dynasty to the early days of the founding of New China, it had been the commercial and political center of Jianyang, and had gradually developed into a financial center, water transport terminal and trade center in central Sichuan. According to the *Records of Shiqiao Town*, "13 banks across the country have set up branches here. There are 6 guildhalls, 9 wharves, and more than 100 tea shops in the town. There are more than 300 merchants of the 'eight merchants' which are rice, sugar, tobacco, wine, salt, cotton, oil, and mountain products. There are more than 1,000 ships of all sizes docked at the Shiqiao Wharf." The ancient Shiqiao Town, which was in its heyday for a time, represents Jianyang's active business contacts and also precipitates Jianyang's commercial road culture. From the perspective of history to examine the commercial road culture of Jianyang, the once prosperous commercial scene of the ancient Shiqiao town cannot be avoided, and should even be interpreted as the key thing of a period. It can be said that the appearance of the ancient town of Shiqiao has built a bridge for the orderly inheritance of the Jianyang commercial road culture, with a bright background.

In addition, the Dongda Road in Chengdu is the only way which must be passed for Chengdu to connect with the east of Sichuan. It was first formed in Shuhan and became prosperous in the Tang and Song Dynasties. In the Ming and Qing Dynasties, the post road began to be popularized. Dongda Road was the main line from Jinguan Post to Longquan Post and then to Yang'an Post. It was the most convenient for people and information to travel through. Passing places of Dongda Road are: Deshengchang, Shahe Fort, Hongmen Pu, Damian Pu, Jiepai Pu, Longquan Post, Shanquan Pu, Liugou Pu, Nanshan Pu, Shipan Pu, Chishui Pu, Jiuqu Pu, etc. And more than half of these post stations are in Jianyang. The exchange of people and information also made Dongda Road prosperous as a commercial road, bringing about increasingly frequent trade. In the ruins of Dongda Road, we can still vaguely imagine the noise of personnel exchanges and the prosperity of business exchanges in those days, and also engraved is a distinctive part of Jianyang commerical road culture that is worth mentioning. Starting from Dongda Road, Jianyang today has already entered the era of aviation, high-speed rail and subway, becoming a world-class "golden port" where people, logistics, capital and information flow converge. This inevitably leads to more frequent and high-level commercial exchanges, and the connotation of the commercial road culture is thus enriched and its extension is thus expanded accordingly.

2. The Connotation and Times Value of Commercial Road Culture

For more than 2,000 years, for the political, economic and cultural activities in the Bashu region, the road connecting Chengdu and Chongqing is undoubtedly the most important one among the transportation arteries in the Sichuan Basin determined by natural geography, economic geography and political geography. The location of Jianyang determines its important position on this road. A unique and colorful commercial road culture is formed, the spiritual and material wealth of post stations, towns and immigrants are gathered, and the humanistic spirit of diligence, integrity, openness and inclusiveness is embodied. Inheriting and carrying forward the commercial road culture, and creating distinctive landscapes and activities can strongly promote Jianyang to become an economic highland and cultural center in the construction of Chengdu Chongqing double city economic circle, and form a golden bridge for exchanges and cooperation within and outside the province and at home and abroad. The commercial road is also part of Jianyang's nostalgia. The making of this cultural character can enhance Jianyang's excellent gift of "being remembered".

3. Personality of Jianyang Commercial Road Culture

In addition to the common characteristics of the general commercial road culture of the cities and counties where Bashu culture and Tianfu culture belong, Because Jianyang has the first gateway in the east of the capital of Sichuan; There are often troops or special security forces stationed; For quite a long time in history, the mission of the military bases based in Chengdu of controlling and pacifying the vast southwestern minority areas; and the diversity of landscapes and scenic spots, we can pay attention to the following aspects in the study and judgment of commercial road culture:

(1) Contribution to the creation and maintenance of the Southern Silk Road. The Southern Silk Road is one of the earliest huge international trade routes. Its development and stability were first based on the effective rule over the southwestern barbarians (in history, there were two forms — the chieftain system dominated by indirect control before the Ming and Qing Dynasties' reform of the land, and the government directly appointed officials to govern and moderately stationed troops at some key nodes). From the ownership of Niubing County and the relationship between Wei Gao's achievements and Jianzhou, as mentioned before, Jianyang has made its own contribution to the establishment of the Southern Silk Road in history. As for whether there is a route of the Southern Silk Road from Chengdu and Chongqing to Jianyang, it remains to be proved by unearthed cultural relics. However, it is possible as Jianyang connected with the southwest barbarians militarily.

(2) Sichuan (especially Chengdu) is the most prosperous literary and artistic highland in China. In the *Biography of Chengdu*, I discussed that Chengdu is the number one city of Chinese poetry. Therefore, poets like to visit Sichuan since ancient times. This makes the Chengdu Chongqing

commercial road with Jianyang as the hub also a cultural road and an artistic road. This kind of coincidence, interweaving and complementing each other, agricultural civilization and industrial and commercial civilization, as well as the religious or humanistic beliefs, poems and songs represented by literati and refined scholars, are harmonious symbiosis. Because of the obvious mobility as a support, Jianyang does have its own elegance with Chengdu, Chongqing or other major cities as the presentation of the fixed landscape of urban civilization. In the construction of the new Jianyang, it can be considered and used in the cultural landscape layout of the two lakes and one mountain, the city central park, Tianfu greenway, and the new transportation network.

(3) Jianyang's history is largely related to its salt. Niubing County is named after Niubing Salt Well, and Yang'an County is named after Yangming Salt Well. In the history of Jianyang for more than 2000 years, the main body of Jianyang commercial road is salt road, and the mainstream of commercial road culture is salt industry culture. Jianyang salt industry has a history of more than 2000 years. In the second year of Yuanding in the Western Han Dynasty (115 BC), Niubing Salt Well and Yangming Salt Well were firstly discovered in the territory. In Sui Dynasty, there were 4 wells, including Yangming Salt Well and Niubing Well. In the Tang Dynasty, there were six wells, including Yangming Salt Well, Niubing Well, Shangjun Well and Xiajun Well. In the seventh year of Chunxi in the Southern Song Dynasty (1180), 19 wells of salt were boiled in Jianzhou, with a production of 135,000kg. During the Hongzhi period, wells including Shangliu produced 1,397,000kg. In addition, in the fourth year of Yongle (1406), the old bamboo tube well in Ziyang Township, Jianxian County reopened to boil salt, and produced more than 5,000kg of salt every year. In the 17th and 18th years of Shunzhi's reign in the Qing Dynasty (1660—1661), the government began to recruit workers to dig 18

bamboo tube wells. In the eighth year of Yongzheng (1730), there were 93 wells. During the reign of Qianlong, four plants were gradually formed: Haiji Plant, Lanyong Plant, Tianchang Plant and Jiangwang Plant. In addition, there was Laojun Well, and the number of salt wells in the territory reached 182. In the 51st year of Qianlong's reign (1786), there were 533 wells. There were 54 salt frying stoves, 84 salt frying pots and 139 warm water pots. In the early Qing Dynasty, household-based salt supply was implemented. In the first year of Qianlong's reign (1736 AD), the deputy governor decided to move to Shiqiao Well in Jianzhou to take charge of and conduct inspection of salt. By the end of the Qing Dynasty, there were 91 people who assumed the position of deputy governor. In the thirtieth year of the reign of Guangxu, the official transportation and distribution was established. The annual output of salt in the territory was more than 7,000 tickets, and the weight of Jianzhou tickets was about 500kg. In the early years of the Republic of China, there were 32 stoves for boiling in the county with more than 260 salt wells. The annual output of hua salt and ba salt in the county was more than 1 million kg. In the first year of the Republic of China, the tax on wells was abolished, with 630 grams for each ticket, 1 gram for two grams of ba salt, and 6 wen for each gram; Three grams of hua salt is one gram, and the tax was 5 wen per gram. In 1915, all factories in the county produced about 200,000 kilograms of salt per month, and the tax was about 6,000 yuan per month. After 1945, there were more than 270 salt wells in the territory. In 1947, there were 39 stoves for boiling distributed in Shiqiao Huojingwan, Shehongba, Waisi, Maliulin, Wuhuang Temple, Shizhong, Chishui Baijiawan, Laojunjing, Ziyang Shuanghechang, etc. The total fund was 114 million yuan. There were 889 salt workers with an annual salt production of 1,911,600kg. In 1949, salt production was 2,062,500kg. In 1950, there were 34 salt households in the county, 322 cattle for production, and 1,494,500kg salt was produced in the county. In 1951, there were 29 private salt wells, distributed near Jiancheng, Shiqiao, Waisi, Shizhong, Wuhuang Cave, Maliulin, Haijing, Laojun Well, etc. There were 45 management personnel, 35 staff and 833 workers. The salt production in the year was 3,366,000kg. In June 1951, according to the decision of the Central Government Council to "gradually reduce salt farms and a number of small wells and stoves with high cost, poor conditions and small output", Jianyang salt farms began to be abandoned and workers were transferred to other industries. Jianyang's long history of salt industry gave birth to a brilliant salt industry culture and formed the main body of commercial road culture.

Section VIII Mass Culture

1. The formation basis of Jianyang mass culture

After we have sorted out the previous seven major cultures, the foundation of Jianyang mass culture has been introduced in many ways, such as farming culture, intangible cultural heritage culture, commercial road culture, and Dongguan culture. These is not only the concentrated embodiment of mass culture in some aspects and at some levels, but also the mass culture that keeps pace with the times. They are the new foundation and resources for realizing transformation and facing reality and the future. To sum up, in addition to the four major cultures mentioned above, the bases for the formation of today's Jianyang mass culture mainly includes:

The infrastructure of urban and rural cultural construction is constantly increased and optimized; The development of routine and characteristic cultural activities in urban and rural streets and communities under the guidance of Party building; Broad mind and vision resulting from participating in and holding cultural, sports and art exchange activities inside and outside the city and at home and abroad.

Historically, the core values represented by benevolence, righteousness, courtesy, wisdom, honesty, loyalty, filial piety, sense of honour and sense of shame, through family education (including family traditions and family instructions), social landscape and customs, private schools and academies, and local sages, transmit positive energy, and form **an atmosphere of kindness and beauty and its inheritance**; In today's society, with the core values of socialism and Tianfu culture as the connotation, through family education, universal school education, urban and rural landscape construction, activity development, selection and recognition of advanced figures, Tianfu cultural action, etc., form and optimize **the trend of the good, beautiful and elegant**; Especially after the "return" of Jianyang to Chengdu, Jianyang faces new development opportunities and challenges. In the context of the improvement of the cultural self-confidence, pride and sense of mission of the urban and rural masses in the city, the people of Jianyang, with the embodiment of the national core values and the inheritance of Tianfu culture, have gradually welcomed, with the attitude of master, the construction of the Chengdu-Chongqing double-city economic circle, the park city, the three cities and three capitals, the world cultural city and the metropolitan area with a new concept, new thinking, new spirit and new atmosphere.

In the past six years, the city has realized that "civilization is the soul and the first brand of the city", formulated and implemented the "Three Year Work Plan of Jianyang City to Build a National Civilized City", and thoroughly implemented the "five major upgrading projects". Its rich and colorful practices include the selection activities of "Sichuan good people", "touching Xiongzhou" moral model and "good people around"; In January 2021, the 17th mutton food culture tourism season was held, during which about 1.7 million tourists were received and the income was 450 million yuan; Held an impressive dragon boat culture festival; The "Donglai Impression" project started holding competitions; Used well the support funds of cultural and creative projects to support the construction of cultural and creative blocks and space; "Internet+" 7 categories of new media construction; "A trip to remote villages and towns" cultural performance activities; "People's Stage" square and square dance competition; Strawberry Picking Festival, Peach Blossom Appreciation Festival, Jiulian Lantern Parade, Square Culture Week activities of the Spring Festival, and folk art performances are deeply rooted in the hearts of the people; "The Cherry is Red", "The Story of Brother Xiang" and "Notes on Seeing and Hearing" won awards in provinces and cities; Business training of civilized units; Organized young and middle-aged literary and artistic backbone people to go outside the city for training, observation, collection, exchange, exhibition and performance activities; Jointly built "Jianyang Quyi Volunteer Teaching Class" with the Provincial Quyi Research Institute; Carried out the selection and commendation of civilized units, villages, communities and service windows; Created the publicity logo of Jianyang city image "Sincere promise · Engraved Jianyang" and promoted its application; Exposure of uncivilized phenomena and order for rectification; Created a fair and honest market environment; Created a healthy and upward humanistic environment; Created a social and cultural environment conducive to the healthy growth of adolescents; Took advantage of the National Day and other time nodes to carry out online memorial activities for heroes and martyrs, and activities of children's hearts saluting the party and the national flag; Held moral lectures covering both urban and rural areas, and further promoted a series of themed activities of civilized etiquette norms such as "civilized dining table", "civilized exchange" with high public attention, strong motivation and great social impact; Multi-themed, down-to-earth collecting and creative activities and activities of benefiting people through literature and art carried out by the literary and artistic circles; Actively carried out education and training for non-public economic personnel, especially paid attention to conveying the spirit of important meetings of the central, provincial and municipal governments to private entrepreneurs, guided them in the correct political direction, and guided them to establish correct ideals and beliefs; Created international and high-quality cultural and tourism scenic spots and projects, and launched a number of high-quality tourism projects for mountain sports, health care and vacation, and ecological leisure; Strengthened the construction of cultural well-off society, protected and carried forward the excellent traditional culture in rural areas, and promoted the standardization construction of cultural infrastructure in villages and towns; In the process of rural revitalization, based on the natural, industrial and cultural foundation, integrated the traditional Chinese cultural elements such as family customs, Han clothes, ancestral temple, etc. into businesses, and created scenic spots and spaces; Actively compiled and published *Meeting Tianfu Xiongzhou*, and *There Is A Zhou Keqin in Jianyang*, and regularly launched *Jianyang Literature and Art*; Successfully held the "performance of the shortlisted songs of the city song of Jianyang" and promoted the city song "Jianyang"; Upgraded tourism activities with the theme of four seasons and made characteristic and quality activities such as "one village, one festival" and "one town (street), one activity"; With online and offline integrated, opened a new mode of cultural activities (art performances, public welfare exhibitions, public welfare lectures); Actively bringing the activities of Tianfu Culture into campuses; Took advantage of the Universiade to plan and launch a series of promotional activities of "sending Jianyang mutton soup to the Universiade", and selected ten brands of mutton soup; Yuan Tingdong, a famous Bashu cultural expert, was invited to talk about Jianyang Big Ear Sheep and Liu Zihua in short videos on Tiktok; Pinned down the publicity theme — "Jianyang is not simple", and closed the psychological distance between Chengdu, the country, the world and Jianyang; Supported the global delivery of mutton soup in Jianyang on the winter solstice day launched by "Haidilao", attracting 300000 people from all over the world to participate… In these active explorations, a large number of beneficial experiences and practices have been formed, combined with learning from the advanced ideas and practical experience of other excellent cities at the same level, supplemented by the latest research and judgment on the deep excavation of the eight major cultures of Jianyang. Under the guidance of the relevant requirements of the 14th Party Congress of Chengdu on the inheritance and innovation of Tianfu culture and the construction of a world famous cultural city, the mass culture of Jianyang, from content to form, can be realized, to a new level, full of high-quality works, allowing the "culture benefiting the people" project in Jianyang to present a different kind of happiness and wonderfulness.

However, we should also see some shortcomings of Jianyang's mass culture. For example, there are many forms of innovation, but few contents closely combined the high-quality resources of Jianyang or presented Jianyang's excellent character; The pursuit of refinement and elegance in urban mass cultural activities is far from enough; There are few masterpieces that are popular with the masses and have the value of dissemination and reference (the overall number of awards for cultural and creative works is relatively small); The cultural and civilized quality of the masses is still obviously uneven; The identity of people in Jianyang formed based on the household knowledge of Jianyang's culture, as well as the self-confidence and pride of citizens in Jianyang, need to be improved.

2. The fine character of Jianyang mass culture

For more than 2,000 years, the people of Jianyang have built their own happy life by relying on their industrious hands, and formed a cultural personality of patriotism, love for the family, helping each other, honesty and kindness, and respect for culture and elegance, which has become the basic cultural background and soil of Jianyang. The excavation and collation of its connotation and typical cases, and the enrichment and addition of its connotation in combination with Jianyang's new positioning and mission, and the creation of a new mass culture in the Internet era, will be an important part of Jianyang people's improvement and optimization of their own quality, and the enhancement of the sense of gain and happiness in cultural life. Externally, the construction of mass culture is also a basic project to enhance Jianyang's excellent character of "being remembered", "being yearned for" and even "being looked up to".